Design for More-Than-Human Futures

This book explores the work of important authors in the search for a transition towards more ethical design focused on more-than-human coexistence.

In a time of environmental crises in which the human species threatens its own survival and the highest level of exacerbation of the idea of a future and technological innovation, it is important to discard certain anthropocentric categories in order to situate design beyond the role that it traditionally held in the capitalist world, creating opportunities to create more just and sustainable worlds. This book is an invitation to travel new paths for design framed by ethics of more-than-human coexistence that breaks with the unsustainability installed in the designs that outfit our lives. Questioning the notion of human-centered design is central to this discussion. It is not only a theoretical and methodological concern, but an ethical need to critically rethink the modern, colonialist, and anthropocentric inheritance that resonates in design culture. The authors in this book explore the ideas oriented to form new relations with the more-than-human and with the planet, using design as a form of political enquiry.

This book will be of interest to academics and students from the world of design and particularly those involved in emerging branches of the field such as speculative design, critical design, non-anthropocentric design, and design for transition.

Martín Tironi is a sociologist at Pontificia Universidad Católica de Chile; holds a master's degree in Sociology from Sorbonne V and a PhD from Center de Sociologie de l'Innovation, École des Mines de Paris; and is post-doctorate, Center de Sociologie de l'Innovation, École des Mines de Paris. He is Visiting Fellow at the Center for Invention and Social Process, Goldsmiths, University of London, 2018. His research areas are anthropology of design, multispecies design, digital devices and technologies, and urban infrastructures. He is currently Director of the School of Design of Pontificia Universidad Católica de Chile and the Head Milenio project 'Futures of Artificial Intelligence Research' (FAIR).

Marcos Chilet is a designer who earned his undergraduate degree from Pontificia Universidad Católica de Chile and an MA from Goldsmith College, University of London. He is now Professor of Future Scenarios at the School of Design, Pontificia Universidad Católica de Chile. His practice and research areas are critical design, the relationship between politics, designers, and media technologies. He recently published the book *Materiales Televisivos: hacia una economía digital de los contenidos* about the impact of international streaming services in the Chilean TV culture. He was part of the curatorial team of the Chilean pavilion entitled *Tectonic Resonances* that won the London Design Biennale in 2021. He is currently Sub-Director of the School of Design of Pontificia Universidad Católica de Chile.

Carola Ureta Marín is a designer and visual communicator based in London, specialized in editorial design, cultural development, and historical research projects. She obtained her BA in Design (2012), an MA in Cultural Management (2015) in Chile, and an MA in Visual Communication from Royal College of Art, London (2022). She was part of the curatorial team of the Chilean pavilion entitled Tectonic Resonances that won the London Design Biennale in 2021. She is a frequent speaker at international congresses on Design Studies and Design History: Taipei (2016), Barcelona (2018), New York (2020), Quebec (2021), and Melbourne (2022). She is Director and Creator of The City as Text (La Ciudad como Texto), a collaborative digital platform that allows online visitors to partake in a virtual walk through 2.4 km of Santiago de Chile's main avenue during a specific date and time.

Pablo Hermansen is a designer who holds a PhD in Architecture and Urban Studies from Pontificia Universidad Católica de Chile. Dr. Hermansen's research and publications focus on the material conditions of interspecies coexistence, prototyping as a more-than-human research device, and performative strategies for the political visibility of counter-hegemonic groups in public space. He works in the fields of digital museography and interactive installation and provides consulting services in the area of critical service design for public institutions.

Routledge Research in Design, Technology and Society

Series Editors: Daniel Cardoso Llach (*Carnegie Mellon University, USA*) and Terry Knight (*Massachusetts Institute of Technology, USA*)

The Routledge Research in Design, Technology and Society series offers new critical perspectives and creative insights into the roles of technological systems and discourses in the design and production of our built environment. As computation, software, simulations, digital fabrication, robotics, 'big data,' artificial intelligence and machine learning configure new imaginaries of designing and making across fields, the series approaches these subjects critically from enriched socio-material, technical and historical perspectives—revealing how conceptions of creativity, materiality and labor have shifted and continue to shift in conjunction with technological change.

Computer Architectures
Constructing the Common Ground
Edited by Theodora Vardouli and Olga Touloumi

Data Publics
Public Plurality in an Era of Data Determinacy
Edited by Peter Mörtenböck and Helge Mooshammer

The Digital Bespoke?
Promises and Pitfalls of Mass Customization
ginger coons

The Architectural Imagination at the Digital Turn
Nathalie Bredella

Design for More-Than-Human Futures
Towards Post-Anthropocentric Worlding
Edited by Martín Tironi, Marcos Chilet, Carola Ureta Marín and Pablo Hermansen

For more information about the series, please visit: https://www.routledge.com/Routledge-Research-in-Design-Technology-and-Society/book-series/RRDTS

Design for More-Than-Human Futures

Towards Post-Anthropocentric Worlding

Edited by
Martín Tironi, Marcos Chilet, Carola Ureta Marín and Pablo Hermansen

LONDON AND NEW YORK

Designed cover image: Created by Design System International

First published 2024
by Routledge
4 Park Square, Milton Park, Abingdon, Oxon OX14 4RN

and by Routledge
605 Third Avenue, New York, NY 10158

Routledge is an imprint of the Taylor & Francis Group, an informa business

© 2024 selection and editorial matter, Martín Tironi, Marcos Chilet, Carola Ureta Marín and Pablo Hermansen; individual chapters, the contributors

The right of Martín Tironi, Marcos Chilet, Carola Ureta Marín and Pablo Hermansen to be identified as the authors of the editorial material, and of the authors for their individual chapters, has been asserted in accordance with sections 77 and 78 of the Copyright, Designs and Patents Act 1988.

All rights reserved. No part of this book may be reprinted or reproduced or utilised in any form or by any electronic, mechanical, or other means, now known or hereafter invented, including photocopying and recording, or in any information storage or retrieval system, without permission in writing from the publishers.

Trademark notice: Product or corporate names may be trademarks or registered trademarks, and are used only for identification and explanation without intent to infringe.

British Library Cataloguing-in-Publication Data
A catalogue record for this book is available from the British Library

Library of Congress Cataloging-in-Publication Data
Names: Tironi, Martín, 1979– editor. | Chilet, Marcos, editor. | Ureta Marín, Carola, editor. | Hermansen, Pablo, editor.
Title: Design for more-than-human futures : towards post-anthropocentric worlding / edited by Martín Tironi, Marcos Chilet, Carola Ureta Marín, Pablo Hermansen.
Description: New York : Routledge, 2023. |
Series: Research in design, technology and society | Includes bibliographical references and index.
Identifiers: LCCN 2023015075 | ISBN 9781032334394 (hardback) | ISBN 9781032334400 (paperback) | ISBN 9781003319689 (ebook)
Subjects: LCSH: Design—Environmental aspects. | Human ecology.
Classification: LCC NK1525 .D425 2023 | DDC 744.01—dc23/eng/20230609
LC record available at https://lccn.loc.gov/2023015075

ISBN: 978-1-032-33439-4 (hbk)
ISBN: 978-1-032-33440-0 (pbk)
ISBN: 978-1-003-31968-9 (ebk)

DOI: 10.4324/9781003319689

Typeset in Sabon
by codeMantra

In Memory of Dr. Bruno Latour (1947–2022)

We dedicate this book to the more-than-human resonances that brought us together. We hope they will help us out of the Anthropocene.

Contents

List of Figures	*xi*
List of Contributors	*xiii*
Acknowledgements	*xvii*
Prologue	*xix*

Introduction: Design for more-than-human futures: towards
post-anthropocentric and decolonial perspectives   1
MARTÍN TIRONI

1   Notes on excess: towards pluriversal design   29
MARISOL DE LA CADENA AND ARTURO ESCOBAR

2   Anticipations of more-than-human futures: social innovation
as a decentring, engendering, reframing, and caring practice   51
EZIO MANZINI AND VIRGINIA TASSINARI

3   Design's intimacies: the indeterminacy of design with
machines and mushrooms   58
LAURA FORLANO

4   Growing materials: technical and caring processes as rooted
design practices   72
NICOLE CRISTI

5   Learning from accidental abundance   88
CARL DISALVO

x *Contents*

6 How would animals and architects co-design if we built the right contract? 92
IGNACIO FARÍAS, TOMÁS SÁNCHEZ CRIADO AND FELIX REMTER

7 Before the idiot, the poet? Aesthetic figures and design 103
ALEX WILKIE AND MIKE MICHAEL

8 Revisiting empathy by gentrifying our guts: exploring design as a cosmopolitical diplomacy practice through microbial fruits of Istanbul 112
URIEL FOGUÉ, ORKAN TELHAN, EVA GIL LOPESINO AND CARLOS PALACIOS RODRÍGUEZ

9 Design beyond human concerns: a sancocho-style approach 130
LEONARDO PARRA-AGUDELO AND EDGARD DAVID RINCÓN QUIJANO

10 Furrowing the *Maraña*: designing to sail out of the Anthropocene 141
PABLO HERMANSEN AND JOSÉ GUERRA SOLANO

Index *169*

Figures

6.1 Co-worker suit (left) and beaver experience suit (right). CC BY 2017 Katharina Meenenga, Laura Krohn, Marie Van Tricht, Pedro Racha-Pacheco, Seppe Verhaegen, and Victoria Schulz. Used with permission
Source: https://thedesignincrisis.wixsite.com/designincrisis/submission   97

6.2 The last protocol. CC BY 2017 Katharina Meenenga, Laura Krohn, Marie Van Tricht, Pedro Racha-Pacheco, Seppe Verhaegen, and Victoria Schulz. Used with permission
Source: https://thedesignincrisis.wixsite.com/designincrisis/5-weeks)   99

6.3 Action and reaction plan. CC BY 2017 Katharina Meenenga, Laura Krohn, Marie Van Tricht, Pedro Racha-Pacheco, Seppe Verhaegen, and Victoria Schulz. Used with permission
Source: https://thedesignincrisis.wixsite.com/designincrisis/5-weeks   100

8.1 An Istanbul of many Istanbuls, 2021
Source: elii [architecture office]   115

8.2 MFoI as a contact zone, 2021
Source: elii [architecture office]   117

8.3 Kiosks as points of constant exchange of microorganisms, 2021
Source: elii [architecture office]   118

8.4 Kiosks as points of constant exchange of microorganisms, 2021
Source: elii [architecture office]   119

8.5 The point of encounter as a strange totemic structure in Özgürlük Park, 2021
Source: Engin Gerçek   120

xii *Figures*

8.6 Structure for a point of encounter between the macro and micro worlds
Source: Engin Gerçek 121

8.7 Multiple format: Platform, petri dishes, fables, robotic parrot, workshops, website, periodical publications, articles, plans, and drawings
Source: elii [architecture office] 122

8.8 From the city to the guts: Transcalar condition of urban phenomena, 2021
Source: elii [architecture office] 124

8.9 MFoI recycled at Tarlataban and bostans
Source: Eda Hisarlıoğlu 125

8.10 Could design be a form of cosmopolitical diplomacy?
Source: [architecture office] 127

9.1 Bone Sancocho
Source: DISCA Lab Archive 137

10.1 Alexander's campaign trail
Source: Martín Pastenes 151

10.2 Huilo and Maqui meet through the fence, which is a point of encounter and separation
Source: Mora (2020, p. 69). In "Condiciones materiales para un espacio relacional enriquecido con Huilo y Maqui". Investigación aplicada desde una perspectiva autoetnográfica en el recinto de dos Pumas con color. Pontificia Universidad Católica de Chile 160

10.3 Planimetry of Huilo's and Maqui's enclosures, this was made during the research
Source: Mora (2020, p. 77). In "Condiciones materiales para un espacio relacional enriquecido con Huilo y Maqui". Investigación aplicada desde una perspectiva autoetnográfica en el recinto de dos Pumas con color. Pontificia Universidad Católica de Chile 162

10.4 Maqui played with the braids repeatedly. He rubbed himself with the parsley braid constantly, which was recorded with the hairs impregnated in it
Source: Mora (2020, p. 86). In "Condiciones materiales para un espacio relacional enriquecido con Huilo y Maqui". Investigación aplicada desde una perspectiva autoetnográfica en el recinto de dos Pumas con color. Pontificia Universidad Católica de Chile 163

Contributors

Emanuele Coccia is a philosopher. He did a doctorate in medieval philosophy and philology at the University of Florence. He received post-doctoral grants from the Max Planck Institute in Frankfurt am Main, the CNRS, and the Universitat Autonoma di Barcelona. He is the author of influential books like *The Life of Plants: A Metaphysics of Mixture and Metamorphoses*.

Nicole Cristi is a PhD candidate, Anthropology, University College of London. MA Material and Visual Culture Studies, UCL. Centre for the Anthropology of Technics and Technodiversity (CATT). Designer and BA in Aesthetics, Pontifical Catholic University of Chile (PUC).

Marisol de la Cadena is Professor of Anthropology and Science and Technology Studies at the University of California-Davis, author of *Earth Beings. Ecologies of Practice across Andean worlds* (2015), and co-author of *A world of Many Worlds* (2018).

Carl DiSalvo holds a PhD in Design from Carnegie Mellon University and is Associate Professor in the College of Computing at the Georgia Institute of Technology.

Arturo Escobar is Professor of Anthropology Emeritus at the University of North Carolina, Chapel Hill, author of *Designs for the Pluriverse: Radical Interdependence, Autonomy, and the Making of Worlds* (2018), and co-author of *Relationality: Making and Restor(y)ing Life* (2023).

Ignacio Farías holds a PhD in European Ethnology from Humboldt University and is Professor of Urban Anthropology at the Institute of European Ethnology and Co-Director of the Georg-Simmel Center for Metropolitan Studies at Humboldt University.

Uriel Fogué is an architect and holds a PhD in architecture from UPM. He is Associate Professor at the Escuela Técnica Superior de Arquitectura de Madrid (Universidad Politécnica de Madrid, UPM), Visiting Professor at the École Polytechnique Fédérale de Lausanne (EPFL), Principal at elii (architecture office), and Director of the Political Fictions Crisis Cabinet.

xiv *Contributors*

Laura Forlano is a Fulbright award-winning and National Science Foundation funded scholar, and is a disabled writer, social scientist, and design researcher. She is Professor in the departments of Art + Design and Communication Studies in the College of Arts, Media, and Design at Northeastern University. She received her PhD in communications from Columbia University.

Eva Gil Lopesino is an architect, a PhD candidate in architecture from the UPM, Associate Professor at the Escuela Técnica Superior de Arquitectura de Madrid (Universidad Politécnica de Madrid, UPM), Visiting Professor at the École Polytechnique Fédérale de Lausanne (EPFL), and Principal at elii [architecture office].

José Guerra Solano is a social anthropologist and holds an MA in American aesthetics from Pontifical Catholic University of Chile. Prof. Guerra has developed his investigation in the presence of more-than-human in the subjectivation process. Currently, he's investigating using autoethnography and design at the service of gender studies.

Pablo Hermansen is a designer who holds a PhD in Architecture and Urban Studies from Pontificia Universidad Católica de Chile. Dr. Hermansen's research and publications focus on the material conditions of interspecies coexistence, prototyping as a more-than-human research device, and performative strategies for the political visibility of counter-hegemonic groups in public space. He works in the fields of digital museography and interactive installation and provides consulting services in the area of critical service design for public institutions.

Ezio Manzini is an eco-social activist, Founder of DESIS Network, and Honorary Professor at Politecnico di Milano.

Mike Michael is a sociologist of science and technology and a professor at the University of Exeter. Research interests have touched on the relation of everyday life to technoscience, the use of design to develop a 'speculative methodology,' and the role of aesthetics and affect in the making of publics. Recent publications include *Actor-Network Theory: Trials, Trails and Translations* (Sage, 2017) and *The Research Event: Towards Prospective Methodologies in Sociology* (Routledge, 2021).

Carlos Palacios Rodríguez is an architect, a PhD candidate in architecture from the UPM, Associate Professor at the Escuela Técnica Superior de Arquitectura de Madrid (Universidad Politécnica de Madrid, UPM), Visiting Professor at the École Polytechnique Fédérale de Lausanne (EPFL), and Principal at elii [architecture office].

Leonardo Parra Agudelo holds a PhD in urban development and social transformation from QUT, Brisbane, Australia, an MFA in Design and Technology from Parsons the New School for Design, New York, USA, and a bachelor's degree in industrial design from Universidad de los Andes, and is Associate Professor in the Design Department, Faculty of Architecture and Design at Universidad de los Andes (Bogota, Colombia).

Felix Remter studied cultural anthropology and social sciences at LMU, Munich and Enroled at the integrative Graduate Center "TechnoScienceStudies" (TU Munich) and is Researcher at the Munich University of Applied Sciences (KSH).

Edgard David Rincón Quijano is a PhD candidate in Design and Creation from the University of Caldas, is Industrial Designer from the National University of Colombia, holds a master's degree in Industrial Design from ISTHMUS, School of Architecture and Design of Latin America and the Caribbean, and is Assistant Professor of the Design department at the Universidad del Norte.

Tomás Sánchez Criado holds a PhD in Social Anthropology from Universidad Autónoma de Madrid and is Ramón y Cajal Senior Research Fellow at the Open University of Catalonia's CareNet-IN3 group.

Virginia Tassinari is a design researcher and co-initiator of the DESIS Philosophy Talks format, and researcher and lecturer at Politecnico di Milano.

Orkan Telhan is an interdisciplinary artist, designer, and researcher; holds a PhD in Design and Computation from MIT's Department of Architecture; and is Associate Professor of Fine Arts, Emerging Design Practices in the Weitzman School of Design at the University of Pennsylvania.

Alex Wilkie is a professor of design and a sociologist of science and technology at Goldsmiths, University of London. His research has been variously located at the intersections of design (as topic and resource) and science and technology studies for over 25 years, addressing issue mapping, user-centered and human-computer interaction design, studio studies, energy-demand reduction, and public engagement with science and technology. Alex is currently working on the scope and implications of more-than-human aesthetics for inventive methods, knowledge practices, and the climate crisis. Recent publications include *Speculative research: The lure of possible futures* (Routledge, 2018) and *Inventing the Social* (Mattering Press, 2018).

Acknowledgements

This book is the result of different convergences. It began to be wrought almost eight years ago when Martín Tironi and Pablo Hermansen had the opportunity to start working in the Design Interaction Workshop at the Pontificia Universidad Católica de Chile, recognizing in more-than-human relationships a way to redesign and make worlds. In 2019, they had the first opportunity to leave papers and academic classrooms and develop the installation *Cenizas de coexistencia* at the Museo de Arte Contemporáneo (MAC) in Chile. It became evident for the need to seek more sensitive and material languages to reimagine the anthropocentric matrices of design.

Nevertheless, the most important starting point for this publication was the Chilean Pavilion at the London Design Biennale 2021, where the heart of the curatorial team was made up of the designers Pablo Hermansen, Marcos Chilet, and Carola Ureta Marín and the sociologist Martín Tironi. Titled *Tectonic resonances from the south: from user-centered design to planet-oriented design*, this Pavilion was the great catalyst for the dedication and intention of this book. Had it not been for this collective curatorial work, this book – whose flaws and omissions are certainly innumerable – would not have come to light. While this publication is not the perfect translation of a material exhibition into a written text, we do owe the Pavilion almost two years of conversation and debates around design as a place to rethink our modes of habitability.

We would first like to thank all the more-than-human entities that made this project possible. We would also like to thank our families, who have to bear the resonances of what we do and don't do.

We would also like to thank the Ministry of Culture of Chile; Miryam Singer; the Director of Arts and Culture of the PUC; and Mario Ubilla, Dean of FADEU. But perhaps our greatest debt is to the PUC School of Design. Its entire community, from students, professors, and staff, have been the container and sounding board for many of our reflections and interventions. Directly or indirectly, the PUC Design has been our most fierce critic, and at the same time, an inexhaustible source of possibilities to deepen in the challenges for a design from the South and post-anthropocentric. We also want to thank John Dunn and Catalina Marshall for the accurate work of xviii *Acknowledgements*

reviewing the manuscript. To Martín Bravo and Design System International for capturing the essence of the London Design Biennale 2021 pavilion and translating it into an incredible cover image for this book.

We hope that this series of convergences helps to explain in part the genesis of this book. Much more than a monolithic dogmatic, they are partially articulated proposals for beginning to project new ways of doing design in a damaged planet, considering the interventions and forces that develop other species and agencies.

Thanks.
Martín Tironi, Pablo Hemansen, Marcos Chilet,
and Carola Ureta Marín.
September, Chile and United Kingdom, 2022.

Prologue

We still have no real idea of what design is and what it can do. The discipline that was born barely a century and a half ago has just begun to explore the power it has. Yet, some misconceptions still make its full maturation difficult. Indeed, a twofold prejudice has so far defined the exercise of design, or rather a twofold limitation, which concerns together the object on which it is exercised and its object. Indeed, it has been thought that design is a set of human and only human practices and that precisely because of this the domain of its application is limited to a set of objects and contexts with which human beings have to deal.

In fact, the object of design is always the planet in its totality, and first of all in a very literal sense of the word: that there is no place or area on the planet that cannot or has not been the object of design, conception. This is a way of expressing the very fact of the Anthropocene. Because of the staggering expansion of the human species on the planet, no square inch of the Earth's flesh (and it matters little whether it is the lithosphere, atmosphere, or hydrosphere) not only bears the mark and trace of the presence of the human species but has been voluntarily changed by it. The Anthropocene confronts us with a planet that is the product of species design. But precisely because of this, precisely because there is nothing that we can think of as "natural" and non-anthropogenic, the opposite is also and especially true: any act of design can only now have the totality of the planet as its object. When you manipulate or redesign a single portion, what you are manipulating is always the totality of the planet. To design a cup or a sofa is to shape, again and again, the flesh of the whole planet.

In fact, this willingness of the planet to be manipulated by those who inhabit it is something much more radical than we think. We are used to thinking that outside the human sphere nothing is artificial, that everything is a given and a "natural" fact. We are used to thinking that the environment is what living things have to adapt to and not an artifact of the living things themselves. Actually, every living thing, by the very fact of living, is radically changing its environment and also radically changing the planet. Plants have no hands, no tools, but their very existence is a modification of planet Earth on a local and global sphere. The whole planet, from this point of view, is a

xx *Prologue*

garden of which the living are the designers, the landscape architects. One
of the greatest biologists of the past, Lamarck – one of the first to use the
term "biology" – allowed this aspect to be grasped. Indeed, in a treatise
on hydrogeology, he asked whether living things exert an influence on the
geological texture of the planet. His answer is astounding: every tiny portion
of the Earth's space is either the result of transformation wrought by a living being or is itself the remnant, the corpse, the graveyard of ancient living
things.[1] Nothing on this planet is a "mere natural environment," untouched,
illiberated. Everything has been produced, manipulated, chiselled, remade by
the living. For that matter, one only has to look at the "original state of this
planet," four and a half billion years ago: the Earth was then a huge mass of
fire, unsuitable for any form of life. It was only through the design and transformation activity of the countless number of living species that preceded us
and radically transformed its surface that the Earth became liveable, habit-
able for each of the species that inhabit it. If it is essential to emphasize this,
it is certainly not to legitimize the horrors carried out by the human species
in recent decades. It is to show that the solution to these errors is not a return
to a dreamy form of naturalness: everything in nature is artificial, everything
has been made, manufactured by other living things for other living things.
Indeed, in the face of the climate crisis, the solution can never be to reduce or
eliminate design: as living, we can never stop acting, stop transforming the
Earth. We must not choose between design and non-design but understand
through what design form the Earth was created and designed by those who
inhabited it.

Actually, if you look closely, if living things modify the Earth and do not
cease to manipulate and transform it, it is because they are nothing but modi-
fications, transformations of the planet itself. Everything living is made of the
same matter as the planet and is the act of transformation, of design of the
planet upon itself. It matters little whether they are plants, animals, viruses,
bacteria, or archaea: everything that lives is the result of a transformation of
one and the same flesh, the flesh of Gaia. That is why, in the end, the only
true designer is always and only the Earth itself: it is the Earth that transforms itself, in every act of modification of the world. And it is only when we
come to integrate this idea that design can be all the way eco-responsible or
rather geo-responsible, responsible to Gaia.

This is why design can no longer think of itself as being in opposition to
nature but must think of itself as coinciding with nature itself. We pay too
little attention to it, but the word nature comes from the Latin verb to be
born (nasci). Nature is not the collection of things that are different from us,
it is not even the collection of things that are not artificial, produced, because
even animals or plants are somehow made, produced. Nature is the collection of things that come into being by birth: of all those things that have to
be born in order to exist. What is common between pandas or pangolins,
oaks or porcini, tomatoes, wheat, humans, bacteria, archaea, dogs, cats, or

Prologue xxi

mice is the fact that they are all born. Now, it is by no means trivial to have to be born in order to exist and being born is by no means a synonym for existing. In fact, to be born means that a living thing had to take matter that was already alive: to be forced to take the flesh and life of another living thing in order to exist, or rather literally recycle the flesh of others. Being part of nature means this: having to be born in order to exist, not being able to afford anything other than second-hand life, life already used, flesh already lived, even if for other purposes, and use it for other desires, for other experiences. Individuals (but actually also species) do not stop passing flesh to each other. Birth is this recycling process whereby each living thing uses the forms set up by others and each species uses the bodies of other species in order to build itself up. It is this carnal continuity of all living things and all species that makes life and technology (or life and design) synonymous: living always means inheriting and rehashing another's form, having to readjust and redesign a life, a body, a planet that was not born for us.

I am reminded of an observation made by a German philosopher of the last century, Alfred Sohn Rethel, who on a visit to Naples wrote an illuminating essay on the relationship of Neapolitans to technology: observing the way in which a broken object was used for purposes totally different from the one for which it was made, Sohn Rethel wrote that things in Naples begin to function when they are broken. It is the same in nature: flesh – the flesh of the living and the flesh of the Earth – functions when it is broken, when it is able to pass from one subject to another, when, in short, it is recycled. The flesh of all living things has nothing private; it is currency of exchange between living things belonging to the most diverse kingdoms, because it is the only flesh on the planet, with which we build ourselves, others, and modify with our most imperceptible breath the Earth.

In short, there is no difference between life and technique. It cannot be given because of the fact that we are born: technique is the consequence, the fate to which the fact that we are born compels us, that is, the fact that we have had to take on someone else's form, and in the human case, a mixed form, an already broken form. Everything is already repair and readjustment. If life and design coincide, it is because everything is always broken, everything is always already used. That is why a pure form is never given but always and only renegotiation of a form. And it is only through this renegotiation that living things can give life to one another.

Giving birth is this active production of continuity, this design of continuity: to be a mother is to be able to circulate one's flesh in the life of one who does not say I in the same way as her, to make the same flesh the site of a multiplicity of I's. Conversely, birth is this: to say I in a flesh that had already said I differently. Birth is this carnal, physical continuity with bodies we have nothing to do with. My flesh belonged to my mother and father and before that to my grandmother and grandfather. Which means, for example, that the life that animates my body is much older than my own body: I am

xxii *Prologue*

46 now, but the life that allows me to speak was already 30 when I was born because my mother was that age. But she was also born, meaning she inherited a life that was already alive. And so on to the first mother, to the first Eve. But she too was born, she was not created out of nothing: she had to appropriate an already living life that belonged to another species, to that of a primate. Birth therefore produces a continuity not only between mother and son or daughter but between an individual and an infinite number of other individuals who do not belong to the same species. Which means that our age is that of life on Earth. We are both very young and very ancient. And that is why every act of design (that is, every act of life) is a form of rewriting the entire history of the planet.

However, this also means that each of us broods a flesh whose origins have nothing human about them. Each and every one of you because of this continuity produced by birth finds pieces of infinite other species within your body. Because of birth, each species transmits a life that began before it into other forms, just as each man transmits not only lives but also forms that existed before his birth. These previous lives live in us and are present. We are the reincarnation of other species. We are the recycling, the second time of other species. We are the design act of all species in evolutionary history. To experience this, just look in the mirror: the eyes, the mouth, the nose, the ears – we share all these organs with thousands of other species. This means, for example, that our bodies give us access to a life that is not essentially human. We are a kind of walking zoo. We are biodiverse in ourselves; we do not need to relate to other living things to experience biodiversity.

From this point of view, the identity between life and design allows us to also understand the scope, power, and therefore also the responsibility of design. If every time we manipulate any portion of matter all we are doing is borrowing and using the agency of the one and only true designer who is the planet, in what we do what is at stake is the very form and life of all species. The set of these essays charts a series of pathways to design that is thought of as the very movement through which living things, for billions of years, have been trying to shape themselves and the world around them. And it is by the ability to follow the paths traced in these pages that the future of the planet will be decided.

Emanuele Coccia, October, 2022

Note

1 Lamarck, Hydrogéologie, ou Recherches sur l'influence qu'ont les eaux sur la surface du globe terrestre, sur les causes de l'existence du bassin des mers, de son déplacement et de son transport successif sur les différens points de la surface de ce globe, enfin sur les changemens que les corps vivans exercent sur la nature et l'état de cette surface, Paris 1802.

Introduction: Design for more-than-human futures

Towards post-anthropocentric and decolonial perspectives

Martín Tironi

In June 2021, the Chilean Pavilion won first place at the London Design Biennale. Titled "Tectonic Resonances from the South: From User-Centred Design to Planet-Centred Design," the pavilion explored opportunities to redefine our ways of relating to the planet through design. Through a sonorous intervention with lithophones sourced from several Chilean quarries, the pavilion's creators sought to reconnect the practice of design to the materiality of the planet using one of its earliest technologies: stones tools. This curatorial experience of a radical return to the past sought to revitalise a decolonial way of feeling and thinking, proposing a language that expands design opportunities in the face of our current environmental unsustainability. While the origins of design are traditionally anchored in the European industrial revolution, to a modern narrative of linear progress that has proposed instrumentalising the planet to achieve more human worlds, the pavilion was conceived as an invitation to situate design in a more-than human horizon: a practice that should explore ways of coexisting in correspondence (Ingold, 2020) with the designs, interventions, and forces developed by other species and agencies. There is certainly an ironic gesture here: a pavilion on a decolonial and not anthropocentric design exhibited in London, the epicentre of European imperialism and modern rationality. However, rather than attempting a sort of return to postcolonial purism, we are interested in generating border interventions and hybrid spaces in which the conceptualisation and practices of design emerge from the co-construction of forms of knowledge and gazes.

The intention of this book is to expand on some of the premises and reflections behind the construction of that pavilion. It brings together authors from different fields and disciplines to address opportunities for engaging in a form of design that is involved with new narratives that interrogate the reign of the anthropocentric and blaze paths towards protecting other post-extractivist epistemologies. At a time of environmental crises in which the human species is threatening its own survival and the highest level of exacerbation of the idea of a future and technological innovation, it is important to discard certain anthropocentric categories in order to situate design beyond the role

DOI: 10.4324/9781003319689-1

2 Martín Tironi

that it has traditionally held in the capitalist world, creating opportunities to build more just and sustainable worlds.

Design for more-than-human futures is an invitation to travel new paths for design framed by an ethics of more-than-human coexistence that breaks with the unsustainability installed in the designs that outfit our lives. In the face of increasingly uncertain futures monopolised by techno-intelligent prediction which tends to limit the conversation around opportunities to those which currently exist, it is crucial to develop undisciplined and pluriversal approaches (Escobar, 2018) that allow us to project shared life alternatives. While today more than ever the speed and radicalness of socio-environmental changes make it increasingly difficult to be part of them (Latour, 2017a), design cannot be a mere spectator, nor can it continue to replicate clientelist and instrumentalist strategies for relating to the world.

Questioning the notion of *human-centred design* is central to this discussion. It is not only a theoretical and methodological concern, but an ethical need to critically rethink the modern, colonialist, and anthropocentric inheritance that resonates in design culture. As its various chapters demonstrate, the book is situated in the contemporary discussion regarding how to rethink design from a post-anthropocentric and decolonial way of making, thinking, and feeling. The authors share the need to interrupt what design has been doing from a modern-colonial epistemological matrix.

One of the premises that cuts across this book is that the scenario of multi-system crisis that we are moving through (social, environmental, public health, economic, etc.) demands a renewed capacity for design to imagine and make possible alternative futures. The unsustainability and environmental crisis that we are experiencing is not the fortuitous result of bad decisions. Rather, it is the product of specific designs that are deeply rooted in our ways of relating to and inhabiting the world, materialised in products, services or experiences. This points to the importance of generating a process of "inverse engineering" or ontological detoxification (De la Cadena and Escobar, in this book), which allow us to undesign the elements behind the dynamics of unsustainability.

The practice of design should explore and experiment with new sustainable ways of relating to and being in the world, forming different modes of problematising the present and imagining futures. As other authors (Escobar, 2018; Fry, 2020) have argued, there is a need to interrogate or, rather, *redesign* the culture of design in its ontological, methodological, and ethical spheres. If we truly want to counteract the process of defuturing that we are experiencing, which consists of creating futures without futures, as Tony Fry (2020) puts it, we cannot continue to inform design using ways of thinking that have already been structured, classified, and disciplined in the modern-colonialist cannon. On the contrary—and this is the call made in this book—we believe that design must be capable of developing speculative thought (Coccia, 2018), thought based on a break with the current

Introduction: Design for more-than-human futures 3

development model that manages to make available ways of projecting more inclusive environments with the various entities that co-inhabit our planet.

This introduction is organised as follows: the first section addresses the ecological crisis that forces us to question the suppositions, practices, and values upon which modern design was founded. In the second section, I propose three operations or displacements: (a) planet-oriented design; (b) pluralising future regimes; and (c) decolonising the practices of design for an ethics of reparation. I seek to use these displacements to explore how design can become a means to imagine other ways of inhabiting the world and containing the damage associated with the modern-colonialist system. Finally, I describe the chapters included in this book.

Designing on a planetary disaster

The escalating ecosystemic crisis that we have experienced over the past few years has generated an urgent need to examine the foundations of design (Fry & Nocek, 2020). Furthermore, the COVID-19 pandemic, which has shaken the social and economic order in an unprecedented manner, has exacerbated the experience of global civilising crisis and revealed the need to mobilise alternatives to the dominant ways of projecting lifestyles (Manzini & Menichinelli, 2021).

Various forces have developed over the past few years to understand the importance of human activity in the acceleration of the dynamics of crisis and deterioration of the land macro-environment. As many academics have noted, one important concept for understanding the scope and impacts of this process—due to the lack of a more adequate one—is the Anthropocene (Crutzen, 2006; Bonneuil & Fressoz, 2013; Latour, 2017b; Ferrando, 2016), the most recent geological period on Earth which has been influenced by humans, or anthropogenised.

This notion gives way to attempts to explain or give meaning to the capacity that we have as a species to leave a scar on our planet's geological history. Scholars have argued that humans have been capable of moving from being just another biological agent to being a geological force, marking a stratigraphic layer on the terrestrial mantle (Bonneuil & Fressoz, 2013). Humans have ceased to be conditioned by the environment, and our species has now become an agent that conditions the land system. This notion places humans alongside the forces that participated in forming the planet as we know it and led to a present in ruins that will inevitably end without us (Stengers & Goffey, 2015). Or, as the late Latour states, what happens to the planet is not in the future, but is happening now, and no matter what we do to contain it, the threat will remain with us for centuries (2015).

Recognising the usefulness of the concept coined as the basis for the construction of ways of making and thinking that are more sensitive to the environmental crisis, it seems important to clarify the limits that this

4 Martín Tironi

notion presents for rethinking possible futures (Haraway, 2016, 2018). The homogenisation of responsibility is the first problem, in that it tends to assume a universalisation of a life system. We must remember that we would need five Earths if we were to maintain the level of consumption of the average US citizen and we continue to move forward with this development model. As such, various authors speak to the need to recognise different levels of responsibility that fall on human action, making the necessary distinctions to understand the modes of life that reaffirm ecological damage (Bonneuil & Fressoz, 2013; Altvater et al., 2016). It is not a question of listing and assigning blame, but of recognising that it is a unique and contextualised—both ontologically and epistemologically—form of being human and making a world that is in crisis and turning around this loss of relational worlds of being in the world (Escobar, 2018; Fry & Nocek, 2020). As such, while the influence of humanity on the environment has always existed, many point to capitalist modernity as the accelerator of this dynamic of ecosystem transformation. In a strict sense, we should be discussing the capitalocene period (Haraway, 2016).

Several authors have shown that our capitalist modernity is inseparable from the process of colonisation (De la Cadena, 2015; Escobar, 2018) and its capacity to expand a particular understanding and valorisation of the planet and all of its more-than-human components, in which the latter are conceived of as mere resources for the satisfaction of human needs.[1] From this perspective, the Earth becomes an object of appropriation, exploitation, and consumption, forgetting, as Tim Ingold would say, its condition as the foundation for all that lives (2020). In his book *Facing Gaia* (2017) regarding the new climate system that the Anthropocene represents, Bruno Latour shows a willingness to emancipate humans from Earth, excluding or denying the relationship of mutual co-dependence and relational interdependence between humans and the environment.

There is no question that the position that design has occupied in this context is marked by its function as a tool for acting out and executing this specific way of understanding, defining, and exploiting Earth. Unsustainability is not limited to a matter of ideological principles. It is also designed and expressed through concrete designs. Some authors argue that the modern-colonial system has imposed certain limits on the way in which design is practiced, turning design into a negative ontology, that is, a design that does not problematise its strategies of production, intervention, and relationships that it establishes with its surroundings (Tlostanova, 2017; Vazquez, 2017; Fry, 2020). This Anthropocene perspective focused on the satisfaction of human desires of certain characteristics has impacted the socio-ecological dynamics on multiple scales, to the point that many aspects of biodiversity have been reconfigured and even eliminated because of our intervention (Altvater et al., 2016).

The history and urgency are clear: environmental degradation, prolonged droughts, the advance of desertification, the extinction of multiple species

Introduction: Design for more-than-human futures 5

due to the loss of ecosystems, pollution, higher temperatures, the expansion of pandemics and their consequences for social gaps. The stamp of modern living has been structured under an expectation of exponential growth that is directly related to a need to increase industrial capacity to support consumption and population growth patterns (Altvater et al., 2016). This world view of linear growth and a future based on consumption also implies an expansion of a fictitious experience in which the border of possibilities continues to extend itself based on a sanctification of technological development, leading us to believe that the planet and its multiple ecosystems are capable of absorbing everything we decide to throw at it and design. To put it more directly, we live under the idea that the development model will deploy technical tools that can compensate for environmental losses and damages without questioning the ethical and moral exigencies that this challenge poses (Pelluchon, 2020).

This techno-optimist illusion that has developed over the past few years has not only crumbled through the accumulation of catastrophic events that surpass the limits of the technological capacity to understand them. It also has created a driving need to identify conceptual tools and actions that can make us project futures for coexistence with Earth, alternative and more sustainable ways of inhabiting. However, it is important to note that to date the ecological crisis has mainly been considered a technical problem under the expectation that technological development will provide answers to the multi-systemic crisis that we are facing. We know that the current environmental crisis makes us examine our models for making and inhabiting the world in a much deeper way and that the discussion of their solutions cannot be reduced.

This is where design can play a key role, developing tools for creating worlds and rethinking our relationship with the environment. There are currently many initiatives and projects that show that design is experiencing a particularly vital and generative moment, expanding the political discussion on possible worlds, and contributing to counteracting the negative effects of the extractivist and instrumental logic of our relationship with the environment. Everything suggests that the current socio-environmental crisis requires reimagining or de-designing nearly every aspect of modern lifestyle, exploring actions that allow us to project more sustainable and inclusive futures.

In this regard, approaches such as decolonial design (Tlostanova, 2017; Fry, 2020), autonomous design (Escobar, 2018), transition design (Irwin et al., 2015) and design justice (Costanza-Chock, 2018) as well as interspecies approaches (Coccia, 2018; Tironi & Hermansen, 2020) are of particular interest. Without overlooking the differences between these approaches, one interest that these perspectives share is the importance of challenging the conventional role that design has been given as a decorative technique or functional action. Instead, we must position it as a political role in discussions on social justice, social innovation, ecological or decolonial transitions,

6 *Martín Tironi*

etc. In short, design must become involved with efforts to problematise how we inhabit the world and connect with others. As Escobar argues in *Design for Pluriverse*, today design must participate more actively in questioning the social systems that nurture our current anthropocentric development system, generating conditions for projecting plural, post-capitalist, post-patriarchal and post-human communities.

In the pages that follow, I propose four displacements or operations that design can activate to contain/respond to the damage associated with the modern-colonial way of conceiving of design.

Towards a planetary design

Over the past few years, the idea of human-centred design has invaded the practices, discourses, and discussions about design. This approach has become one of the most influential axioms over the past few years and has catapulted design into the sphere of public policy (Holeman & Kane, 2020), organisations and services (Meroni & Sangiorgi, 2011).

The idea of user-centred design does not only circulate as one of the epistemological foundations of the main schools of design around the world but has also become the bar used to measure good design. This has led to the development of all manner of products, solutions and innovations based on this approach. This trend has managed to amplify itself through the introduction of the design thinking approach, which proposes various steps (empathise, define, ideate, prototype and test) for identifying problems, needs and possible solutions (Giacomin, 2014).

One of the main theories of this axiom is that design should respond to the needs, concerns, and desires of the user, responding through products, services and solutions that are friendly to users' needs. Under this premise, all design processes must define the identity, interactions, and visions of the receivers' world prior to engaging in any formal development. This allows design to inscribe scenarios of action or scripts (Akrich, 1987) on the product that are appropriate for the needs of the people involved. In the end, this translates into the formulation of a certain type of "compatible" user. We could thus say that this turn has humanised design, seeking to translate, represent, interpret, and intervene in the material and symbolic environments in which humans act.

While user-centred design has created important contributions and innovations, everything suggests that this paradigm should be questioned in the context of our current environmental crisis. The complexity of the current challenges suggests that the notion of human-centred—and its focus on human protagonists—is insufficient to think and make in the face of the challenges of the Anthropocene and digital society, making it necessary to begin to design from relational and ecological approaches that are more open to unforeseeable events and the changing stakeholders that are to come.

Introduction: Design for more-than-human futures 7

Beyond the legitimate critiques that have been made in this regard that user-centred design tends to label participants as relatively stable and static entities (Ricci, 2019), it seems fundamental to recognise the need to decentre design from the human, rethinking its capacities and scopes in the face of interspecies environments and worlds. The idea of a constant linear evolution in which the future of inhabiting depends on human design is called into question when human inhabitants seem to have come to the brink of collapse and are pushed by other forces and more-than-human agents. Concretely, we question the idea of viewing major cities as the pinnacle of humanity and focusing the design of inhabitable orbits on the capacity to build and expand cities as centres of consumption.

While over the past few decades the interest in exploring the notion of coexistence beyond human limits (Stengers, 2005; Latour, 2007; Coccia, 2018) has been highlighted, in the design field we find limited work on exploring forms of coexistence between humans and more-than-humans. The efforts that exist in this area share a desire to explore experimental and speculative tools to understand the citizenship of more-than-human entities (Binder et al., 2015; Lenskjold & Jönsson, 2017; Forlano, 2017) or understand how more-than-human agencies become part of the design process (Rice, 2018; Tironi & Hermansen, 2018; Wakkary, 2021). These studies also share the assessment regarding the marked instrumental, individualist, and anthropocentric nature of human-centred design, encouraging us to question community-oriented designs and more-than-human environments. This leads to questions such as: How can one approach design not merely from the idea of "design opportunity" or that of "users' needs," but from the alignments and intersections between humans and the environment (Ingold, 2020)? How can we incorporate the making of design into a relational world and go beyond the human (Kohn, 2013), where multiple epistemes and cosmos participate at the same time?

The notion of planet-oriented design developed in the context of the Chilean Pavilion at the 2021 London Biennale takes up the need to expand the scale and range of political action of design, exploring the epistemic and ontological bases of human-oriented design.[2] That is, a design that is no longer oriented towards stable and discrete human entities, but that is open to the composition of relational and "other-than-human" worlds (Lien & Pálsson, 2019; Savransky, 2021) in which the focus is on the ecology of human and more-than-human relationships that sustain the diversity of life. Given that the notion of modern design has mainly been based on an individualist and utilitarian logic, the question is how to project post-anthropocentric design guided by an ethics of coexistence between the diversity of experiences, materialities and beings that inhabit the planet (Latour, 2012; De La Bellacasa, 2017; Vazquez, 2017). Such a design would make it possible to move from a rationalist logic that understands beings as static to a logic of becoming (Ingold, 2017) in which the value is placed on the web of partial interdependencies and interconnections that comprise the problem.

8   *Martín Tironi*

Moving from human-centred design to planet-oriented design is not a call to forget human problems or much less to turn it into a matter of an elite that is exhibited in galleries. On the contrary, it is a question of recognising that worlds "exceed" modern categories (De la Cadena, 2015) and thus require other designs to offer a mechanism for listening to realities that cannot be reduced to the nomenclature of "user," "service," or "strategy." As such, it is a question of establishing a more determined commitment between design and the multi-systemic and interrelated crises that we are experiencing, generating the actions necessary to project a more inclusive and relational emerging civilisation (Manzini, 2015). Repositioning design beyond the human means opening up the possibility of exploring instruments, practices and theories that allow one to think or repair the world in the face of increasingly devastating anthropogenic forces (Pelluchon, 2020) in which humans and more-than-humans, technologies and vegetables, tsunamis and animals, data and viruses are involved. Recognising the incapacity of Eurocentric critical thinking to project post-capitalist alternatives or to define the possible beyond the frameworks established by the current development system (Escobar, 2018), design presents a speculative capacity to open multiple futures in harmony with the heterogeneous realities and height of contemporary ecosystemic challenges in which the very notion of humanity is challenged by technological developments and ongoing socio-ecological disasters.

Isabelle Stengers' cosmopolitical proposal (2005) is a fundamental reference for thinking through the implications and reaches of the notion of planet-oriented design. Stengers (2005) and Latour (2007) have argued in favour of opening the traditional notion of politics to a "cosmopolitics." This forces us to rethink political action from an "ontological pluralism," opening itself up to new types of human-environmental relationships. It is a more-than-human concept of politics in which instead of limiting this notion to a substantialist enunciation, it analyses how other entities (animals, rivers, technologies, rocks, vegetables, etc.) can be invested with certain qualities that allow them to resist, diagram and produce political events. This involves challenging how materiality (and other entities) are conceived of as elements subjected to human purposes and, on the contrary, taking the autonomy that objects and more-than-human entities may present seriously. As Isabelle Stengers notes, the cosmopolitical proposal contains a question regarding how "designing the political scene" protects us from anthropocentric egotism according to which "humans of good will decide in the name of the general interest" (Stengers, 2005: 1002).

As such, rethinking a notion of politics that is not limited to managing exclusively human interests is not only a philosophical matter, but a matter of design (Tironi & Hermansen, 2018). The idea of planet-oriented design seeks to address this need and to explore a form of decentring through co-design operations that allow other entities that have become invisible to be included. The invitation is thus to project a design not for the problems of a particular

Introduction: Design for more-than-human futures 9

body that has been posited as universal (male, white, heterosexual, of a certain socio-cultural and economic condition) that lives in a specific context (the modern city). Rather, we should understand design's potential as a relational space in which each of our interventions have both positive and negative impacts that go beyond our own corporality, episteme, and ontology. It is therefore necessary to become conscious of how our way of designing and living in the world comes up against and conflicts with other more-than-human entities and bodies with whom we share the planet.

The work of Ståhl et al. (2017) shows us how archaeology has found evidence of complex forms of humans inhabiting the world that emerged before capitalism and allowed for creation and design that sought balance with those more-than-human agencies and agents, allowing us to identify and come back together with design projects that were silenced by capitalism. This exercise presented by the authors allows us to break with the concept of Design as a discipline that comes from the consolidation of capitalism and gives us an opening onto referents that we were ignoring and that can shed light on lines of communication that can be established with other ways of making and living in the world.

Over the past few years, we have seen how these ontological clashes continue to grow and become more radical. Together with the series of catastrophic events that have taken place over the past few years, the COVID-19 pandemic has shown how more-than-human agencies and bodies can inundate the reality that we have built and designed thinking only of our bodies and ways of being. Like most of the bodies and beings that are hardly perceived (Lewis et al., 2018), the virus often has no name in our world system and goes beyond the ontological parameters that define the limits of the real and possible (De la Cadena, 2018). However, as these entities and beings manifest, they call into question our ways of living, as we have seen with the pandemic. The experience of the past few years shows us how these agencies of invisible beings and bodies become an uncontrollable problem for institutions. They escape our epistemologies, and we make the decision to ignore them until it becomes impossible to continue to do so. These agencies are often placed in a subordinate position because our categories cannot translate and capture them (Blaser, 2012). As Helmreich (2008) argues, the nature of beings that are hardly perceived such as bacteria or viruses has a complexity that escapes the capacity for human understanding. However, upon becoming aware of their implications for our ways of living -as is the case of COVID-19 we can understand the fragility of our own existence, showing how these subjects can destroy our world without even wanting to.

From this perspective, Latour's proposal of creating spaces for listening to and addressing these agencies as "matters of concern" (2004), suggests the need to mobilise design as a mechanism for projecting and experiencing modes of coexistence on earth. Recognising that we are earthly before we are human, as we constantly evolve with other beings that co-inhabit the earth

10 *Martín Tironi*

(Latour, 2017b), the question is how to establish alliances and collaborations with other earthly actors, respecting their singularities and not reducing them to human designs. As such, one of the challenges of planet-oriented design is precisely to promote modes through which these ignored agencies and corporalities can be incorporated into the political debate. It is not only a question of anticipating conflicts and establishing patterns of peaceful coexistence (Latour, 2017a), but also of designs that allow us to recognise how these same agencies and bodies can redesign the environments that we inhabit (Coccia, 2018). As a continuation of this proposal, philosopher Maria Puig de la Bellacasa (2017) presents the notion of "matters of care," endowing these agencies with a presence and importance in daily human life and recognising their role as agents that can escape and impact human corporalities. When we recognise that the question of habitability no longer only depends on human rationalities and interests, but on relearning to establish alliances and collaborations with earthly actors that co-inhabit the planet, an ethical responsibility for design to activate forms of attachment with this heterogeneous territory that cannot be reduced to human logics emerges.

Pluralising regimes of the future

The second displacement that I will develop to contain the damage associated with the modern-colonialist system of understanding design has to do with problematising the notion of future that informs and has guided most of the practice of design.

Over the past few years, we have experienced an inflation of analysis of the idea of future. In the current context of social, economic, and environmental crisis, a rich discussion of the futures that are possible for humanity has opened, and various assessments and ideas about what could be done to address these crises have been developed. While there has always been significant interest in understanding and estimating the future, we are in the presence of a true market of futures, with all manner of sophisticated technologies, protocols and methodologies focused on understanding and anticipating futures.

The pandemic has radicalised this need to pre-design the future given the growing sensation of a lack of reference for a certain and stable tomorrow. Various authors have noted that contemporary society has probably never been as future oriented as it is now due to the growing uncertainty regarding the future of society and the collapse of the planet (Bryant & Knight, 2019).

Between the various spaces of development and the emergence of "futurological work," we find two fields that are undergoing significant expansion: the first linked to the development of predictive systems based on artificial intelligence (AI) and the second is a renewed interest in what are called Future Studies (Mazé, 2019) in different fields of knowledge.

Introduction: Design for more-than-human futures 11

Over the past few years, we have seen a true socio-technical imaginary emerge around the predictive and anticipatory capacities of algorithmic systems based on AI. Thanks to the progress made by algorithmic systems that estimate future behaviours based on current or past data (Big Data) left behind by people or events, it is said that we are experiencing new "systems of anticipation" (Adams et al., 2009) in which the idea of future becomes something that can be manipulated and calculated through the prediction of smart systems. Authors like Rouvroy and Berns (2013) have noted that AI systems are computing all possible futures and preparing actions in the present in order to neutralise risks. These "defuturisation techniques" that provide greater security do not only tend to reduce the variety of future possibilities, but also lead to a process of rationalisation and economisation of the future. "Products of prediction" or "futures markets" (Zuboff, 2019) thus usher in the expansion of mechanisms of predicting the future. While the promoters of these predictive systems present their operations as "objective" and perfectly democratic facts (without references to exclusions based on class, religion, or gender), it is essential to politicise and pluralise future systems at a time that is increasingly controlled by these automated systems. In other words, we must critically examine the hierarchies, biases and concepts of the world that materialise in these initiatives based on algorithmic prediction, recognising the role that they can play in design to generate future alternatives.

But together with the expansion of these predictive systems based on Big Data and AI, over the past few years there has been a great deal of interest in crossing design with the field of Future Studies, developing different approaches and methods for prospecting and packaging futures. These future design methods are being used a great deal in the world of innovation, design thinking and policymaking, and have allowed design to successfully enter the realm of prospecting and forecasting. However, and without intending to be exhaustive, these future studies demonstrate clear limitations when it comes to exploring problematising paths that allow future systems to be decolonised and pluralised.

First, recognising the potential that these approaches have for decision-making in the organisational field, these perspectives focus on creating certainties about the future instead of tensing or questioning it (Ricci, 2019). Along these lines, these studies are dominated by an effort to "package" methodologies -many of them hyper-rationalist- that allow experts to capture scenarios and identify the plausibility of certain trends in terms of being reproduced in the future. For example, the "futures cone" (from Voros, 2008) is very common in business circuits and prospective studies, and there are four types of them: possible (might happen), plausible (could happen), probable (likely to happen) and preferred (want to happen).

As several authors have shown (Forlano & Mathew, 2014; Angheloiu et al., 2017), these studies tend to be limited to the exploration of future

12 Martín Tironi

products or services for commercial purposes or for the development of business strategies, and they tend to leave aside the political and performative aspects involved in the mobilisation of images of the future. As Mazé (2019) states, the exercise of projecting futures is a political act in that it involves a valorisation, certain moral, cultural and social preferences, and conditions what could be. In other words, there is a trend in these approaches to reproduce the status quo and not think from alterity, from futures discarded by certain hegemonic cannons. In their effort to generate or package certain certainties about future trends to generate comparative advantages or minimise risks, many of these approaches lose sight of the discussion of the implications of mobilising socio-material configurations of futures, moving away from the transformative and problematising objective that we need in our current time of crisis.

Tensing futures

If we really wish to take the socio-environmental causes of the global pandemic and environmental crisis seriously, we cannot continue to inform the prefiguration of futures from the same thought systems that are being questioned in innovation, unlimited growth, and technological development. It is thus necessary to critique the dominant notion of the future that governs the world of innovation and design.

A concept of the future is circulating that is anchored to the modern and colonial idea of an always prosperous future that offers growing opportunities. Here future is nearly synonymous with progress and development (Escobar, 2014), emphasising an abstract and abundant future emancipated from the tradition and the past, where the modern surpasses the non-modern, denying attachments and relationships to the Earth and the past. This hegemonic concept of time that is unique to modernity as a monoculture because it excludes the differences, multiplicity, and other modes of experiencing temporalities.

In his latest book, *Oú atterrir* (2017b), Bruno Latour discusses the new climate regime that the Anthropocene represents, a planet that this particular universalist and linear concept that is part of the project of the moderns has taken to the will of emancipating humans from earth, excluding or denying a mutual relationship of co- and interdependence between humans and the environment. It is thus a unidirectional and profoundly Anthropocene concept of the future in which the value of the future is oriented towards generating a world at the service of human interests.

The installation of this hegemonic future anchored to the idea of progress and promoted by the extraordinary force of modern capitalism does not only cancel out the creation of alternative futures, but also eliminates the critical capacity to prefigure alternatives. In its permanent capacity to reinvent itself (Boltanski & Chiapello, 1999), modern capitalism defines the limits of the real and the possible. The installation of this concept of totalising

Introduction: Design for more-than-human futures 13

future stands as an obstacle to alterity, projecting from other world views, aesthetics, and realities.

A decolonial view of the future or, if one prefers, the task of challenging the globalising coloniality, should start from assuming that the deficit or lack of future does not only have to do with exhausting the modern idea of progress (Latour, 2013) but also is related to a situation in which the future folds or is encapsulated by an omnipresent present. This is a future that does not require a project and becomes a form of expansion of the present in which there is really no alternative to that which exists. This becomes totalising—a "continuous present," as Day (2023) call it, that captures the ability to narrate and desire other possible worlds. It is a presentified future in which the present becomes everything that exists in the real, generating futures that are already exhausted.

Projecting decolonial futures or futures from the South also involves taking seriously the idea developed by the anthropologist Arjun Appadurai (2013): the future is neither unique nor shared by everyone, nor is it a political matter. Rather, it is a contested field, as multiple socio-material configurations seek to organise and mobilise ideas of the future.

In this regard, the design philosopher Tony Fry (2020) calls on the design world to produce "futures that have futures" by stopping the process of "defuturisation" that tends to cancel the emergence of other worlds, eliminating the opportunity to access counter-hegemonic futures. We must build tools that make it possible to open those windows onto alternative futures, not to anticipate, calculate or capitalise them, but to create alternatives to unsustainable or inequitable ways of inhabiting the planet (De la Cadena & Blaser, 2018). The strategies developed in the fields of fiction and speculative design (Dunne & Raby, 2013; Smith et al., 2016; Wilkie et al., 2017; Tharp & Tharp, 2019) that seek to create experiences of defamiliarisation, alienation or tension to redirect norms and provoke discussions of alternative futures or presents are very interesting for prefiguring those decolonial future alternatives. On a more pragmatic level, some are creating tools to visualise sustainable transitions (Fuad-Luke, 2013; Irwin et al., 2015; Wilkie et al., 2015; Gaziulusoy et al., 2019), or to generate fictional prototypes that help question the relationship with the given (Forlano & Mathew, 2014) or to create relational spaces between humans and more-than-humans (Binder et al., 2015; Lenskjold & Jönsson 2017; Tironi & Hermansen, 2020).

More-than-human futures

A decolonial design or design from the South, as Escobar (2018) puts it, should generate tools for moving towards the idea of more-than-human futures (Tironi & Hermansen, 2018, 2020; Granjou & Salazar, 2016; De la Cadena, 2018). That is, questioning the future category confined to the 'human club' (Stengers, 2005) is undoubtedly one of the most important shifts if we want to think about our conditions of habitability.

14 *Martín Tironi*

The practice of design has depended on an anthropocentric modern tradition to a great extent, taking up the ontological dualism between nature and society (Latour, 2013) and responding critically to the impetus of appropriation and dominion of nature. This dualism, which tends to address nature as an object and society as a subject (Descola, 1996, 2001) finds its maximum expression in the advent of the Anthropocene, producing a loss of relational and ecological modes of inhabiting (Coccia, 2018).

One of the pending challenges is to explore a design for futures oriented in a post-dualist practice and ethics in which the designed futures are not solely for human purposes. In other words, it involves projecting worlds in which humans, and more-than-humans can coexist, enriching each other in an interspecies process of correspondence (De la Cadena & Blaser, 2018; Ingold, 2020). If design traditionally points to how to achieve more human futures, favouring white men and seriously impacting the nature of the planet, a challenge for decolonial design would be assuming that futures are not exclusively designed by humans or for humans, but for multi-species, shared futures and designed with technological agencies, plants, viruses, telluric forces, rivers, traditions, etc. in mind (Granjou & Salazar, 2016; Coccia, 2018). Looking at the worldmaking capacity of different entities (Tsing, 2015) is not only a call to humility in design, but also a matter of being open to projecting new modes of more just and sustainable coexistence.

Repositioning design in discussions of more-than-human futures is an unavoidable ethical responsibility. It is also an invitation to explore design's capacities to repair the world in the face of increasingly devastating anthropogenic forces. Designing for more-than-human futures means moving from a techno-paternalist logic that seeks to domesticate the planet, and move to a relational logic, in which heterogeneous actors can collaborate to create interspecies connections or disconnection.

Decolonising design practices for an ethics of reparations

At a time of searching for modes of emancipation from industrial design and new epistemologies that allow us to rethink our modes of habitability, there is a renewed interest in developing design practices from critical and decolonial approaches. It has become urgent to gather epistemologies and practices framed by plural ethics that recognise worlds and world views that are often excluded from what is now hegemonic design. As Escobar (2018) argues, the challenge of moving towards decolonial design is not only a theoretical issue. Rather, it points to facing and taking up the socio-environmental responsibilities that design has had in the damages that we currently experience as planet.

However, one cannot continue to think about design's "responsibility" from mere diligence or professional correctness when developing a product or service. Design should engage with power relations that are established in the same form of producing and projecting and that are constantly expressed

Introduction: Design for more-than-human futures   15

in certain decisions and the consequences of using design. This problem is what Sasha Costanza-Chock attempts to address in her study *Design Justice* (2018), where design is conceived of as a tool for liberation of oppressed groups even as she recognises the intersectionality of perspectives for discussion and the web of injustices present in the context in which it is inserted. As Arturo Escobar (2018) argues, the configuration of relationships of subordination has its roots in an epistemology and ontology that determines the type of solutions that are developed in the face of the ecological crisis.

Many of the solutions that circulate in conscious consumption, responsible design, or circular design today, inevitably fall into the parameters inscribed in this extractivist matrix. These theoretical attempts to resolve the socio-environmental crisis aligning with the dominant ontology—and responsible for many of our problems—end up reproducing the conditions that limit our understanding to address and explore problems (Haraway, 2016). This leads to the search for the solution being captured by that which is its cause, imposing limitations for taking up and repairing the damages created by human activity.

The attempts that have emerged from the global South in response to the project of the late capitalism of the Global North and its unique form of design claim those ontologies and epistemologies that are sought out and invisible and that modernisation and development projects tried to eradicate after the consolidation of postcolonial states. Authors like Colombia's Arturo Escobar (see also Gutiérrez Borrero, 2015, 2020) have been part of the theoretical line of thought that has tried to reposition ontologies and epistemologies from the South, defying the modern/colonial parameters of relating to the world and the earth. One of the hypotheses that emerge from these works is that Euro-Western design, which has gone hand in hand with the capitalist model of development, installed a canonical and universal idea of design that expands, subsuming other forms of making. This leads to an invisibilisation of "designs otherwise," which existed and continue to exist under names and concepts that are different from those of modern design (Gutiérrez Borrero, 2015).

This process of resurgences brings with it new Design proposals. In his book *designs for the pluriverse* (2018), Escobar introduces us to the concept of ontological design—using works by authors like Winograd and Flores (1986) and Willis (2006)—as the conversation between opportunities for active participation in the understanding and creation of subjects (Winograd & Flores, 1986), giving way to new ritual forms, ways of being and modes of making. The main question posed in this proposal revolves around the recognition that the existence of worlds beyond the dualist tradition that relates to the world from instrumentalisation to make room for local designs that help to project pluriversal ways of life oriented towards saving life and the planet instead of its appropriation and domination. In this way, "decolonial pluriversality is decentred and stresses the provinciality of

16 *Martín Tironi*

the universalised Western concepts by constantly juxtaposing them with their incommensurable non-Western parallels and opposites" (Tlostanova, 2017).

This proposal also stems from the work of Tony Fry in his book *Becoming Human by Design* (2012). He argues that the modernising project and its hegemonic consolidation through its unique form of design perpetuates a systemic suppression of forms of relating that do not fit into existing ontological and epistemological parameters, denying other futures and alternatives the opportunity to come into being. In their study *Design and the Question of History* (2015), Fry, Dilnot, and Stewart present us their proposal of "futurisation" as a new system in which multiple futures and thus the agents that make them possible can actively participate in a new pact of inhabitability, counteracting the negative effects of colonisation processes of modernity and their ontology. To put it differently, how can design contribute to decolonising that instrumental and extractivist relationship with the environment and recognise the voice and rights of more-than-human entities, offering more just and sustainable futures?

Designs of care and reparation

There is no doubt that one of the most persistent characteristics of modern/colonial design has been its insistent fascination with innovation (Mohamed et al., 2020). The idea of design for innovation became the mark of contemporary design, and it circulates, conquering spaces in organisations, companies, and academia. As DiSalvo says in his chapter in this book, today more than ever, design is pushed by the need to make something new, to make something that did not exist before, to offer innovation regardless of the contexts or causes. More generally, the discourse of modernisation that has guided design is installed as a world in constant openness to innovation in all fields, always at the service of greater progress for humanity.

Various authors (Gudynas, 2010; De la Cadena, 2015; Escobar, 2018) have insisted that if we want to rethink the extractivist relationship that design establishes with the world and thus halt the ecosystemic damage that we are producing, we must interrogate this cult to the idea of innovation that is unique to the modern story in which humans are located at the cusp of project production. The issue of futures understood under the imperative of indefinite innovation and progress is that they leave aside other modes of approaching and getting involved with the inhabitability of the world, renouncing other ontologies of making the world. When we understand the future as innovation, we only reproduce the modern-colonial and presentist logic of a future that advances, eliminating the relationship with the multiplicity and potential of the past.

This is where the idea of care, maintenance and reparations takes on a central role as a heuristic and political tool to project other, more sustainable forms of inhabiting (De La Bellacasa, 2017). Designing more inhabitable futures in the face of the damage produced by the industrial/extractivist logic should reconsider the practice of maintaining and repairing the world. Developing a more ecological future cannot involve continuing to celebrate innovation and the idea of the project. Rather, it involves thinking about how to de-design the unsustainable ways of life that we have created, calling for an interspecies ethics of care (Haraway, 2016). In response to the dominant *modus operandi* of design culture, which is focused on creation and construction, some authors (Tonkinwise, 2018; Bonnet et al., 2019; Callén & López, 2019; Fry, 2020; Latour, 2020; Lindström & Ståhl, 2020) are examining how design can contribute through "not doing," "elimination," "redoing" or "de-projecting," recreating the conditions for a form of habitability that is coherent with the limitations of the planet. These perspectives are highlighting a shift in design, which is ceasing to be conceived of solely through the prism of production. Scholars are beginning to explore another repertoire of practices and modes of making the world that can contribute to protecting the fragility of the beings that inhabit the planet. In contrast to a culture of design that is focused on the ongoing construction of futures that are decoupled from earthly conditions, there is a need for a design that contributes to slowing down, repairing, or emptying out logics that do not align with the geological trajectory of Earth.

In the face of a planetary ecological crisis, we must challenge the idea of design for innovation and production of the new and explore designs for materialising an ethics of reciprocal care among the entities that live in our environments. As De la Bellacasa says, care is the recognition of an unavoidable condition: we are beings in interdependence who are vulnerable and radically relational. Or, following Ingold (2017), inhabiting is entering into careful correspondence with the development of things. Although it sounds paradoxical, it is likely that we will find the most radical innovation in the practices of reparations and care. We need acts of care, especially when it is urgent to cultivate "the art of living" in a damaged world (Savransky, 2021). There are no inhabitable relationships and places without objects that persist, without ongoing care and repair of our ecologies. The existences that populate our spaces do not persist naturally: if they last, it is because they are cared for, transmitted, and repaired. Inhabiting the world is not about innovating and producing, consuming, and extracting only. It is also about caring and maintaining. We must call for maintenance and care as a design practice that represents a way of being responsible for the relationships that we develop in our environment. It also constitutes a tool for decolonising methods that have limited our opportunities to access natures and ontologies other than human ones (Latour, 2012). It is a mode of recognising what comes before us, of restoring the relationship with alterity and, finally, of building alternative futures.

We could say that these ethics of repair are part of the resurgence of the notions of "Buen Vivir" (Gudynas 2010, 2011; Hidalgo Capitán & Cubillos Guevara, 2014) as a foundation for the relationships that are built with the environment. The Buen Vivir as platform can be understood as a

18 Martín Tironi

political proposal that breaks with the instrumental and extractivist forms of presenting the need for development of Latin America. The recovery of the values of AmerIndian peoples and forms of mutual care that they establish to relate to the environment provide an opportunity to project ways of inhabiting that are not based on over-exploiting our surroundings (Gudynas, 2010).

From this perspective, the ontological and epistemological systems of AmerIndian groups offer an opportunity to dispute and question the modernising-instrumental project and subvert the dependencies built from the Global North. The resurgence of these ontologies contributes to the re-emergence of ways of relating to and transforming the world that are built through mutual care and balance. It is not a question of romanticising or stereotyping the type of relationship that AmerIndian groups had with their surroundings, but one of recognising forms of knowledge that are different from those that are currently dominant. The idea is one of disconnecting design from the uniformity of its expansionist ethos and approaching other world views and forms of coexistence between humans and other species. If the dominant forms of relating to the environment have been designed and inspired by a modern-colonial matrix, it is a matter of beginning to nourish the practice of design from other traditions and spaces.

Questioning projects of accumulation, innovation, and concentration of resources as a Dionysian exercise to satisfy our drives implies projecting new "arts of living." These relationships which are not built on production can be observed in the work of Descola with Ecuador's Ashuar groups (2005). Descola shows that the project of the moderns has a strong tendency to privilege production as a key element for the material conditions of social life, as a central line through which humans can transform nature (Descola, 2001). Descola's argument is that this productivist paradigm of human action in which action appears as a synonymous for manufacturing is not universal or applicable to all communities (Descola, 2001). He shows how the Ashuar present an ontological system in which humanity is understood as one actor in a complex web of bodies that must maintain an equilibrium for the survival of the world. In other words, for that community, the term "agricultural production" would make no sense because the purpose of their activities is not necessarily to create a consumable product that is ontologically separate from the environment that generated it (Wagner, 1991). As Descola says, Ashuar women do not "produce" the plants they grow. Rather, they use them to sustain a relationship of reciprocity and interact with these living beings in an effort to reconcile with their "souls" and promote growth (Descola, 1996, 2001).

The paradigm of production and innovation thus does not allow us to consider this relationship of mutual correspondence that Descola describes, in which the imperative is mutual maintenance and care. AmerIndian groups understand ecosystemic relationships from a holistic perspective. They understand that their needs and ways of intervening with their own life have impacts on the multiple ontologies that coexist and depend on harmonious

Introduction: Design for more-than-human futures 19

coexistence (Descola, 2001). For AmerIndian worlds, all the entities that live together share a common soul that offers the opportunity to be social subjects. From that perspective, bodies are permeated by the relationships that they establish with others and are thus constantly changing based on interactions and effects.

Thinking about design from the idea of care thus implies paying attention to that more-than-human network that sustains life (Puig de la Bella Casa, 2017), evoking a form of design co-constructed and advanced by multiple bodies and agencies. This capacity allows one to leave aside the unidirectionality of modern industrial design, understanding it as a discipline that is no longer focused on the production of a specific object, but on the relationships that it attracts and produces.

In short, on a damaged planet (as Anna Tsing says in Tsing et al., 2017), we must question the idea of a future guided by the ethos of production and innovation and explore futures guided by the art of rehabilitation and reparation, addressing the task of making our world inhabitable and sustainable. Understanding connections of maintenance and care as a practice of future is a form of redesigning our relationship with the world, recognising what precedes us and restoring the relationship with alterity.

Design can serve as a platform for beginning to think about futures for care, that is, a design that is no longer centred on the idea of the individual and autonomous user, but that is oriented towards the different entities that co-inhabit and make our planet. Simply looking at the socio-environmental impacts of capitalist development and production, limited to the epistemology of modern-colonial design guided by the logic of hypergrowth, we can observe the need to generate forms of design that invite detachment, care, de-design, that let us identify the unsustainable elements of our society. We are surprised by the increased frequency of what we decide to call natural disasters—assuming that they escape our control—without recognising that our own designs and projects are causing the imbalance.

The challenge of beginning to repair the consequences of modern design implies recognising all the practices and voices that were made invisible by the Euro-Western order and the beings and ecosystems that have not been considered as design agents and subjects. When we speak of reparation as a possible heuristic alternative for questioning the instrumental relationship between human beings and the Earth, we must consider the need to repair the relationship with other subordinate groups and species. The processes of harm caused by certain dominant design logics can be reversed by all those forms of creative life that mobilise corrections and open up paths of ontological openness to different design forms that can recompose the living.

Prototyping coexistence from fragility

Moving design towards the discussion of a more-than-human future is an ethical responsibility given the disaster that we are facing as a planet. The crises that we are experiencing, and the collapse of the ideas of progress,

20 Martín Tironi

rationality, and universality (Debaise & Stengers, 2015) have created a need for other *world-making* that can generate the conditions required for just cohabitation among all the entities that constitute our worlds.

But how can this transition be activated? How can forms of knowledge and coexistence be created with ontologically diverse participants? There is no question that one of the most interesting devices that design culture has to offer is prototypes. If we move away from a definition that reduces prototypes to a purely provisional testing technique to arrive at a final product, the prototype can constitute a privileged space of research and creation that can be used to rethink our forms of relating to the environment, generating specific more-than-human design situations (Tironi & Hermansen, 2018, 2020). In the face of the planetary dimension of the problems we are experiencing, and the disorientation caused by the crisis of inhabitability, the prototyping tool can place a fundamental role for exploring situated forms of connecting to the more-than-human. Understood as an epistemic tool that has the potential to create cultures of experimental *making* (Corsín Jiménez, 2014), the prototype emerges as a space of ontological opening for reimagining our forms of relating to the world. At the same time, it is a conceptual figure that contributes to rethinking more inclusive and fair futures. Below, I present three properties that can be activated through prototyping and that open up the spaces of experimentation necessary to go beyond anthropocentric design.

The first characteristic that makes this device a privileged place for generating more-than-human futures is its *fragility*. Prototypes are designed to create knowledge and learning based on the failures that they experience. The material fragility and malleability of the prototype allows it to make available events and situations that are revealed in mistakes. Contemporary society has made resilience and innovation one of its most prized *telos*, but prototyping processes make fragility and temporariness its reason for being. Facing the absence of reflection from and with fragility (De la Bellacasa, 2017; Denis and Pontille, 2022), the prototype is open to what we could call an *ecology of fragility*. It does not only legitimate failure as a mode of knowledge. The fragility inherent to the prototype sharpens the attention to the set of connections and resistances that emerge from the testing process. The trial-and-error tests conducted as part of this process make visible the properties of the agencies that come into play. Before the tests that lead to the prototyping process, the properties that agencies have are ignored. Or, as Latour put it, reality is what resist the test (Latour, 1984).

A second characteristic derived from this fragile mode of existence of the prototype is the *ontological opening* that this device makes possible. The prototype allows for the inclusion of more-than-human agencies in the reflection on the constitution of the social, to the power to be used to think through the relationship with energy (Wilkie et al., 2015), ecosystems, or animals (Lenskjold & Jönsson, 2017; Tironi & Hermansen, 2018; Ávila, 2022). The provisional and fragile nature of the prototyping process allows

Introduction: Design for more-than-human futures   21

us to speak of a form of ontological diplomacy or hospitality of this testing technology (Tironi & Hermansen, 2018; Ávila, 2022), as it allows relationships with agencies, forms of thought and ways of feeling that go beyond human discourse to be created. While one of the challenges that the environmental crisis poses is how to open ourselves up to listen to other species and more-than-human agencies, the prototype allows for an opening up to multiple forms of existence. The prototype makes "the other" visible through the traces that agencies leave in the process of trial-and-error, articulating negotiations and associations that cannot be reduced to the word.

The third characteristic of the prototype that I wish to highlight is its capacity to prefigure _"what could be"_ that is, a form of anti-normative and speculative intervention. The prototype understood as an open process and not as a static object activates alternatives to what "is" or "should be" in order to explore uncertain, inconclusive or undefined possibilities. The fluctuating and iterative activity of prototyping is invested with a certain transformative vitality that allows it to challenge the pre-established idea of having to think that things are as they are. It invites us to inhabit failures and multiply the possibilities of futures. The prototype as a dialogic platform allows forms of knowledge and perspectives that are often divergent to be integrated and taken up, opening the possibility of design that is involved in processes of change.

The capacity of the prototype is not limited to packaging or setting the characteristics of a product. It has the potential to generate open and experimental forms of knowledge, facilitating social transitions towards more just and sustainable societies and multiplying possible worlds instead of unifying them. The power of prototyping as an epistemic tool is its capacity to articulate the "what if," to not close problems. It is an incomplete and unfinished form of knowledge that is open to possible futures, to what could come into being. The "what if" is a way to generate questions and forms of knowledge that are in process of being defined. If the work of diplomacy that Latour (2012) proposed involves creating dialogues with different modes of existence that humans do not yet know of, prototyping as a research technology invites us to open ourselves up to these activities of experimentation and exploration. It is not a matter of turning prototyping into a depoliticised tool of possible futures, but rather a question of mobilising this tool to decolonise our modes of approaching reality, expanding forms of epistemic equity. In short, prototyping allows modes of description and association of different entities to operate, including the voices of more-than-human worlds.

Book chapters

The chapter **"Notes on Excess: Towards Pluriversal Design"** that opens this book is written by Marisol de la Cadena and Arturo Escobar, two authors central to thinking and making design for transitions toward the pluriverse. They develop certain premises and questions to challenge the hegemony of

22 Martín Tironi

one-world or one-world making design and begin to explore a design for the pluriverse, contributing to a "world of many worlds." For de la Cadena and Escobar, globalisation, development, and colonialism can be understood as a mono-ontological concern (a world made from a world). They call on us to practice design that contributes to "ontological detoxification," that is, a design that is less preoccupied with optimisation and productivity and more concerned with projecting pluriversally, where humans and more-than-humans can flourish in mutually enriching ways.

The text by Ezio Manzini and Virginia Tassinari, **"Anticipations of more-than-human futures,"** addresses experiences of social innovation, which the authors have long explored. They recognise in them radical forms of disruption that reveal anti-hegemonic cultural actions. The authors invite us to consider these innovation movements "from below" as opportunities to destabilise dominant anthropocentric cannons, anticipating scenarios and actions necessary to project more-than-human forms of coexistence.

Laura Forlano's study (**"Design's Intimacies: The Indeterminacy of Design with Machines and Mushrooms"**) features a delicate reflection on design in times of radical indetermination. Starting from the premise that the planetary crisis calls for a redesign of many of the foundations that sustain our society, Forlano proposes an interesting reflexive intersection between the ontological uncertainty caused by algorithmic machines and the loss of biodiversity that characterises our contemporary world. The chapter invites us to see today's ecosystemic crises not as a call to hide in fear, but as an opportunity to learn to design in the face of the incommensurable qualities of the more-than-human.

Nicole Cristi in her chapter **"Growing Materials: Technical and Caring Processes as Rooted Design Practices"** explores the idea and experience of 'growing materials' as a design practice based on caring and deeply rooted in a more-than-human approach to design. Her research is grounded on a 16-month collaborative ethnography on biofabrication practices. The present text approach the experience with the *Laboratorio de Biomateriales de Valdivia* in southern Chile.

In his chapter **"Learning from Accidental Abundance,"** Carl DiSalvo offers incisive reflections on how to understand the design of unmaking, of detaching from the vocation of creating newness and innovation, deploying new practices of decentring that allow us to reconsider the pre-existing and previous, in this case, by reusing discarded products. Using the case of a foraging collective in Atlanta, the author proposes certain premises for unlearning the design that we have inherited from a certain modern-productivist tradition, creating conditions for transformative and collective learning of our conditions of inhabitability.

The chapter **"How would animals and architects co-design if we built the right contract?"** by Ignacio Farías, Tomás Sanchez Criado, and Felix Remter addresses the need to place the practice of design in crisis, examining the role that this discipline has played in the production of a catastrophic present.

Introduction: Design for more-than-human futures 23

The authors narrate an experience of teaching design with urban animals in which the latter are understood as epistemic and methodological partners for rethinking the ontology of the practice of design, involving their capacities to transform design and repair the damage that anthropocentrism and certain universalist designs have produced for the planets.

In the chapter, "Before the idiot, the poet? Aesthetic figures and design," Alex Wilkie and Mike Michael address the qualities and potential of the "figure of the poet" for thinking and projecting the design process. Continuing with previous studies by the authors on the figure of the idiot, Wilkie and Michael analyse how the aesthetic figure can be combined to endow design with new inventive and generative capacities, promoting research that is more committed to questions than to certainties, and with the potential for speculative interventions in the world.

In the chapter "Revisiting Empathy by Gentrifying Our Guts: Exploring Design as a Cosmopolitical Diplomacy Practice Through Microbial Fruits of Istanbul," the authors Uriel Fogué, Orkan Telhan, Eva Gil Lopesino, and Carlos Palacios Rodríguez of the text discuss a design project for more-than-human futures, entitled Microbial Fruits of Istanbul (MFoI). Here, they present the shared narrative that allowed the design team to bring together their diverse knowledge(s) as well as the team's learnings and questions that were raised throughout the project's process, some of which, we think, entail big challenges to the discipline of design. Throughout the text, we intended to ask how a project for more-than-human futures may bring design methodology closer to a cosmopolitical diplomatic task rather than a human-centric creation process and allow us to see architectural design as a point of encounter for multiple species rather than a platform that primarily serves human interests.

The chapter "Design Beyond Human Concerns: A Sancocho-Style Approach" by Leonardo Parra-Agudelo and Edgard David Rincón Quijano proposes more-than-human design that the authors call 'sancocho style.' The emphasis is placed on the web of relationships that create interworlds, overcoming the dualism unique to modern-colonial methods. The chapter calls on us to create a design culture that incorporates more rational ways of intervening in and making worlds, a design practice focused on the creation of more sustainable modes of inhabiting that go beyond universalist anthropocentric strategies.

The closing chapter of the book is "Furrowing the Maraña: Designing to sail out of the Anthropocene" by Pablo Hermansen and Jose Guerra. The authors explore the concept of *maraña* as a tool for thinking about possible futures beyond the epistemological limits of modernity and offering a path to advance towards a design entangled (*enmarañado*) with the planet. The chapter calls us to look into the myth of Alexander and the Gordian Knot as the myth of origin for an episteme of dissection that acts as a point of origin to a culture of cutting the *marañas* of the planet.

24 Martín Tironi

Notes

1 Following authors like Stengers (2005), Latour (2005), and De la Cadena (2015), I understand the notion of more-than-human as all of the other entities and agencies (animate and inanimate) that interact in the world. This perspective seeks to break with the modern hierarchy that views humans as the only subjects with the capacity for political agency. The goal is to begin to explore a "cosmopolitics" (Stengers, 2005) in which beings and entities that transcend human action are recognised as political material. The concept of more-than-human allows us to extend the social to other entities and to emphasise the move away from understanding sociability solely as a human issue in order to explore associations between humans and other-than-humans.
2 For more information on the pavilion, see www.londondesignbiennale.com/participant/chile-0.

Bibliography

Adams, V., Murphy, M., & Clarke, A. E. (2009). Anticipation: Technoscience, life, affect, temporality. *Subjectivity, 28*(1), pp. 246–265.

Akrich, M. (1987). Comment décrire les objets techniques? *Techniques et culture, 9*, pp. 49–64.

Altvater, E., Crist, E. C., Haraway, D. J., Hartley, D., Parenti, C., & McBrien, J. (2016). *Anthropocene or capitalocene?: Nature, history, and the crisis of capitalism.* Binghamton, NY: PM Press.

Angheloiu, C., Chaudhuri, G., & Sheldrick, L. (2017). Future tense: Alternative futures as a design method for sustainability transitions. *The Design Journal, 20*(supp1), S3213–S3225.

Appadurai, A. (2013). The future as cultural fact: Essays on the global condition. *Rassegna Italiana di Sociologia, 14*(4), pp. 649–650.

Ávila, M. (2022). *Designing for interdependence: A poetics of relating.* London: Bloomsbury Publishing.

Binder, T., Brandt, E., Ehn, P., & Halse, J. (2015). Democratic design experiments: Between parliament and laboratory. *CoDesign, 11*(3–4), pp. 152–165.

Blaser, M. (2012). Ontology and indigeneity: On the political ontology of heterogeneous assemblages. *Cultural Geographies, 21*(1), pp. 49–58.

Boltanski, L., & Chiapello, E. (1999). *Le nouvel esprit du capitalism* (Vol. 10). Paris: Gallimard.

Bonnet, E., Landivar, D., Monnin, A., & Allard, L. (2019). Le design, une cosmologie sans monde face à l'Anthropocène. *Sciences du Design, 10*(2), pp. 97–104.

Bonneuil, C., & Fressoz, J. B. (2013). *L'événement Anthropocène: la Terre, l'histoire et nous.* Paris: Éditions du Seuil.

Bryant, R., & Knight, D. M. (2019). *The anthropology of the future.* Cambridge: Cambridge University Press.

Callén Moreu, B., & López Gómez, D. (2019). Intimate with your junk! A waste management experiment for a material world. *The Sociological Review, 67*(2), pp. 318–339.

Cano Raміréz, O. (2017). Capitaloceno y adaptación elitista. *Ecología Política, 2017*(53), pp. 8–11.

Carrasco, C., Borderías, C., & Torns, T. (Eds.) (2011). *El trabajo de cuidados. Historia, teoría y políticas.* Madrid: Catarata.

Coccia, E. (2018). *La vie des plantes: une métaphysique du mélange*. Paris: Éditions Payot & Rivages.

Corsín Jiménez, A. (2014). Introduction: The prototype: more than many and less than one. *Journal of Cultural Economy*, 7(4), pp. 381–398.

Costanza-Chock, S. (2018). Design justice: Towards an intersectional feminist framework for design theory and practice. *Proceedings of the Design Research Society*.

Crutzen, P. J. (2006). The "anthropocene". In E. Ehlers & T. Krafft (Eds.), *Earth system science in the anthropocene* . Berlin, Heidelberg: Springer.

Dator, J. (2019). *Jim Dator: A noticer in time: Selected work , 1967-2018* (pp. 3–5). Cham: Springer.

Day, S., Lury, C., & Ward, H. (2023). Personalization: A new political arithmetic?. *Distinktion: Journal of Social Theory*, pp. 1–28.

De La Bellacasa, M. P. (2017). *Matters of care: Speculative ethics in more than human worlds* (Vol. 41). Minneapolis: University of Minnesota Press.

Denis, J., & Pontille, D. (2022) *Le Soin des choses. Politiques de la maintenance*. Paris: La Découverte.

De la Cadena, M. (2015). Chamanismo andino in the third millennium: Multiculturalism meets earth-beings. In *Earth beings: Ecologies of practice across Andean worlds* (pp. 179–208). Durham: Duke University Press.

De la Cadena, M., & Blaser, M. (Eds.) (2018). *A world of many worlds*. Durham: Duke University Press.

Debaise, D., & Stengers, I. (2015). *Gestes spéculatifs: colloque de Cersy*. Dijon: Les Presses du reel.

Descola, P. (1996). *The Spears of twilight: Life and death in the Amazon jungle*. New York: New Press.

Descola, P. (2001). Par-delà la nature et la culture. *Le débat, 144*, pp. 86–101.

Dunne, A., & Raby, F. (2013). *Speculative everything: Design, fiction, and social dreaming*. Cambridge: MIT Press.

Escobar, A. (1994) Welcome to Cyberia: Notes on the anthropology of cyberculture. *Current Anthropology*, 35(3), pp. 211–231.

Escobar, A. (2014). *La invención del desarrollo*. Cali, CO: Editorial Universidad del Cauca.

Escobar, A. (2018). *Designs for the Pluriverse*. Durham: Duke University Press.

Ferrando, F. (2016). The party of the anthropocene: Post-humanism, environmentalism and the post-anthropocentric paradigm shift. *Rel.: Beyond Anthropocentrism*, 4, p. 159.

Forlano, L. (2017). Posthumanism and design. *She Ji: The Journal of Design, Economics, and Innovation*, 3(1), pp. 16–29.

Forlano, L., & Mathew, A. (2014). From design fiction to design friction: Speculative and participatory design of values-embedded urban technology. *Journal of Urban Technology*, 21(4), pp. 7–24.

Fry, T. (2012). *Becoming human by design*. London: Bloomsbury Academic.

Fry, T. (2020). *Defuturing: A new design philosophy*. London: Bloomsbury Publishing.

Fry, T., Dilnot, C., & Stewart, S. (2015). *Design and the question of history*. London: Bloomsbury.

Fry, T., & Nocek, A. (Eds.) (2020). *Design in crisis: New worlds, philosophies and practices*. London: Routledge.

Fuad-Luke, A. (2013). *Design activism beautiful strangeness for a sustainable world*. London: Routledge.

26 *Martín Tironi*

Gaziulusoy, I., & Erdoğan Öztekin, E. (2019). Design for sustainability transitions: Origins, attitudes and future directions. *Sustainability*, *11*(13), p. 3601.

Giacomin, J. (2014). What is human centred design? *The Design Journal*, *17*(4), pp. 606–623.

Goffey, A., & Stengers, I. (2015). *In catastrophic times: Resisting the coming barbarism*. London: Open Humanities Press.

Granjou, C., & Salazar, J. F. (2016). Future. *Environmental Humanities*, *8*(2), pp. 240–244.

Gudynas, E. (2010). La ecología política de la crisis global y los límites del capitalismo benévolo. *Íconos: publicación de FLACSO-Ecuador Íconos - Revista De Ciencias Sociales*, *36*, pp. 53–67.

Gudynas, E. (2011). Buen vivir: Today´s tomorrow. *Development (Society for International Development)*, *54*(4), pp. 441–447.

Gutiérrez Borrero, A. (2015). Resurgimientos: sures como diseños y diseños otros. In *Nómadas* (Col), No. 43, October (pp. 113–129). Colombia: Universidad Central Bogotá.

Gutiérrez Borrero, A. (2020). When design goes south: From decoloniality, through declassification to dessobons. In T. Fry & A. Nocek (Eds.), *Design in crisis* (pp. 56–73). London: Routledge.

Haraway, D. J. (2016). *Staying with the trouble*. Durham: Duke University Press.

Haraway, D. J. (2018). Staying with the trouble for multispecies environmental justice. *Dialogues in Human Geography*, *8*(1), pp. 102–105.

Helmreich, S. (2008). Species of biocapital. *Science as culture*, *17*(4), pp. 463–478.

Hidalgo Capitan, A., & Cubillo Guevara, A. (2014). Seis debates abiertos sobre el sumak kawsay. *Íconos: Revista de Ciencias Sociales*, *48*, pp. 25–40.

Holeman, I., & Kane, D. (2020). Human-centered design for global health equity. *Information Technology for Development*, *26*(3), pp. 477–505.

Ingold, T. (2017). On human correspondence. *Journal of the Royal Anthropological Institute*, *23*(1), pp. 9–27.

Ingold, T. (2020). *Correspondences*. Cambridge: John Wiley & Sons.

Irwin, T., Kossoff, G., & Tonkinwise, C. (2015). Transition design provocation. *Design Philosophy Papers*, *13*(1), pp. 3–11.

Kohn, E. (2013). *How forests think: Toward an anthropology beyond the human*. Berkeley: University of California Press.

Latour, B. (1984). Les Microbes: Guerre Et Paix; suivi de, Irréductions. Paris: A.M. Métailié.

Latour, B. (2004). Why has critique run out of steam? From matters of fact to matters of concern. *Critical Inquiry*, *30*(2), pp. 225–248.

Latour, B. (2005). *Reassembling the social: An introduction to actor-network theory*. Oxford: Oxford University Press.

Latour, B. (2007). 2. Quel cosmos? Quelles cosmopolitiques?. In J. Lolive & O. Soubeyran (Eds.), *L'emergence des cosmopolitiques* (pp. 69–84). Paris: La découverte.

Latour, B. (2012). *Enquête sur les modes d'existence: une anthropologie des modernes*. Paris: La Découverte.

Latour, B. (2013). *Nous n'avons jamais été modernes: essai d'anthropologie symétrique*. Paris: La découverte.

Latour, B. (2017a). *Facing Gaia: Eight lectures on the new climatic regime*. Chichester: John Wiley & Sons.

Introduction: Design for more-than-human futures 27

Latour, B. (2017b). *Où atterrir? Comment s' orienter en politique*. Paris: La découverte.

Latour, B. (2020). *Imaginer les gestes-barrières contre le retour à la production d'avant-crise*. AOC media - Analyse Opinion Critique. http://www.bruno-latour.fr/fr/node/849

Lenskjold, T. U., & Jönsson, L. (2017). Speculative prototypes and alien ethnographies: Experimenting with relations beyond the human. *Diseña*, *1*(11), pp. 134–147.

Lewis, L., Gottschalk-Druschke, C., Saldías, C., Mackenzie, R., Malebrán, J., Goffinet, B., & Rozzi, R. (2018). Cultivando un jardín de nombres en los bosques en miniatura del Cabo de Hornos: extensión de la conservación biocultural y la ética a seres vivos poco percibidos. *Magallania (Punta Arenas)*, *46*(1), pp. 103–123.

Lien, M., and Pálsson, G. (2019). Ethnography beyond the human: The 'other-than-human' in ethnographic work. *Ethnos*, *86*, pp. 1–20. DOI: 10.1080/00141844.2019.1628796

Lindström, K., & Ståhl, Å. (2020, June). Un/making in the aftermath of design. In *Proceedings of the 16th Participatory Design Conference 2020-Participation (s) Otherwise-Volume 1* (pp. 12–21).

Manzini, E. (2015). *Design, when everybody designs: An introduction to design for social innovation*. Cambridge: MIT press.

Manzini, E., & Menichinelli, M. (2021). Platforms for re-localization: Communities and places in the post-pandemic hybrid spaces. *Strategic Design Research Journal*, *14*(1), pp. 351–360.

Mazé, R. (2019). Politics of designing visions of the future. *Journal of Futures Studies*, *23*(3), pp. 23–38.

Meroni, A., & Sangiorgi, D. (2011). *Design for services*. Farnham: Gower Publishing, Ltd.

Mohamed, S., Png, M. T., & Isaac, W. (2020). Decolonial AI: Decolonial theory as sociotechnical foresight in artificial intelligence. *Philosophy & Technology*, *33*(4), pp. 659–684.

Pelluchon, C. (2020). *Réparons le monde: Humains, animaux, nature*. Paris: Éditions Payot & Rivages.

Ricci, D. (2019). Tensing the present: An annotated anthology of design techniques to inquire into public issues. *Diseña*, *1*(14), pp. 68–99.

Rice, L. (2018). Nonhumans in participatory design. *CoDesign*, *14*(3), pp. 238–257.

Rouvroy, A., & Berns, T. (2013). Gouvernementalité algorithmique et perspectives d'émancipation. *Réseaux*, *177*(1), pp. 163–196.

Savransky, M. (2021). *Around the day in eighty worlds: Politics of the pluriverse*. Durham: Duke University Press.

Smith, R. C., Vangkilde, K. T., Otto, T., Kjaersgaard, M. G., Halse, J., & Binder, T. (Eds.) (2016). *Design anthropological futures*. London: Bloomsbury Publishing.

Ståhl, O., Tham, M., & Holtorf, C. (2017). Towards a post-anthropocentric speculative archaeology (through design). *Journal of Contemporary Archaeology*, *4*(2), pp. 238–246.

Stengers, I. (2005). The cosmopolitical proposal. In B. Latour & P. Weibel (Eds.), *Making things public: Atmospheres of democracy* (p. 994). Cambridge: MIT Press.

Stengers, I. (2010). Including nonhumans in political theory: Opening pandora's box? In B. Braun, S. Whatmore, & I. Stengers (Eds.), *Political Matter: Technoscience, Democracy, and Public Life* (pp. 3–33). Minneapolis: University of Minnesota Press.

28   *Martín Tironi*

Stengers, I., & Goffey, A. (2015). *In catastrophic times: Resisting the coming barbarism*. Critical climate change. S.l. London: Open Humanities Press.

Tharp, B. M., & Tharp, S. M. (2019). *Discursive design: Critical, speculative, and alternative things*. Cambridge: MIT Press.

Tironi, M., & Hermansen, P. (2018). Cosmopolitical encounters: Prototyping at the National Zoo in Santiago, Chile. *Journal of Cultural Economy, 11*(4), pp. 330–347.

Tironi, M., & Hermansen, P. (2020). Prototipando la coexistencia: Diseños para futuros interespecie. *ARQ (Santiago)*, (106), pp. 38–47.

Tlostanova, M. (2017). On decolonizing design. *Design Philosophy Papers, 15*(1), pp. 51–61.

Tonkinwise, C. (2018). 'I prefer not to': Anti-progressive designing. In Gretchen Coombs, Andrew McNamara, Gavin Sade (Eds.), *Undesign* (pp. 74–84). London: Routledge.

Tsing, A. L., Bubandt, N., Gan, E., & Swanson, H. A. (Eds.) (2017). *Arts of living on a damaged planet: Ghosts and monsters of the anthropocene*. Minneapolis: University of Minnesota Press.

Tsing, A. L. (2015). *The mushroom at the end of the world*. Princeton: Princeton University Press.

Vazquez, R. (2017). Precedence, earth and the anthropocene: Decolonizing design. *Design Philosophy Papers, 15*(1), pp. 77–91.

Voros, J. (2008). Integral futures: An approach to futures inquiry. *Futures, 40*(2), pp. 190–201.

Wagner, R. (1991). The fractal person. In M. Godelier & M. Strathern (Eds.), *Big men and great men: personifications of power in Melanesia* (pp. 159–173). Cambridge: Cambridge University Press.

Wakkary, R. (2021). *Things we could design: For more than human-centered worlds*. Cambridge: MIT press.

Wilkie, A., Michael, M., & Plummer-Fernandez, M. (2015). Speculative method and Twitter: Bots, energy and three conceptual characters. *The Sociological Review, 63*(1), pp. 79–101.

Wilkie, A., Savransky, M., & Rosengarten, M. (Eds.) (2017). *Speculative research: The lure of possible futures*. London: Routledge.

Willis, Anne-Marie (2006). Ontological designing–laying the ground. See: https://www.academia.edu/888457/Ontological_designing.

Winograd, T. & Flores, F. (1986). *Understanding computers and cognition: A new foundation for design*. Norwood: Ablex Publishing Corporation.

Zuboff, S. (2019). *The age of surveillance capitalism: The fight for the future at the new frontier of power*. New York: Profile Books.

1 Notes on excess

Towards pluriversal design

Marisol de la Cadena and Arturo Escobar

We want to start by letting our readers know two things about the piece they will read. One is that the intention of our writing is to contribute towards "a world of many worlds." This is our rewording of the refrain that the Zapatistas made popular; they also live by it as do a multitude of people, usually marked ethnically or racially as "indigenous" or of "African descent," but of course they are not the only ones. So, the refrain is not our academic "invention"—we use it to name practices of life that make worlds and from where the noun (world) can also emerge as a verb and an adjective: worlding practices or worldings. These and the worlds they make are intra-connected, not even inter-connected, a phrasing that would imply their separation and later connection. Instead, the composition that our writing wants our readers to imagine is akin to an ecology where entities intra-live in divergence: that is, each through their distinct ways, with their distinct requirements. Coloniality is also part of this ecology; its practices shape the worlds as only one world (containing many separate cultural worldviews of the one world) without undoing their many-ness, nor the intra-connection that complicates their plurality and makes it less than many.[1]

This complex dynamic is what surfaces through the phrase "a world of many worlds"—or the pluriverse; we offer it as an analytical tool to meet (in creative tension, yet not replacing) analyses inspired by and performed with the tools of the one-world world (Law, 2015). And this is the second: we both have said this in previous writings (de la Cadena, 2010, 2015, 2018; Escobar 2014, 2018, 2020), but we have done so separately; while we have been in conversation more years than we want to recall, this is the first attempt for the two of us at writing together. We want to do so ecologically: that is, showing the connections across the differences that motivate each of us. Through our many years of intellectual partnership, mutual influence is palpably making unclear which ideas are whose; this, which includes Mario Blaser, is a most cherished achievement. But we are not a seamless unity, and the reader may feel the seams that weave us together, while also marking us individually—but not completely!

DOI: 10.4324/9781003319689-2

Excess

So back to the ecology of divergent worldings. A salient analytical characteristic of this composition is what Marisol calls excess, and which she conceptualises as what *is* beyond the limit of what *can be*. This obviously brief conceptualisation only gets us started, and while abstract, it is grounded in the conversations she engaged in with Mariano and Nazario Turpo, two *runakuna* (the word male Quechua indigenous persons use to self-identify) with whom she thought for almost ten years.[2] The conversations were replete with what all three understood from each other and with what they could not understand because what was talked about onto-epistemically *exceeded* their respective worlding practices (including thought of course). For example, that a rock was a person, that potato seeds feel, that hail can be mean—Marisol grasped neither statement without turning them into "cultural beliefs about nature" which in turn would signal that those statements expressed a reality of second order (beliefs are not *really* real, right?) and that her interlocutors believed, while she—the anthropologist—knew. This, indeed, indexes the coloniality of the discipline and, importantly for our writing here, manifests one of the epistemic practices that makes the world one, and cancels the possibility of practices that are in divergence with the one-world world. Prompted by Mariano and Nazario in a journey that took several years, Marisol chose to "not know" as her epistemic position. *Thus became* "excess": a conceptual tool to name presences that appeared in their conversations and that she did not grasp because they *were* beyond the limit of her onto-epistemic purview both as an anthropologist and a Peruvian citizen (the latter, a condition that she shared with Turpo).[3]

Beyond the specific conversation between Mariano, Nazario, and Marisol, excess is also a feature between many people (indigenous, afro-descendant, and neither) and modern politics and economies (the state, political parties, the market). These relations are textured—as in woven and as in sensed—by matters that neither side can grasp about the other but nevertheless compose their encounter. Not surprisingly, excess can be ignored by all sides enacting it; sometimes, in so doing, it can be cancelled as not-being, as in the example above: using culture, anthropology knows as *belief* (i.e., as "not really" being) what *is* without the requirements of the regime of reality that effects the translation, and it offers such knowledge for circulation—creatively or destructively—in its own epistemic regime. And thus moved, what would otherwise appear as "unknown yet possible" through the analytics of "excess"—the mountain *as person*, the river *as relative*—becomes *not-being*: it *is* as impossible. To be clear: not recognising "excess" is not the problem. The problem is denying possibility to what cannot be within—and thus cannot be thought from—the worlding practices of the modern episteme because it does not meet its requirements. Such denial—itself a worlding practice—fits a specific world inaugurated more than 500 years ago; it was endowed at birth with a will to expansion that devours and metabolises into itself what it is not.

Notes on excess: towards pluriversal design 31

"Excess" allows us to think what is beyond our onto-epistemic ability; it is a tool towards the colossal task of thinking pluriversally. This way of thinking presents a challenge to all disciplines and their disciplined practitioners—design included. Like anthropology, design is a practice that abides by the requirements of the one-world world. Like anthropology, it has beautifully learned from different cultures and translated "their practices" to its own (the scare quotes will make sense momentarily). In so doing, it has ignored excess. How *is* design when the feeling of excess—for example, through encounters with entities recalcitrant to representation—impinges on its practices? Can designing decidedly move towards a non-representational understanding of humans and other than humans that is inherently relational? Can there be a pluriversal design that does not rely on the onto-epistemology of already existent subjects and objects, and hence, can design be without representation? We will tackle these questions in the last sections of this text.

Pluriversal contact zones and care of excess

Many years ago, Mary Louise Pratt used the term "contact zones" to conceptualise "the space in which peoples geographically and historically *separated* come into contact with each other and establish ongoing relations, usually involving conditions of coercion, radical inequality, and intractable conflict" (1992, p. 8). Our emphasis in Pratt's quote has a reason: she used "contact zone" to call attention to processes through which divergent worlds (our word) encountered each other and composed a pidgin togetherness. She writes: "A 'contact' perspective emphasises how subjects get constituted in and by their relations to each other. It treats the relations among colonisers and colonised, or travellers and 'travelees,' *not in terms of separateness*, but in terms of co-presence, interaction, interlocking understandings and practices, and often within radically asymmetrical relations of power" (ibid., emphasis added). Accordingly, encounters across previously separate people were sites where their worlds inflected each other but not to simply become a newly formed "third." Instead, each became self-different from what it had been, while continuing to be itself and also *with* the other.

We borrow Pratt's term to write about co-presence as well. Like in her work, our terms are not those of separateness, but the more than half a millennia co-presence among worlds old and new has not produced simple togetherness. Instead, the encounter that contact zones are is also a site of excess among those that inhabit it and throughout which *divergence* can be felt. We borrow divergence from Isabelle Stengers. She uses it to think of entities or practices that may come together, even become through each other, and yet share no sameness whatsoever: like the orchid and the wasp to use Deleuze and Guattari's figure (1987, p. 12). They have an interest in common that is specific to each of them, and thus, it is not the same interest (Stengers, 2011). Notwithstanding the convergence, orchid and wasp diverge. Clarification: divergent entities—orchid and wasp—are incommensurable to

32 Marisol de la Cadena and Arturo Escobar

each other, and they cannot be compared; this is unlike "difference" where entities can be compared through formulas of equivalence.

Grounding the above commentary in fieldwork and following Pratt's inspiration, we propose the idea of pluriversal contact zones: as sites of encounter among divergent worlds that are suffused with excess; nevertheless, emerging beyond the onto-epistemic limits of the one-world world (present at the contact zone as well) excess oftentimes goes unfelt or is dismissed *even by those to whom it matters.* The event through which Marisol initially thought "excess" in pluriversal contact zones happened in Cuzco, Peru; it brought together a coalition of urban environmentalists and indigenous peasants to defend an entity called Ausangate against a mining corporation who wanted to translate it into a repository of ores. Ausangate is a mountain and, also, an earth-being; the practices that make each of them diverge as does their respective resulting entity: Ausangate is a complex self-excessive entity that occupies a space that Euclidian coordinates cannot encompass. Becoming through a pluriversal contact zone, the alliance to defend the entity was equally complex: urban activists defended the mountain and indigenous peasants defended the earth-being. Their interests diverged (ontologically so), and while many on the indigenous side were aware of this condition, they chose to continue in the alliance: it was sustained by a common interest, namely the joint (environmentalist and indigenous activists) defence of Ausangate (earth-being and mountain) against its conversion into an open-pit mine. Their interest in common which was not the same interest proved effective both as an environmental success (it sustained the alliance that defeated the mine) and as an onto-epistemic tool that smothered the excess. That those who cared for the earth-being participated in preventing the excess from appearing in public is not surprising: earth-beings are hegemonically impossible, their presence could have hindered the alliance even with good-hearted people like those who care for the environment.

Pluriversal contact zones are uncertain as political terrain; the "coming out" of excess may summon the imposition of modern onto-epistemic limits, but it can also open up the latter to conversations of care and wisdom across divergent worlding practices. The presence of excess makes pluriversal contact zones tangible; they suggest an unknown togetherness which worlds have to learn—some of them from scratch and all with prudent attention to the coloniality of practices that made the world one. Scary as this endeavour feels, it needs to be undertaken, for if we open our senses to current events, we may feel the presence of the pluriverse and its contact zones proliferate. Opportunities at feeling them tend to follow the pace of their encroachment and attempts at their destruction by practices of the Anthropocene–Capitalocene–Plantationocene.

Pluriversal contact zones may erupt in—interrupt we should say—modern practices of all kinds: films and judiciary courts, for example, and not by chance, the combination of both, as in *Forest Law/Selva Jurídica*, an artistic documentary (Biemann and Tavares, 2014). Among the themes in the film

Notes on excess: towards pluriversal design 33

were the deliberations to save an area of the Amazonian rain forest that coincided with what was within what is known as *territorio Sarayaku* in Spanish and Sarayaku territory in English; in Kichwa, this area is named as *Kawsay Sacha*, which translates to English as "living forest" and as "selva viviente" to Spanish. We would like to slow down this translation with two intentions. One, is relatively obvious: following Walter Benjamin's well-known recommendation, the intention would be to make the language of origin (Amazonian Kichwa) inflect the languages of destiny (English and Spanish) (Benjamin, 1969). Our second intention is to listen to this inflection in the contact zone where all three languages overlap even if only one is spoken: Spanish, for example.[4] This condition is not infrequent in public settings (courts, newspapers, political demonstrations when indigenous spokespersons engaging in conversations with, or are themselves, lawyers, journalists, environmentalists). At these pluriversal contact zones, if we listen carefully, we may feel *another ontological grammar* within the hegemonic one: one that by speaking of humans-with-nature (another way of being person) stubbornly refuses the ontological distinctions that enable the capitalocenic practices that currently devastate the planet. Having this in mind, we want you to read/listen to José Gualinga's words. He is a Sarayaku spokesperson; in the film he talks about explosives that some oil prospecting corporation buried within what the judge made present (at the court) as "the territory of the Sarayaku people." While meeting the court's terms, Gualinga's speech also transforms its grammar—let's listen:

> The state tried to minimize the presence of the explosives on Sarayaku territory. It indicated that an explosive is dangerous when it is attached to a human body that is classification A. Classification B is when an explosive is left in a building; in that case you can evacuate people. And classification C is when explosives are somewhere far away. The state said that the presence of explosives in Sarayaku falls into category C because they're far from the main dwelling place of Sarayaku people and they don't present a threat; hence, there is no need to remove them. But for us their presence represents category A, and that is what we told the state: that *the explosives are attached to the body of the Sarayaku.*
> (Emphasis added, José Gualiga in Biemann and Tavares, 2014)

Gualinga's words are spoken in Spanish, *and* they are also inextricable from a Kichwa understanding that refuses separations between territory and people. Sarayaku territory is a space that *can be mapped into two (or three) dimensional coordinates*, as the judge suggested, *and* it is also an entanglement of persons—not only human persons—in practices that inherently relate the entities that compose Kawsay Sacha, the Kichwa naming of living forest that Sarayaku is: territory indivisible from persons and vice versa. If we listen carefully—with an ear towards what *exceeds* the legal grammar of

34   Marisol de la Cadena and Arturo Escobar

the state (and the ontology prescribed by hegemonic grammars)—we may hear that the judiciary deliberations about the place in the Amazon named Sarayaku enacted a pluriversal event. In it, the rainforest was present in the court as a biological organism, and *not only* such: present in the courts was also Sarayaku living forest, an entanglement of persons that does not add up because while individually identifiable, they are also inseparable. Perhaps unknowingly, *Selva Jurídica*-Forest Law, the film, offered to our senses the possibility of sensing a pluriversal contact zone.[5]

Political excess: from negation to pluriversal contact zones

As of the turn of the 21st century, the denial of the possibility of being to what cannot exist within the worlding practices of the modern onto-episteme because it does not meet its requirements has reached an unprecedented destructive capacity, one that is even self-destructive. Academics have named it variously: Anthropocene, Plantationocene, and Capitalocene—all apposite terms to describe the bundled actors that have historically composed its might. At the same time, those that such mighty will was supposed to have been destroyed perhaps centuries ago, have reminded it of its localised history, a condition that the will to a one-world world (a world without many worlds) thinks is universal (and practises it, as in universal history). Performed through heterogeneous actions emerging from many worlds, the reminder expresses an adversarial will: to mark the limit of the actions of the one-world world. Hence, the historical moment variously named as mentioned is also a pluriversal moment: one in which the many worlds, their worlding practices, and their allegedly impossible entities acquire visibility, bringing them fully into the domain of politics. Politics—and most specifically environmental politics—is arguably inhabited by what exceeds it, and, in cases, publicly so. If we displace, even if momentarily, the will that historically inhabits us and summon our attention towards what we have learned is impossible, we may feel the ecology of divergent worldings' proposals reclaiming its possibility. Perhaps the world that makes itself as one is coming to an end, to become one among many intra-connected worlds, or what we think through the notion of "pluriverse."

We find support for garnering attention to those worlds that have been rendered impossible in the work of Argentinian anthropologist and philosopher Rodolfo Kusch, particularly his 1975 essay, *La negación en el pensamiento popular*. Preceding our proposal by almost half a century, Kusch interests us because as he works to make visible that which by modernity's decree cannot exist, he productively follows this denial to find within its assertions housed in the complexity of the worlding practices of what he calls *lo popular* or *grupos populares* (popular groups) in Latin America. He proposes that such practices enact the affirmation "I exist, therefore I think, and not the other way round" or in Spanish *"existo, luego pienso y no al revés"* (p. 58). This reverses the Cartesian dictum (I think, therefore I am), and in

Notes on excess: towards pluriversal design 35

so doing alters the preeminence of the thinking subject over the inert object and thus the representational relation between both. Kusch proposes that on enacting this reversal, popular practitioners assert the preeminence of *estar* over *ser*. While the latter, *ser*, conveys abstract being (anywhere), *estar* is to be in/with place and signals a mode of worlding in which entities are always in and through relations. Intriguingly, this includes assemblages of people and things. For instance: the rituals through which Aymara truck drivers in Bolivia bless their brand-new trucks are both a tradition to ensure the favour of local divinities and a practice through which the truck ceases to be a mere object (as it would be in, say, Buenos Aires) and becomes embedded in a local web of existence, into which via the ritual it is now relationally woven: *"El camión esta instalado en la **pacha** indígena, en tanto este término significa todo lo referente al vivir mismo, al habitar en el mundo"* ("The truck gets thus embedded in the indigenous *pacha*, a term that refers to life itself, to a mode of dwelling in the world"; p. 60).

These relational practices, which alter the subject–object relation, also perform a "reduction of the object" aspect of the truck (p. 60). Moreover, considering that the truck is a modern invention (as is also the job of a driver and even the property of the truck), the same practices also evince that the evolutionary temporality of the European civilising–colonising project (whereby "popular groups" would "leave superstition behind") is hard to achieve to say the least. "There is no progress from one to the other" (*no hay progreso de uno hacia otro*, p. 61), and instead, both (the modern and the popular, to say it quickly) co-exist in an encounter replete with tensions where modern and popular constantly re-create themselves. This re-creation constitutes *lo criollo*, not a simple hybrid (a third condition resulting from the combination of the pre-existing two) but a "double vector" of thoughts and practices complexly combining into, and sustaining, each other. He says, *lo criollo concilia a ambos, porque salva todo lo referente a las cosas, o sea la relación sujeto-objeto, aunque sea a nivel de picardía, de tal modo que igual sostiene el otro vector, como un área de la plegaria siempre disponible, en donde se afianza la fe, la ética o la política popular* (p. 61; we may add that this applies to human/more-than-human and observer/observed relations).[6] We surmise that this cunning is an always present source of forms of resistance that foster pluriversal contact zones that, at times, become articulated in terms of explicit political projects, as we shall see shortly with the example of Colombia.

Kusch's investigation of the potential recombination between inextricably entangled but divergent ways of worlding—modern and popular, as a shorthand—is revealing in terms of understanding the notion of PCZs (as well as the possibility of objectless-oriented designing, to be discussed in the last section). By ascertaining the ascendancy in popular practice of *estar* over *ser*, he ponders whether the West, with its unilateral affirmation of being, has failed to understand the meaning of estar. From here follows that the West's uprootedness ("desarraigo"; a separation from place that is

36 Marisol de la Cadena and Arturo Escobar

inherent to designing) reflects a type of thought distanced from existence itself. The vector or logic of modern thought ends up privileging abstraction and the objectification of things, while shunning emotionality and contradiction, which, according to Kusch, are central to popular thought. As he adds, speaking about these two logics, "si la primera [pensamiento culto] es el producto de una seria inquietud respecto a la ciencia, la otra [el pensamiento popular] surge de una no menor preocupación por el puro hecho de vivir ... es probable que sea también la oposición entre una lógica utilizada por los colonizadores y otra empleada por los colonizados" (p. 50).[7] While discussing the steady will to impose the former over the latter, he explains these contrasting ontologies and phenomenologies in various ways, for instance, by differentiating *la amanualidad* (the *amanual*, or the absence of the hand, thought as distinct from action in modern thought, primarily concerned with the "utility of the world," which Kusch, leaning on Heidegger, considers inauthentic) from *la no-amanualidad*, centred on "the installation of the truthfulness of existence ... the truth of being that lies behind the theater of tools" (pp. 67–69). As he hastens to say, however, *amanualidad y no-amanualidad* do not exclude themselves completely, for both are *aperturas del existente* (openings of what exists; p. 67).

It is thus not a question of choosing one over the other but of attempting to comprehend "toda la verdad" (the whole truth) through a veritable integration of both logics in their multiple instantiations, something that the modern West seems incapable of doing. At issue is *comprensión* (comprehension) more than knowledge. Comprehension does not function under the representational assumption of the separation between the observer and the observed or of thought over action.[8] As such, it constitutes a negation of the weighty and imposing *affirmation* of being (over estar) that is the mode of existence that the West imagines for itself, and that the West itself registers through historical thought and re-enacts with its beliefs about scientific knowledge. But, Kusch continues, the logo-centred attitude cannot efface the reality of the world ("puedo hacer como si no tuviese vigencia el árbol sobre mí, pero no puedo suprimir su existencia"; "I can pretend the tree doesn't have any relevance to me, but I cannot suppress its existence"; p. 82). And it is this reality "being-with-tree" that popular thought affirms,[9] thus denying the *prevalence* of the assertion "being-without-tree," *without cancelling the assertion itself.*

One can say that for Kusch popular practices disrupt the prevalence of *pensamiento culto*; the popular becomes through an affirmation crafted out of the negation of the ontological *imposition* of Western trajectories that it, the popular, nevertheless encounters and is partially connected to in myriad ways. This negation is of utmost existential and philosophical importance:

> La negación rescata aquello que se está, las frustraciones diarias, los proyectos no efectivizados, *todo eso que hace la imposibilidad de ser a nivel de occidente.* ... El proyecto de existir surge de la inmersión en

Notes on excess: towards pluriversal design 37

lo negativo mismo. ... La negación se introduce en el estar simple, en tanto sumerge a uno en la totalidad real del existente. ... Esta diferenciación entre la negación y la afirmación en América [Latina] conduce a la delimitación entre lo que es y lo que está. Esta a su vez, no puede ser sino ontológica. No puedo tomar como verdadero lo que es, sino lo que además está (pp. 89, 92, our emphasis)[10]

How to think "lo americano," then? As *estar-siendo* (to be-being). But there is a consequence, and this consequence is, he says, the generalised resentment that arises from rejecting what is offered to Latin America, including redemption through material things, objects, development, and technology—design, one could say—in short, everything that Latin America is not or is insufficiently. This situation causes a *desgarramiento ontológico entre mi estar y el ser* (an ontological tearing apart between to be and being; p. 98), since there is always something that stands on the way of fully being what/who you are. The popular ethos questions the object-centred "being" of modern technology (*tecnologías de la clase media*, middle-class technologies, such as the jet airplane, for instance; nowadays one could mention digital devices) by refusing to become fully habituated to them rationally; this would amount to completely accepting the project of *ser para estar* (to be in order to exist alive). In this refusal, there appears the possibility of the affirmation of being through the formula of *estar-siendo*, o *estar para ser* (to exist in order to be).[11]

"Esto explica el problema americano"—he surmises. "Esto no es sino en apariencia un problema de ciencia, ya que es ante todo, un problema de existencia, de posibilidad de ser" (p. 110). As some Colombian activists put it, "el problema [crisis civilizatoria] no es de ciencia, sino de las condiciones de la existencia y la re-existencia." Moreover, science (e.g., economics) can simply—and allegedly legitimately—ignore the world-making practices of the *pueblo*. Commenting on the long and well-known Argentinian poem *Martín Fierro*, an epic of gaucho and rural life of the second half of the 19th century that depicts the gaucho as a residualised category in the making of the modern nation (that time of the "historia montada en el extranjero"), and its attempt at redemption by Peronism, he intuits the possibility of the irruption of *what cannot be* according to the dominant onto-epistemic regime, as suggested in this quote from the epic's opening stanzas:

Yo no soy cantor letrao
mas si me pongo a cantar
no tengo cuando acabar
y me envejezco cantando,
las coplas me van brotando
como agua de manantial.[12]

Sing we must, according to Kusch, if Latin Americans want to embrace a liberatory existential-political project. For "una cosa es **cantar** y otra **decir**. Decir es colocar una frase *fuera de uno mismo* para que otros la escuchen ...

No es lo mismo que cantar, sino que es menos" ("One thing is to sing, to say is something else altogether. To say is to place a sentence *outside of oneself* so that others listen to it … . It's not the same as singing, it is actually less," p. 136; our emphasis). With Kusch, we propose that "cantar" is a practice of estar-siendo, a disobedience to the mandate to just "say" and leave what you said behind. Cantar is always attached to bodies that are in place. It is an excess of "decir"—it is a rejection of abstracting oneself from speech. And it is not a coincidence that singing and art are as central to Latin American contemporary forms of protest; their affect goes beyond "information," and perhaps, it is in this respect that Kusch writes: "el canto expresa toda la verdad del existir" (the song expresses the entire truth of existence; p. 138).[13] Can designing-in-place sing in this sense? Or has design become fatally incapacitated to create without knowing? Will it always fall short of understanding popular rationalities and ways of worlding, as the Latin American middle and upper classes and intellectuals, trapped in the project of civilisation and, moreover, with José Faustino Sarmiento, decrying when not persecuting that/those which do not want to conform to such project? Could *cantar* be the enactment of a certain strategic primitivism, as Viveiros de Castro would have it, and if so, what might be the implications for an onto-epistemically autonomous practice of designing (de Castro and Hui, 2021).

Puerto Resistencia, Colombia, April–July 2021

April 28, 2021, marked the onset of a *paro nacional*—akin to a general strike—in Colombia, an event that reverberated throughout the country, with a political epicentre in Cali, a city with a multi-ethnic population of 2.3 million inhabitants, about 40% of them Afrodescendant. The "paro" started as mobilisations against a regressive tax reform that affected impoverished sectors and the middle classes. These groups had already been deadly hit, biologically and economically, by 12 long months of restrictions imposed by the COVID-19 pandemic; they were also emotionally devastated by the spectacle of constant assassinations of social leaders, mostly environmentalists, indigenous, and black activists. In Colombia, defending the environment is to defend life—the deaths of these leaders make it obvious. "*Nos están matando*/they are killing us," this phrase became sadly famous throughout Colombia in denunciation of the assassinations of activists and those in the frontline of the 2021 wave of protests. Yet, it goes beyond that: it asserts the everyday killing effected by the denial of life stemming from the abhorrent inequality that sustains the Colombian state; this is foundationally related with its brutal monopoly of decisions concerning land and now, what we know as nature: the extraction of its resources promises unlimited economic growth. Opposing this is a confrontation that the state cannot tolerate, and rather than engaging in politics, it transforms adversaries into enemies and declares the death sentence of the latter.

Notes on excess: towards pluriversal design   39

Life was already at stake when those opposing the tax reform took to the streets and continued fighting when the might of the state was unleashed to quell what were actually demands to be alive and live with dignity, for the right to breathe, and clean air at that. Thus, we suggest that what started as opposition to neoliberal tax reforms was never merely such: it was an outburst of cries demanding to count. As Kusch might have it, it was, and is, the irruption of what cannot be by modern mandate or, as the black activist and vice-presidential candidate for the Historical Pact progressive coalition Francia Márquez were to put it as a central principle of her campaign throughout the ensuing months, it was the irruption of "los nadies y las nadies" (the nobodies). Irruptions of this sort had surely happened before in Colombia and throughout the continent, but this time, it involved a refusal to be denied, since what is at stake is a potential transition to another Colombia altogether, quite different from the current one, often classified in international rankings as one of the most unequal, corrupt, and violent in the world, and with the largest internally displaced population in the planet, close to eight million.

Using Rancière's terms—with which Kusch may have found some coincidence—we can say that it was the insurgence of politics: those that *count as not counting* demand to be included in the counted. Yet, this time, the cries were insistently public and remained on the streets longer than ever, defying the absolute danger of being killed by state forces. "They messed with those that have nothing to lose" is how the insurgents explained their defiance of death. Peoples of all colours, and young and old, men, women, and neither one, have come together in defence of life, and they do so collectively in a Cali neighbourhood tellingly re-baptised as *Puerto Resistencia*. There, a container has been transformed into a bunker, a police station into a library, and a community meeting room into a medical station. This is how the BBC reported the first few weeks of the protests:

> Por primera vez en décadas los **obreros, campesinos, indígenas y estudiantes** se organizaron para protestar al tiempo; la caída de la reforma tributaria en medio de una emergencia fiscal mostró grietas en un modelo económico hasta ahora sólido y la capacidad de los políticos para generar confianza y resoluciones parece más limitada que nunca (Emphasis in the original).[14]

Puerto Resistencia—and many sectors in Cali—shelters peoples from the whole region. In many instances, as in the case of the indigenous Minga or organisations from the Pacific Littoral, their presence is not disconnected from rivers, mountains, forests, for they *are with* those entities that they defend as they defend their lives. This ability to be in inseparable relation *with* what the state covets for "economic growth" defies the state monopoly over land and nature indeed. But it also does more than that: it challenges the

40 *Marisol de la Cadena and Arturo Escobar*

state's onto-epistemic constitution which can recognise "obreros, indígenas, campesinos, estudiantes" (like the BBC does) but is unable to fathom—and thus negates—their inseparable being with what they defend. And this is where we want to add to Rancière, opening the limits of the Modern Constitution to what exceeds it: we propose that what was/is at stake with the mobilisations is the emergence of pluriversal contact zones, perhaps of a new kind, an emergent politics with an impending potential to modify what the modern deems impossible and can make it such *within its own limits*. The unprecedented *paro* (as the months-long wave of strikes in 2019 Chile) opened up possibility in ways previously unimaginable for what exists negatively within the limits and affirms itself beyond those limits, as Kusch intuited.[15]

We suggest that the breakdown that occurred may have been an unprecedented insurgence: one that housed an emergence, a novel kind of gathering for which no name yet exists as it exceeds the possible within the historically usual politics in Colombia. For a short time, this emergence opened up a pluriversal zone between deeply entangled but contrasting worlding projects (capitalist, modernist, and developmentalist, on one side; and multiple visions of justice, equality, care, non-humans, and life, on the other side), creating the opportunity for the various worlds to discover themselves in a shared space. The state, however, could not allow such possibility to come to fruition, heavily repressing its presence, militarily, discursively, onto-epistemically, with the unfailing support of conventional mass media.[16] By all counts, while the state continued to think about the emergence as something to be controlled (so as to re-establish the norm as soon as possible), those mobilised, we suggest, were thinking *in* the emergence, thus creating thought beyond the established given, intuiting a transition to a different kind of society, beyond the abnormal normalcy of the present. *No volveremos a la normalidad, porque la normalidad era el problema* (We shall not go back to normality because normality was the problem to begin with), was loudly heard in Chile in October 2019; this slogan reverberated and reappeared in Colombia with the pandemic and the paro. The Colombian emergence was improvised, a politics that was proposed as it was being practised. So as its participants protested and marched, they made music, and danced, and performed, and designed all the paraphernalia needed for the protests. Puerto Resistencia itself became a site for the lively practice of counter-design of sorts.

The spatial, emotional, and political heart of Puerto Resistencia was/is a ten-meter-high impressive sculpture in the shape of an arm culminating in a fist holding a sign stating simply: Resist! Built collectively throughout the span of several weeks, it coincided with the taking down by indigenous people of monumental statutes of Spanish Conquistadors in Cali, Popayán, Bogotá, and other cities. This act seemed to be saying: "Here we are, we are not done with, and we are rising." Constructed of multiple materials including sand, cement, metal, and cardboard, among others, it was even deemed safe by city inspectors in terms of its structural integrity; it may mean that the structure is there to stay, announcing that another Colombia is possible. It became the space of congregation for "first line protesters" but also for children and older adults, grandmas, medical volunteers, musicians, performers, and all those that, even as the insurgence has quelled, have kept the emergence alive. Concerts were held at its foot, summoning those attending to keep up and be a presence for the long haul.

In this sense, we venture to propose that the *paro* itself is a kind of design, but one intended to *parar*—to stop the everyday functioning of the abnormal normality that organises life and death—or shall we say the death of life—in "Colombia." It is not an imaginative stretch of mind to propose that the multiple blockages of main roads throughout the country made palpable the demand of the strike to stop the cycle of political and economic violence. For a time at least, in Puerto Resistencia, another worlding was imagined and practised, an example of what has been called "prefigurative politics," the kind of politics that endeavours from the start to practise a desired world. We cannot discuss at length here the implications of the recent forms of protests that have become prominent in Latin America, particularly since 2019 (in countries like Chile, Colombia, Peru, and others), much less their possible outcomes in the short and medium terms; yet, we believe they propose an onto-epistemic re-design of politics. To offer what we mean, we turn to design as we end this text.[17]

On pluriversal designing

Kusch relocates objects within the stream of existence, where they re-acquire their character of always entangled, and hence agential, things. As he ponders (demarcating his argument from Heidegger's), "¿No será la filosofía del tiempo un simple recurso para salvar la originalidad de una cultura que, como la occidental, *ha creado los objetos?*" ("Could it be the case that the philosophy of [linear, cumulative] time is a simple trick to save Western culture, *which has created the object?*"; our emphasis, p. 73). There is no doubt that design has played an important role in the consolidation of an ontology of inherently existing objects, and of individual subjects' intent on creating and using them, rendering them into "scarce" commodities, extracting value from them, hoarding and discarding them, turning them into waste, and so forth. Design has contributed hugely to laying down the social orders that naturalise and enact such an ontology. Today, the results are everywhere for all to see: in the treatment of most humans, Earth, and life, as objects, i.e., as entities which need to be subjected to the requirements of such an ontology, by force if necessary but preferably through biopolitical management, technoscience, politics, and design—all of which has resulted in a world of obscene social inequalities, untold destruction of the Earth, profligate consumption and waste, and a paroxysm of profit making; in short, a threat to life.

42 Marisol de la Cadena and Arturo Escobar

Argentinean anthropologist Rita Segato counterposes two historical projects: *el proyecto histórico de las cosas* (the historical project of things) and *el proyecto histórico de la vincularidad* or the project of relations. While the former is the materialisation of capitalism and the state-form of the world—with their coloniality and mandate of masculinity—the latter is the realisation of a communal-form of world making. As she clarifies, "we only have intermediate situations, interfaces, transitions between the State-reality and the place-world," although the fact of being in between-worlds can be regressive or progressive, enabling or disabling of relational and communal forms of life (2015, pp. 78, 79). For Segato, the project of things instaurates a "pedagogy of cruelty" functional to dispossession (2018); it arrests life while enshrining the realm of the object, essential to capitalism. These orders can be dismantled by building on the relational and communal practices that still inhabit, in fragmentary and contradictory ways, many Afro-Latin American, indigenous, peasant, and urban marginal worlds. As she concludes (2016, p. 106):

> We need to remake our ways of living, to reconstruct the strong links existing in communities with the help of the 'technologies of sociability' commanded by women in their domains; these locally rooted practices are embedded in the dense symbolic fabric of an alternative cosmos, dysfunctional to capital, and proper of the *pueblos* (peoples) in the political journey that has allowed them to survive throughout five-hundred years of continued conquest. We need to advance this politics day by day, outside the State: to re-weave the communal fabric as to restore the political character of domesticity proper of the communal … *To choose the relational path is to opt for the historical project of being community* … It means to endow relationality and the communal forms of happiness with a grammar of value and resistance capable of counteracting the powerful developmentalist, exploitative, and productivist rhetoric of things with its alleged meritocracy. *La estrategia a partir de ahora es femenina* (the strategy, from now own, is a feminine one; our emphasis).

We may say that for Segato, as for Kusch, practices of collectively being-through-relations continue to exist in Latin America, defying the history of their destruction, despite the inimical conditions that tear apart the communities that such relations build. Segato's quote above constitutes a statement of radical relational–communal politics that can foster pluriversal designing. She calls for counter-pedagogies to cruelty, which she sees as pedagogies against patriarchal powers (wherever they may be, we add) to enable a dis-identification with the historical project of things. Following Mexican feminist sociologist Raquel Gutiérrez Aguilar (2017), we see in this dis-identification a *politics in the feminine:* an ethical practice of power centred on the care and reproduction of life as a whole, in tandem with the post-capitalist social

Notes on excess: towards pluriversal design 43

re-appropriation of collectively produced goods, and beyond the masculinist/ patriarchal canonical practice of the political, linked to capital accumulation and the state and articulating profits through destruction and death.

Before concluding with some implications for designing, there is one more aspect we would like to discuss. What we know as "objects" arise from a dualist ontology that separates mind and body, observer and observed, humans and non-humans. Representation is a required feature of such an ontology; in the realist and rationalistic tradition, "I think, therefore I am" implies "I represent, therefore I am." Such tradition posits a correspondence between representation and reality, between language and things, and this correspondence exhausts the field of knowledge-as-science (Escobar, 2018; Winograd and Flores, 1986). It is quite different from an epistemology of comprehension (holistic understanding), *sentipensamiento* (feeling-thinking), *co-razonar* (co-reasoning through the heart), and embodied knowledge fundamental to some relational ontologies. Representation and the object are required by what Colombian design theorist Alfredo Gutiérrez conceptualises as "project"—an imagination, an ethos, and indeed a practice—which he considers the pillar of modern design and which, in his view, designers consider "the only one." His critique is worth quoting at length (2021, p. 57):

> Modern design (the only one) monopolizes the relationships with tomorrow under the idea of 'project.' The future can only be reached through project, which ends up capturing every possibility of existence. ... [T]he invasive monoculture of a single species of design spreads, 'projecting' over the entire Earth, like a disease, the unique Western world which denies all others. Because for the West there are no other worlds, only unfinished fragments of itself. But in the lands of prefiguration, many plant species distinct from 'design' grow; in the other worlds, which do exist, many things are relationally brought into life by the others of design, by design with other names.

Gutiérrez's protestation against reducing the human and more-than-human histories of what he terms artifice and prefiguration to manifestations of the "will to project" (indelibly linked to the will to power) and, hence, to the modern understanding of design is more than a cautionary note. Surely, it applies to the need to resist bringing the rest of the world into project-driven design through "development"; it also warns against reducing "other-than-Western design" to second-class design or to the category of "craft." In bringing into light an entire new domain of alternatives *to* design rather than alternative designs, through what he calls "Dessobons"—a panoply of practices that include "DEsigns of the South, the Souths, Others, by other NameS" (p. 66)—and by going beyond "designorance" (by which he means those other practices that design ignores and that it ignores it ignores) he invites designers to a decolonial reflection that heals design from its

44 *Marisol de la Cadena and Arturo Escobar*

Occidentosis and *Westoxification* (p. 65) while opening up to the multiple other traditions that brings entities relationally into life.[18]

Our inquiry above suggests the following questions for designing: what would become of designing if it were to be based on the fundamental insight that the world does not exist "out there," separate from us, but that we construct it with every one of our actions and perceptions? That worlds co-emerge with actions—even the one-world world—within a complex dynamic of causality, contingency, and drift? Such an awareness would require a practice of design in which objects, representations, and projects cease to be foundational to the understanding of life and the making of the world/worlds: designing as a practice that contributes to weaken those ways of making life that prioritise measurement, optimisation, productivity, efficiency, and control, *in practical (not just theoretical) terms.* We propose that such practice of design would contribute to a sort of "ontological detox" of worlding practices that make the world one and instead engage in making (aka designing) pluriversally with, but also problematising and displacing, object-centred world making and design. This non-representational thrust of pluriversal designing would become (at least partially) a grounding to challenge the might of the one-world and of one-world making design.

We do not want to underestimate the practical challenges posed by pluriversality and the ontological excess we have described for designing. We emphasise the need to go beyond design as a noun—a singularly identifiable practice—that takes place (literally!) within an also singularly identifiable network of subjects and objects, to act towards design as a verb—a practice that is in a constant process of reimagining itself collectively and pluriversally, that is, as taking place within the relational fields that make up localised worlds; designing as made up of weavings of situated practices and tools that differ from the object-oriented routines that go under the banner of design thinking and user-human-centred design; designing that strays from the fashionable notions of the day, such as smartness, innovation, branding, and, of course, all the trends having to do with digitalisation and AI. The challenge is real also in the sense that it demands from practitioners to let go of, or at least bracket, the glamour that often accompanies the persona of the designer-creator. By comparison, the feats to be pursued through pluriversal designing will likely appear as small and even banal. Designing praxes understood as the healing and caring for the web of interrelations that make up the bodies, places, landscapes, and communities that we all *are* and inhabit might not look that glamorous by comparison. But if designing aims to contribute to a world of many worlds within ontologies of estar-siendo and praxes of healing and care, it will have to broach the task of creating and experimenting collectively in a situated, relational manner. Such renewed understanding might allow feeling the excess that may interrupt colonising, Anthropocenic/capitalocenic forces, while fostering sites to collective experiment with tools appropriate to relational modes of creating. The task of pluriversal designing may need to imagine and experiment with

Notes on excess: towards pluriversal design   45

tools, artefacts, materialities, and infrastructures conducive to open-ended designing endeavours hospitable of those that do not recognise themselves in "design" and welcoming of what they may make of designing.[19] A pluriversal design opens to the undesigned and without designer indeed.

To end, we attempt a succinct answer to these questions in the form of the following set of propositions (some of these are further elaborated in Escobar, 2021; Escobar, Osterweil & Sharma, 2015):

1 Designing pluriversally means designing with/in/from a world of many worlds, with an active awareness that knowing, being, and making life under the premise of dualism has the power to negate possibility to that which ontologically exceeds such premise.
2 Designing pluriversally implies designing relationally, that is, based on the premise that life is constituted by the radical interdependence of everything that exists. Thus, it has to start from and dwell in "not knowing" as epistemic stance to become with such immeasurable, always emergent relationality. Designing pluriversally has to be humble, a practice among other practices.
3 Designing pluriversally places in parenthesis the modern notions of representation, object and project and their associated practices, opening possibility to non-representational, non-object centred, and non-projectual designing praxes.
4 Designing pluriversally works for the reconstitution, healing and caring for the web of interrelations that make up the bodies, places, and landscapes that we are and inhabit.
5 Designing pluriversally is mindful of the conditions of generalised individuation, de-localisation, de-communalisation, and de-placing effected by modern forces; conversely, it contributes to the relational recommunalisation of social life and relocalisation of activities such as eating ("food"), healing ("health"), learning ("education"), dwelling ("housing"), and livelihood provisioning ("economy").
6 Designing pluriversally aims to heal the ontological *desarraigo* (uprootedness) from (of?) body, place, and landscape through forms of making that contribute to re-embodying, replacing, and re-earthing life.
7 Designing pluriversally means regaining the capacity for making life autonomously, instead of outsourcing it to institutions, experts, the state, and the capitalist economy. It strays away from a world centred on dualistic being and having—the historical project of objects/things—while favouring an ontology of *estar-siendo*—the historical project of relations and *arraigo* or attachment to place.
8 Designing pluriversally fosters a departure from anthropocentrism figuring modes of being with forms of life and non-life, fostering conditions for all earth-beings to flourish. It instils an ethics and politics that confer a sense of being at home in a world of aliveness. It creates spaces for reimagining ourselves as pluriverse and as community.

46 *Marisol de la Cadena and Arturo Escobar*

9 Designing pluriversally contributes to dismantle the mandate of masculinity that is at the core of the object-driven ontology of modernity. It practises a politics in the feminine that emphasises collective modes of making and acting, pragmatically privileging communitarian forms of rootedness.
10 Designing pluriversally thrives within pluriversal contact zones, defined as sites of encounter among divergent worlds that are suffused with relations of mutual excess. PCZs open up designing to conversations of care across divergent worlding practices.
11 Designing pluriversally takes seriously the struggles for social justice, respect for the Earth, and the rights to life and being of human and non-human entities.
12 Designing pluriversally involves learning to walk with entities—human and other-than-human persons—nourished by relational existence, as they rise in defence of their life territories, strengthening their life-making and autonomy-oriented practices.
13 Designing pluriversally requires a renewed awareness of how the creation of conditions for life-sustaining co-existence will necessarily have to engage with the dominant logic of unsustainability and defuturing (Fry, 2012, 2021). It thus requires awareness of the ways in which representational practices that want to exclude what does not represent are accomplices of forms of defuturing that lead to destruction.
14 Designing pluriversally understands that it needs to go beyond the grammar of "problems" and "solutions," particularly as it pertains to civilisational challenges such as climate change, which are "ontologically *unframeable, unthinkable* and *incalculable*" (Akomolafe, 2020).
15 Designing pluriversally resists translating the inexhaustible reservoir of non-representational practices into the grammars of modern design, letting them come into the foreground as instances of the relational making of life.
16 Designing pluriversally could become a magnificent key player in the civilisational transitions from toxic to healing existence. This reorientation will take a lot of work. Only slowly will pluriversal designers discover the considerable potential of acting from interdependence and care.

Notes

1 Many discussions of relationality use "radical interdependence" in a way similar to "intra-connected" to indicate the inherent relation among worlds, as in the Southern Africa notion of Ubuntu: I am because you are. By this they mean that nothing has separate, intrinsic existence by itself; everything is mutually constituted; see Escobar, Osterweil and Sharma (2015); Sharma (2015).
2 The book *Earth Beings: Ecologies of Practice across Andean Worlds* was one expression of those conversations (see De la Cadena, 2015).
3 Two PSs: 1. Perhaps, philosophy would call those presences "existents," and also perhaps, it would try and fail to prove their being and proceed to deny it. 2. As an

Notes on excess: towards pluriversal design 47

anthropologist, Marisol could have translated these presences into ethnographic *knowledge* through an analysis of cultural beliefs. This shares episteme with philosophy and accrues to knowledge—not wrong indeed, yet within coloniality as well.

4 This is also in keeping with Pratt's original concept which, she explains, draws from "contact language" as used in linguistics to refer "to an improvised language that develops among speakers of different tongues who need to communicate with each other consistently ..." (Pratt, 1992: 8). We also modify Pratt's original notion for our intention to make audible, not the improvised language, but the ways in which other ontological grammars inflect the one that the hegemonic language(s) presupposes.

5 The work of our friend and co-thinker fellow traveller Mario Blaser with Innu people of Labrador provides another example for exploring the concept of pluriversal contact zones. It concerns the entangled but contrasting explanations for the decline in caribou/*atîku* (which is the Innu word for the Euro-Canadian caribou); the asymmetrical composition of *atîku* and caribou worlds; and the possibility that this case evinced for a time the existence of "interests in common that are not the same interest," in that the Innu and Canadian biologists had a common interest in lessening the decline of *atîku* and caribou. See Blaser (2013, 2016). Such pluriversal approach is being fruitfully explored through ethnographic cases involving forests, mountains, rivers, and many other earth-beings, exploring the possibility of alliances among heterogeneous worlding practices that come together around dissimilar interests in common, in ways that allow for convergences but also divergences among forms of worlding.

6 This is a difficult statement to translate: "*Lo criollo* conciliates both, because it allows all reference to things, that is, the subject-object relation, even if cunningly/naughtily, so that it also ends up sustaining the other [modern] vector, as an always available domain of invocation/prayer in which faith, ethics, and popular politics become strengthened."

7 "If the former (educated thinking) stems from a genuine concern with respect to science, the latter (popular thought) springs from an equally compelling preoccupation with the sheer fact of living ... this opposition could also be related with that between the logic used by the colonizers and that of the colonized."

8 This is one of the stronger points of second-order cybernetics and of the entire view of cognition as enaction pioneered by Francisco Varela; see Escobar (2018) for s discussion and sources.

9 Think, for instance, about so many genres of popular music in Latin America that movingly narrate the co-existence of humans and more-than-humans ("nature"). The brilliant Argentinian poet and singer of place Atahualpa Yupanki embodies this feature at its best.

10 "Negation recues that which exists, the daily frustrations, the projects never realized, *all that which constitutes the impossibility of being from the perspective of the West.* .... The project of existence emerges from the immersion in what is negative itself. ... Negation operates at the level of simply existing, to the extent that it submerges one in the real totality of what exists. .... This differentiation between negation and affirmation in Latin America results in a demarcation of what is from what exists, and this difference cannot be but ontological. I cannot take as true solely what is, but also what exists."

11 Kusch is interested in the question of whether there can be a Latin American, or just another, science founded on what is negated, one based on *el curioso enredo de vivir en la negación* (the curious entanglement of living within the negation) – a non-colonising science (110).

12 "I'm no educated singer, but if I start to sing there's nothing to make me stop and I'll grow old singing—the verses go spouting from me like water from a spring."

48 Marisol de la Cadena and Arturo Escobar

13 Witness the title of one of Pablo Neruda's most famous books of poems, *Canto General* (General Song; 1950), an ode to the continent's epic history since pre-Columbian times.

14 "For the first time in decades, **workers, peasants, indigenous peoples and students** organized to protest collectively. The repeal of the tax reform amid a fiscal emergency showed the fissures in what until then was considered a strong economic model, and politicians' ability to generate trust and provide solutions appeared as more limited than ever." https://www.bbc.com/mundo/noticias-america-latina-57066928 accessed May 25, 2021.

15 In early works, Marisol contended that earth-beings in politics *do not even count as not counting*; they exceed the principle of the count. Rancière's concept of politics, challenging as it is of liberal political thought, thus does not challenge the coloniality of its modern inception.

16 One may wonder whether the process of writing a new Constitution in Chile, and the very composition of the popularly elected Constituent Assembly, cannot be seen as creating such multi onto-epistemic shared space. The Constitution, in this sense, would be a PCZ which could (and should) be capacious enough to harbour the multiple worlds and ways of worlding populating its national territory.

17 As of the time of this writing (July 31, 2021), there are already many sources on the internet on Puerto Resistencia, from both mainstream media services and alternative media outlets.

18 As Gutiérrez states, there are "prefigurative practices aplenty" in the archives of human artifice (p. 63). While indigenous traditions are the clearest case (both past and present!), there are many examples in fields such as dwelling and construction (what moderns call "architecture," which such constructions can also be but not only), food, healing, navigation, learning, technology, and so forth—that is, in so many domains of life in which humans have lived in sufficiency and autonomy.

19 Our gratitude to an anonymous reviewer for suggesting some of these poignant questions. Of course, this does not mean that the task needs to start from scratch. There are many transformative initiatives at present that provide insightful clues. Here, we may locate a diverse set of visions and proposals, such as Chinese philosopher Yuk Hui's appeal to art and cosmotechnics as a way to explore a different relation between technology and nature that engages with Western ontology without becoming techno-logistic; Bayo Akomolafe's (2021) call for "coming down to earth," going into the cracks of the dominant systems, and building sanctuary for the wider living coalitions that refuse to coexist with oppressive systems; design theorist Ezio Manzini's (2022) call for a novel practice of urban dwelling under a novel paradigm of relationality and care based on proximity, which is essential for a place-based and Earth-wise human sociality; and evolving experiments and frameworks for transition design, biodesign, regenerative design (Wahl, 2016, for an inspiring example), and autonomous design. There are also wonderful new insights emerging from interrelated fields such as animism (e.g., Weber, 2020) and plant consciousness. Many of these, of course, will have to be steered ontologically towards more explicit relational and pluriversal understanding and designing possibilities.

Bibliography

Akomolafe, B. (2020). "What Climate Collapse Asks of Us." https://www.bayoakomolafe.net/post/what-climate-collapse-asks-of-us.

Akomolafe, B. (2021). "Coming Down to Earth." March 11, 2021. https://www.bayoakomolafe.net/post/coming-down-to-earth.

Notes on excess: towards pluriversal design 49

Benjamin, W. (1969). *Illuminations*. New York: Schocken Books.

Biemann, U., & Tavares, P. (Directors) (2014). *Forest Law/Selva Jurídica*. Multi-channel video installation and photo-text assemblage.

Blaser, M. (2013). "Ontological Conflicts and the Stories of Peoples in Spite of Europe: Towards a Conversation on Political Ontology." *Current Anthropology* 54(5): 547–568.

Blaser, M. (2016). "Is Another Cosmopolitics Possible?" *Cultural Anthropology* 31(4): 545–570.

de la Cadena, M. (2010). "Indigenous Cosmopolitics in the Andes: Conceptual Reflections beyond 'politics.'" 25(2): 334–370.

de la Cadena, M. (2015). *Earth Being: Ecologies of Practices across Andean worlds*. Durham. Duke University Press.

de la Cadena, M. (2018). "Uncommoning Nature. Stories from the Anthropo-Not-Seen." In *Atnropoos and the Material*. Penny Harvey, Christian Krohn-Hansen and Knut G. Nustad, eds. Durham, Duke University Press, pp. 35–58.

de la Cadena, M. (2021). "Not Knowing: In the Presence of ...." In *Experimenting with Ethnography: A Companion to Analysis*. Andrea Ballestero and Vritt Wintherik, eds. Durham: Duke University Press, pp. 246–256.

Deleuze, G., & Guattari, F. (1987). *A Thousand Plateaus*. Minneapolis: University of Minnesota Press.

Escobar, A. (2014). *Sentipensar con la tierra*. Medellín: UNAULA.

Escobar, A. (2018). *Designs for the Pluriverse: Radical Interdependence, Autonomy, and the Making of Worlds*. Durham: Duke University Press.

Escobar, A. (2020). *Pluriversal Politics: The Real and the Possible*. Durham: Duke University Press.

Escobar, A. (2021). "Designing as a Futural Praxis for the Healing of the Web of Life." In *Design in Crisis: New Worlds, Philosophies and Practices*. T. Fry and A. Nocek, eds. London: Routledge, pp. 25–42.

Escobar, A., Osterweil, M., & Sharma, K. (2015). *Designing Relationally: Making & Restor(y)ing Life*. https://www.gtu.edu/events/designing-relationally-making-and-restorying-life.

Fry, T. (2012). *Becoming Human by Design*. London: Berg.

Fry, T. (2021). *Defuturing: A New Design Philosophy*. London: Bloomsbury.

Gualinga J. (2014). In Biemann, U., & Tavares, P. (Directors) (2014). *Forest Law/Selva Jurídica*. Multi-channel video installation and photo-text assemblage.

Gutiérrez, A. (2021). "When Design Goes South: From Decoloniality, through Declassification, to *Dessobons*." In *Design in Crisis. New Worlds, Philosophies and Practices*. T. Fry and A. Nocek, eds. London: Routledge, pp. 56–74.

Gutiérrez Aguilar, R. (2017). *Horizontes comunitarios-populares*. Madrid: Traficantes de Sueños.

Hui, Y. (2021). *Art and Cosmotechnics*. Brooklyn: e-flux Books; Minneapolis: University of Minnesota Press, 2021.

Kusch, R. (1975). *La negación en el pensamiento popular*. Buenos Aires: Editorial las Cuarenta.

Law, J. (2015). "What's Wrong with a One-World World?" *Distinktion: Scandinavian Journal of Social Theory* 16(1): 126–139.

Manzini, E. (2022). *Livable Proximity: Ideas for the City That Cares*. Milano: Egea.

Pratt, M. L. (1992). *Imperial Eyes, Travel Writing and Transculturation*. London. Routledge.

50 *Marisol de la Cadena and Arturo Escobar*

Rancièr, J. (1999). *Disagreement. Politics and Philosophy*. Minneapolis. University of Minnesota Press.

Segato, R. (2016). *La guerra contra las mujeres*. Madrid: Traficantes de Sueños.

Segato, R. (2018). *Contra-pedagogías de la crueldad*. Buenos Aires: Prometeo Libros.

Sharma, K. (2015). *Interdependence: Biology and Beyond*. New York: Fordham University Press.

Stengers, I. (2011). "Comparison as Matter of Concern." *Common Knowledge* 17(1): 48–63.

Viveiros de Castro, E., & Hui, Y. (2021). "For a Strategic Primitivism: A Dialogue between Eduardo Viveiros de Castro and Yuk Hui." *Philosophy Today* 65(2): 391–400.

Wahl, D. C. (2016). *Designing Regenerative Cultures*. Axminster: Triarchy Press.

Weber, A. (2020). *Sharing Life: The Ecopolitics of Reciprocity*. Delhi: Heinrich Böll Stiftung.

Winograd, T., & Flores, F. (1986). *Understanding Computers and Cognition Norwood: A New Foundation for Design*. Norwood: Ablex Publishing Corporation.

2 Anticipations of more-than-human futures

Social innovation as a decentring, engendering, reframing, and caring practice

Ezio Manzini and Virginia Tassinari

Anticipations of more-than-human futures are already among us. They can be seen by looking carefully into the complexity of contemporary reality: they are examples of practices, and behind them cultural approaches, which counter the dominant anthropocentric mindset. They can be based on traditional ideas and worldviews which have not yet been influenced by modernity, or they can represent moments of rupture within modernity, opposing it from within.

Leaving to others the necessary and complex task to talk (in this volume) about indigenous cultures which have not been influenced by modernity, we will refer here to the ways of being and doing emerging from within this crisis of modernity, as it is the case for forms of social innovation which can be considered radical cultural innovations. Our proposal is to consider these practices and ideas as expressions of ways of being and doing that—by redis-covering the value of collaboration—recognise the complexity of the world we inhabit and the intrinsic limitations of our actions. For this reason, they can be regarded as anticipations of more-than-human futures.

Social innovation as cultural innovation

The beginning of this century has been dominated by the pervasive diffusion of neoliberal economic models and political practices. In their global spread, these practices and ideas have further developed, accelerating the process of destroying the environment as well as the social fabric. Nevertheless, even in their pervasiveness, these neoliberal ways of being and doing do not occupy the entire stage. A careful scrutiny of contemporary reality shows us a com-posite and dynamic social landscape, in which other ways of being and doing actually co-exist. Those are the result of the initiative of creative, entrepre-neurial people who, when facing a problem or an opportunity, come up with new initiatives and put them into practice. Those initiatives are endowed with values which are individual and social at the same time, ranging, for instance, from groups of mutual assistance to care communities, and from small-scale place-based production to the regeneration of urban commons. Such initia-tives tend to (re)connect people in their context, with the places in which

DOI: 10.4324/9781003319689-3

52 Ezio Manzini and Virginia Tassinari

they live, and (re)generate trust and dialogue. In doing so, these initiatives regenerate the social fabric. While these activities are produced at first by small groups of enthusiasts, over time they can evolve and meet with institutional frameworks. The result is that they can end up representing significant countertrends to be found in diverse aspects of everyday life: collaborative social services, various forms of distributed and open production, collaborative welfare, food networks based on new relationships between producers and consumers, and proposals for cities based on new ideas of proximity (Manzini, 2019).

Such bottom-up activities, considered as a whole, are commonly named *social innovation*: a term which has been widely used in the past 15 years, and has become associated with various meanings.[1] Here, it refers to changes in socio-technological systems in which participants break with the individualism proposed by the current dominant neoliberal cultural model and decide to collaborate to enable a social and cultural change for their own context, creating specific value for each of them individually but also for society as a whole.[2]

So far, there have mainly been two different kinds of potential "outcomes" envisioned for social innovation initiatives: the opening of practical possibilities (direct outcome) and the production of social values (indirect outcome). But it seems that there might be another kind of indirect outcome, namely a change in the underlying epistemological paradigm, it can also generate ideas regarding what it might mean to move away from the anthropocentric approach that, until now, has dominated design actions in Western and Westernised societies, moving us closer to a more-than-human approach.[3] The latter implies a move to start recognising the entanglement and interdependencies connecting us to a multiplicity of other agents (human and non-human) beyond ourselves. To acknowledge this means to fully recognise that everything we can possibly do, every action we can engage with, is done from within an intrinsically and irreducibly complex system. This has several implications, of which some might be considered indicators of the steps one needs to undertake to move towards a more-than-human approach, i.e., decentring us as humans, engendering results, reframing systems, and caring for the web of life.

Decentring humans

Recognising complexity means to acknowledge that we are not at the centre of the system. This has to do with the fact that a complex system is a web of interdependencies which, by definition, has no centre. Hence, to recognise complexity implies to adopt a non-anthropocentric approach.

Taking a closer look, one can consider two well-known examples: community gardens (pieces of urban land collectively gardened by groups of citizens) and communities of care (collaborative organisations in which citizens help each other with the support of professional caregivers).

At the heart of each of those social innovation practices, we find people who, in a conscious way, (re)discover and put into practice the possibilities of collaborating to obtain a certain goal: to have a public garden in their neighbourhood and create preconditions for safety and care for elderly and fragile people. In both examples, however, there is something more to it. In the first case, one also experiences the pleasure of gardening, while in the second case, there is the pleasure of doing something for others.

Finally, for both, there is an underlying motivation in feeling part of an initiative that helps to regenerate the city and society. What is important to us here is that both cases cannot be reduced to singular motivations and results: they are always multiple, and their quality depends precisely on this multiplicity. Social innovators recognise this kind of complexity consciously as a core value of what they do as a richness of the experiences they provide. Moreover, the intrinsic complexity of the projects they implement and the results they achieve must also be considered as an expression of their ability to deal with the complexity of their own context (in this case, the neighbourhood in which to establish a community garden or a community of care): a concrete context made up not only of people but also of physical place, infrastructure, artefacts, plants, and animals. This awareness might help to recognise that they are not at the centre of the world, but a mere part of a system of interdependencies which has no real centre (Escobar, 2018).

Engendering the results

Recognising complexity also means to acknowledge that we cannot really control the system of which we are part. This means we cannot define the actual effects of our actions. The reason for this ought to be found in the fact that within a complex system (and each initiative ought to be considered a complex system), each agent interacts with the other agents in an unpredictable way. Therefore, recognising complexity means to recognise that we cannot actually "produce" any kind of outcomes but only contribute to their co-generation. In other words, we can barely do something to make them more possible and probable.

Returning to the aforementioned cases, they cannot be directly produced, as citizens cannot be forced to be gardeners or to take care of someone else. When those projects succeed, this happens because of a multiplicity of converging factors. The intentional action of the promoters of the initiative, who have done something to make them possible, is but one of the elements of the system that guarantees the success of the initiative.

Bruno Latour proposes the word "engendering" to address this kind of processes, i.e., processes considering the complex webs of interdependencies from which the aims of those projects might interdepend:

> To speak of engendering is to establish a distinction between the act of producing—which attributes the undertaking and the central role to

the human agent and the act of *contributing to the generation*—which shifts the center of gravity onto other modes of action.

(Latour, 2015)

Unlike the anthropocentric idea of "production" of which we often make use in our contemporary societies, when referring to engendering processes that we consider to be part of a bigger process and of which we are not in control, we are just one of the many agents interweaving, interacting with others and jointly forming the web of life.

This awareness is in our opinion already present in social innovation initiatives. For instance, a community garden and a community of care which are well integrated in each neighbourhood are not just to be attributed to one singular subject (a subject who decides to do something and implements it). Instead, they exist because of the interactions between every other actor contributing to their realisation. What a single actor can do, rather, is intervene on and within its own ecosystem to give both community gardens and communities of care a greater chance to exist, thrive, and last over time. This means that social innovations cannot really be "produced." All we can do is to intervene to make them possible and more probable (Manzini, 2015). These enabling interventions ought therefore to be considered engendering practices.

Reframing the systems

To make a result possible and probable, it is necessary to operate on a system in which this same result can be achieved. This often implies redefining the system to which we have been referring—in other words—to step into a more extensive one, including agents who were previously not considered.

Those initiatives ought to be considered transformative social innovations because they are based on the redefinition of the system in which and on which they operate. To look closer into this, let us start with a case in which this is particularly evident: community-supported agriculture (CSA). In such initiatives, there is a direct link between groups of citizens and farmers. The most obvious motivation moving citizens is to have access to fresh, local, and affordable food. Farmers instead might find them interesting because they open the opportunity of a more direct and trustful relationship with their customers.

But there is more to it. Each CSA brings together two systems that once used to be separated: that of farms around the city and that of citizens interested in fresh, local, and affordable food. In this case, the system reframing action consists precisely in connecting two systems and two groups of social actors that previously did not interact with one another directly and create a community around food. They form a network of producers and consumers gathered around a shared matter of concern.

The most evident effect of this kind of initiative is a series of advantages for all actors involved. Moreover, the CSA activates a system of interactions between people and places requiring attention and care. What they do is no longer a traditional, linear process of production and consumption, but using Latour's conceptualisation, they approximate an engendering process in which chances of success are given by the change in the system on which they are based: in other words, by reframing their own system.

This redefinition of the system on which to operate is, in our opinion, a key character of social innovation initiatives. For example, if we return to the two aforementioned cases, the creation of a community garden requires a redefinition of its own system (for instance, stepping from the system in which public parks are managed to the one needed to create and maintain a community garden). The same can be said for communities of care that, to exist, must shift from a traditional social and health services system to one based on a collaborative organisation of citizens, volunteers, local associations, and professional caregivers. For both cases, it is necessary to make the strategic move of redefining the system by including the new agents who can and should be involved.

Practices of care

To take steps towards sustainability, it is necessary to establish relationships of care. That is, our activities must work together to reweave the web of life of which we are a part.

Returning to our previous examples, it appears that no community gardens and no communities of care could be possible without *care*. The same is true for CSA initiatives, in which the new systems of food production, distribution, and consumption can work only if and when communities have been built to support them. It is also true that all communities can thrive only if they work to maintain relationships of care. This care is also key to the agricultural and urban environments within which these CSA initiatives are active. Care is key in all those cases not only because there is care for a specific issue, place, or specific kinds of communities but because of a more fundamental reason: in all of them, one can recognise an acknowledgement of how the diverse actors are interdependent within their own specific context and also of how they may contribute to make their own context—and themselves as part of it—more resilient, lively, and rich.

Maria Puig de la Bellacasa says that *"care is everything that is done (rather than everything that 'we' do) to maintain, continue and re-pair 'the world' so that all (rather than 'we') can live in it as well as possible. That world includes ... all that we seek to interweave in a complex, life-sustaining web"* (modified from Tronto 1993, 103) (De la Bellacasa, 2017). Once acknowledged the radical interdependence connecting all actors together, one cannot but care. Given this extended definition of care, in all three cases proposed,

56 Ezio Manzini and Virginia Tassinari

those who choose to collaborate do not only engage with the concrete issues they want to tackle but also with social values such as empathy, trust, and willingness to collaborate. In other words, they do so with the social value of *care*: care for people but also for places and for other actors, acknowledging their interdependence. By caring, they reweave the web of life which has been previously damaged.

This means that social innovation initiatives might be considered practices of care: regenerative practices working to reweave the radical interdependence which has been violated by our anthropocentric choices.

From practice to theory and vice versa

Transformative social innovations can show us ways of being and doing—and therefore also of designing—capable of recognising complexity. This has many implications for design: to decentre humans, engender results, reframe systems, and care for the web of life.

What is proposed here is in relation to a widespread design activity, implemented by a plurality of actors. Among them, there are also those who, due to their skills and abilities, are design experts, that is, *designers*. For them, it is a question of adopting this same approach, but with an additional task and responsibility: to introduce a special contribution of ideas and tools into the tangle of interdependencies in which they are immersed. A way of operating which, until now, we have referred to as "design *for* social innovation," but which perhaps, in the light of what has been said, could be better defined as "design *in* social innovation," considering designers, their ideas and their tools as internal agents of the system they would like to innovate.

We are aware that none of the given cases are perfect examples of what a more-than-human approach could and should be. Nevertheless, we are convinced that many of them can be read and discussed as steps in this direction. They are uncertain and often contradictory steps, but they can be considered meaningful prototypes of this approach: concrete experiences on which it is possible to reflect and from which it is possible to move forward; anticipations of what more-than-human futures could be, when eventually the acknowledgement of radical interdependence will become just common sense.

Besides providing us an anticipation of what it could mean to live and act from within this awareness, these examples can be considered concrete materials for reflection on what it might mean to design from within a deeper acknowledgement of us being part of a larger web of life. By looking at them, much can be learnt to start decentring design, prototyping ways for design to also become an engendering, reframing, and caring practice. By enabling and supporting social innovation, design can both help social innovation practices to thrive and become even more effective as well as learn a new set of values from these practices that might help design in its way out of anthropocentrism.

Furthermore, these social innovation experimentations can also provide the philosophical reflection on some concrete examples of engendering

Anticipations of more-than-human futures 57

practices and contribute to make Latour's itinerary *down to earth* more concrete. The bridge between social innovation and philosophical reflection must therefore be covered in both directions: social innovation can offer materials on which to build a theoretical reflection on how to overcome anthropocentrism and reductivism. Symmetrically, this reflection can lead to shared visions and guidelines for social innovation (and, therefore, also of design for social innovation) which, with more clarity and effectiveness, can operate in a more-than-human perspective. By feeding off each other, social innovation and philosophical reflection can contribute to the generation of a new civilisation to come, of which we are starting to see the first weak signals.

Notes

1 The conceptualisation and diffusion of the social innovation phenomenon, as it appeared at the beginning of this century, has been largely driven by English researchers from the Young Foundation and Nesta. Robin Murray, Julie Caulier Grice, and Geoff Mulgan, *Open Book of Social Innovation* (London: Nesta & the Young Foundation, 2010).
2 In our opinion, "Social innovation" ought to be considered a "transformative social innovation towards sustainability." The expression "transformative social innovation" was introduced in the ambits of the European research project Transit (ended in 2017), whose task was to investigate "transformative social network initiatives and networks in an attempt to understand the process of societal transformation" (in Transit, *Doing Things Differently*. Transit Brief #1, 2017, www.transitsocialinnovation.eu).
3 Many have discussed this issue using these or other expressions. For an overview, see the comprehensive article by Laura Forlano, 'Posthumanism and Design'. *Dhe Ji The Journal of Design, Economics, and Innovation* Volume 3, Number 1, Spring 2017 https://www.journals.elsevier.com/she-ji-the-journal-of-design-economics-and-innovation. For our part, we will take the conceptualisations made by Bruno Latour (Latour, 2015, 2018), Arturo Escobar (Escobar, 2018), and Maria Puig de la Bellacasa (De la Bellacasa, 2017) as our main references here.

Bibliography

De la Bellacasa, M. P. (2017). *Matters of Care*. Minneapolis: University of Minnesota Press.
Escobar, A. (2018). *Designs for the Pluriverse*. Durham: Duke University Press.
Forlano, L. (2017). 'Posthumanism and Design'. *She Ji The Journal of Design, Economics, and Innovation* Volume 3, Number 1: 16–29. https://doi.org/10.1016/j.sheji.2017.08.001.
Latour, B. (2017). *Facing Gaia*. Cambridge: Polity Press.
Latour, B. (2018). *Down to Earth*. Cambridge: Polity Press.
Manzini, E. (2015). *Design, When Everybody Designs*. Cambridge: MIT Press.
Manzini, E. (2019). *Politics of the Everyday*. Designing in Dark Times. London: Bloomsbury.
Murray, R., Caulier Grice, J., & Geoff Mulgan, (2010). *Open Book of Social Innovation*. London: Nesta & the Young Foundation.
Transit. (2017). *Doing Things Differently*. Transit Brief #1, www.transitsocial innovation.eu.

3 Design's intimacies
The indeterminacy of design with machines and mushrooms

Laura Forlano

How do we design in the face of immense technological and planetary uncertainty? When there is no turning back and there are no guarantees, everything must be redesigned—starting with ourselves.

This chapter struggles with the meaning of designing in a world in which both our machines (algorithms) and our natural environment (mushrooms) are characterized by indeterminacy—unknown, uncertain, unpredictable, and indefinite. The algorithms that are embedded in a wide range of computational systems produce results that are difficult to explain, even by the programmer themselves. The climate crisis continues to create unexpected weather patterns that result in hotter, wetter, colder, and dryer temperatures that impact plants, animals, and human life. By considering both machines and mushrooms, the artificial and the natural, as deeply intertwined with what it means to be human, we can begin to think, make, and remake the world in new, more relational ways, revealing the possibility of creating the conditions for living together across difference in ways that reject the binaries of human/nonhuman distinction.

In this rethinking and remaking in the field of design, we might value the more-than-human, advocate for the pluriversal, and aspire towards decolonized practices. This impulse requires that we loosen our desire to obsessively control, plan, and strategize and, rather, embrace our abilities to sense, speculate, experience, create, and anticipate. Taking praxis as a starting point, this chapter draws on a range of knowledge practices including theories from science and technology studies (STS), anthropology, and design as well as critical Black and indigenous studies, gender studies, and disability studies. Specifically, I draw on my own autoethnographic accounts from a research project about living with a "smart" medical device that I have documented in an ongoing book project to inspire the themes that I take up in this text.

I started the year 2020 with a daily 20-minute walk down the hill to Durham University, where I spent 2.5 months as a visiting fellow. On those walks, I was captivated by the language of the audio version of Anna Tsing's *The Mushroom at the End of the World*. At the same time, during those

DOI: 10.4324/9781003319689-4

months, I was struggling with continued problems with my new "smart" insulin pump, which became even more stressful while living abroad. Both algorithms and mushrooms are complex things with which to think. As both algorithms and mushrooms were very much on my mind this year, it is only fitting that, at the end of 2020, they have become characters in this chapter, standing in for broad technological and environmental categories due to their significance in recent debates about the politics of design, which are evident in discussions about topics such as "AI Ethics" and, for example, "The Social Life of Forests," which refers to the communication processes of underground fungi networks.[1]

Much of the past several centuries of Western European thought since the Enlightenment has been obsessed with the colonial quest to conquer vast geographies, dominate both human and nonhuman populations, and quantify knowledge towards an ever more perfect understanding of both computational and living systems, entangled in sociotechnical complexity. Yet, sociotechnical systems can no longer be in terms of 20th-century notions of certainty, prediction, and optimization. In fact, they were never truly grounded in these ideas, as much critical historical writing about science and technology has long argued.

Both algorithms and the multiple ongoing climate crises create potentialities far beyond what may have been previously considered as "possible, plausible, probable or preferable." Instead, we must design for the impossible, implausible, improbable, unpreferable, and unprecedented as well as the imponderable, incommensurable, and incomplete.

Our anthropocentric desires, needs, and preferences—core to the field of human-centred design—are of no concern to algorithms or to the planet. Today, nonhumans—whether machines or mushrooms—have a say, and a stake, in things as uncertain as they are.

Indeterminacy and the perpetual state of "what ifs"

Why compare the worlds of machines and mushrooms at all when it comes to their relationship to indeterminacy? This comparison is not arbitrary—for our machines have come to act in ways that are paralleled in biology. They are dynamic, generative, and evolving—like humans and the natural world—and this is very much *by design*.

In her work on the matsutake mushroom, anthropologist Anna Tsing speaks of "ephemeral glimmer" writing:

> Indeterminacy is not the end of history but rather a node in which many beginnings lie in wait. To listen politically is to detect the traces of not-yet-articulated common agendas...We cannot rely on expert spokesmen, as we have learned in human politics. We need many kinds of alertness to spot potential allies. Worse yet, the hints of common

60 *Laura Forlano*

agendas we detect are undeveloped, thin, spotty, and unstable. At best we are looking for a most ephemeral glimmer. By, living with indeterminacy, such glimmers are the political.

(2015, p. 253)

Similarly, speaking of what we might now think of as "algorithmic creatures" (Choi, Forlano, & Kera, 2020) in her work on "algorithmic architecture," philosopher Luciana Parisi explains:

Algorithms … have become equated with the generative capacities of matter to evolve. It is not by chance that the age of the algorithm has also come to be recognized as an age characterized by forms of emergent behavior that are determined by continual variation and uncertainty … Thus, on the one hand, algorithms are patterns of physical variables that stem from the circulation of the air, gravitational forces, the bearing of weight, volume, the geological nature of the ground, etc.; on the other hand, they are conceptual prehensions: **operators of potentialities** [emphasis mine], not simply calculators of probabilities.

(Parisi, 2013)

Expanding these critical analyses of algorithms, in her book *Cloud Ethics*, geographer Louise Amoore describes algorithms as multiple, relational, and partial "ethicopolitical beings" arguing that they are:

generating active, partial ways of organizing worlds is to substantially challenge notions of their neutral, impartial objectivity. To foreground partiality is also to acknowledge the novel forms of distributed authorship that newly entangles the I who speaks in composite collaborations of human and algorithm.

(Amoore, 2020)

These views of indeterminacy—whether by machine or mushroom—illustrate that we are living in a perpetual state of "what ifs." This state of "what ifs" requires new theories, methods, and practices of designing. Science asks "what is," social science and humanities ask "why is," design asks "how might we," and futures studies asks "what if." Yet, asking "what if" in a world characterized by both technological and environmental indeterminacy creates an endlessly circuitous state of instability. What will we hold onto in this confounding world? How will we make sense of it? How will we design for and live with this world?

Science	What is?
Social Science & Humanities	Why is?
Design	How might we?
Future Studies	What if?

In answer to the "what if" questions posed by our current technological and environmental conditions, critical and speculative design (Dunne & Raby, 2013) has offered a mode of engaging with uncertainty in order to consider and anticipate the social consequences of design using stories, design fictions (Bleecker, 2009), objects and experiences (Candy & Dunagan, 2017) that serve to (or intend to) destabilize (Forlano, 2019) the status quo and envision alternative possible futures. Rather than rushing into designing solutions to problems, critical design invites and provokes us to critique and interrupt business as usual, to pause and disobey the imperative to make viable, desirable, and feasible products. This impulse to slow down reflects what Isabel Stengers (2005) calls the "cosmopolitical proposal" represented by Deleuze's (as mentioned in Stengers) figure of the idiot and defined as a "space for hesitation" in search of careful explorations of what it means to build a good "common world" (and when to opt-out of the constant push towards decisions). She writes: "In the term cosmopolitical, cosmos refers to the unknown constituted by these multiple, divergent worlds and to the articulations of which they could eventually be capable." This critique can be felt acutely in the design field, with the palpable desire to take actions and simultaneously limited attention for reflection.

At the same time, critical design practices are often critiqued for their naivete—reflecting white, male, and wealthy anxieties—as well as their limited notions of participation, which are often restricted to elites that spend their weekends at galleries and museums (DiSalvo, 2012; Prado de O. Martins, 2014). In response to this, a more publicly engaged form of speculation has emerged with a focus on design friction (Forlano & Mathew, 2014), speculative civics (DiSalvo, Jenkins & Lodato, 2016), and community-based participatory design and futuring practices (Harrington, Erete, & Piper, 2019). While these works are oriented towards alternative possible futures and "design otherwise" in order to create new relations between humans, technologies, and things (Ingold, 2010), another discourse in design is oriented towards naming the condition of the world that we have designed as "defuturing," which refers to a loss of relations, a paradox, and an inability to recognize the unsustainability of the world that we have created by design (Dilnot, 2020, pp. 11–13; Fry, 2020).

Intimate infrastructures

My approach to this critical reflection has been to look more closely at my own lived experiences—the everyday, the mundane, and the intimate in order to understand the ways in which my existence literally depends on the ways in which I live with computational systems as well as speculating about the ways in which they (and I) might be made otherwise. This autoethnographic

62 Laura Forlano

approach might be described as "intimacy as method," but as the writer Monica Huerta pointed out in a recent talk about her book, it does not require "a confessional," and it is not necessarily primarily or exclusively about the self (2021), rather it offers a way to shed life on sociotechnical phenomenon. I use this approach because I feel a responsibility to tell the story of the way in which human life and technology are co-constructed in the case of "smart" medical devices. Lauren Fournier describes autotheory as a genre for "Works that exceed existing genre categories and disciplinary bounds, that flourish in the liminal spaces between categories, that reveal the entanglement of research and creation, and that fuse seemingly disparate modes to fresh effects" (2021, p. 2). Recent books by Elizabeth Chin (2016), Tressie McMillan Cottom (2018), McKenzie Wark (2020), and S. Llochlain Jain (2013) are examples of how an autoethnographic approach allows for a deeper understanding of topics from consumption to the intersection of race and medicine to gender identity and, finally, the experience of cancer (in the respective order of the authors).

In design, this is illustrated by practices including first person research (Lucero et al., 2019), soma-aesthetic design (Höök, 2018), embodied design (Wilde, Vallgårda, & Tomico, 2017), and design biography (Wakkary, 2021). By understanding the ways in which we live with computational and natural systems, we can consider our own experiences (and the theories that we make of them) as a kind of new material for design, which requires a reconsideration of who we are becoming as humans, researchers, and designers.

My own interest in the entanglements between computational systems and biological systems draws on my own experience living as a Type 1 diabetic using a "smart" insulin pump. In a way, I've been living in a version of this loop of "what ifs" for the past three years, navigating both the rhythms of an algorithm while, at the same time, being constantly surprised by the patterns present in my own body. As a result, using autoethnographic research methods, I have cultivated my own "arts of noticing" to use Tsing's words in order to document my experiences *living with an algorithm* (or, more accurately, the complex sociotechnical system of software, hardware, data, labour, etc., that allow it to function). While, as a social scientist and design researcher, I have long been interested in the gaps between the claims around computational systems and lived experience, this lived experience fosters a generative (and, sometimes, frustrating) intimacy that I have not been able to achieve with other research projects.

Specifically, I study the "intimate infrastructures" (Forlano, 2017a) that make up my world by describing and analysing the entanglements between myself and my wearable medical devices as well as the ways in which these technologies participate in and co-shape my everyday life. These human–technology relationships are intimate in that they are literally inside, on the surface of and close to my body. But they are also infrastructures in the sense that they shape and create the conditions for my relations with doctors and health-care providers, pharmacies, health insurers, medical device companies, and global supply chains in addition to significant others (through sharing sensor data about blood sugar via a mobile phone application). This juxtaposition of the very small-scale intimacies with the very structures and systems makes this concept all the more relevant for explaining what it means to live as disabled person navigating ableist situations, institutions, and societies. With a focus on themes such as labour, breakdown, and repair, often, I am not sure whether I am taking care of these technologies or whether they are taking care of me.

But things (as in, the research) got a lot more interesting three years ago when I upgraded to a "smart" insulin pump. Suddenly, I was confronted with completely new kinds of questions, challenges, and problems than in the previous five years while using an earlier model of the device. *This new system did not function according to my plans (or to any pre-set logic)*. Instead, I was confronted with algorithmic actions that were quite unexpected, spontaneous, and dynamic. In addition, I would argue that the system is also hostile, abusive, and dehumanizing as I have recently explained in a short article on "The Dangers of Intimate Algorithms" (Forlano, 2020). In it, I describe my experience of sleep deprivation caused by the fact that the system requires my labour in order to function and repeatedly wakes me up many times a night. For legal as well as functional reasons, it must keep the human in the loop.

In my writing on this subject, I have used the notion of the *disabled cyborg* in order to capture specific *posthuman failures* of our computational systems. Thus, it is not only I but also my machine that is disabled through our relations with one another as well as our embeddedness in social structures, systems, and environments. As such, I argue that, rather than hanging on to techno-fixes that fetishize notions of control (over nature, the body, and the human), perfection, and optimization, we might work towards more generous relations between humans and things.

My experience being aggressively nudged awake suggests the ways in which the human–machine relations encoded in these systems require new understandings of agencies, relationalities, and multiplicities. We might consider the following questions: Is this just another version of a cybernetic dream in which all of life is rendered computable? How might these technologies redefine what it means to "make up" ourselves and what it means to be human? How and where are the boundaries between human and technology being reconfigured? How and in what ways will we maintain a sense of agency and autonomy? Will we recognize ourselves at the end of the long experiment called life?

This experience, while oftentimes difficult from a personal perspective, has been interesting from an intellectual, political, and design perspective for a number of reasons. First, it has allowed me to ground my conceptual work on the posthuman in an experience of situated (algorithmic) actions that are not abstract ideas but rather based on my own lived experience of automation, which has allowed me to create new concepts for thinking about

64 *Laura Forlano*

human–machine relations such as *disabled cyborg, intimate infrastructures,* and *posthuman failure* that have been mentioned above to name just a few. Second, it has opened up a host of new research questions, concerns, and communities—both within and outside of universities. Third, it has informed how I think about the role of and relationship between theory, method, and practice. And, finally, while it is not the research project that I had planned upon finishing my PhD, it has allowed me to get much closer to *(and, even, become)* my own research subject, blurring the distinction between the researcher and the researched. These blurred boundaries profoundly complicate traditional understandings of objectivity, hierarchy, and knowledge that typically define academic work.

Such personal approaches that draw on lived experiences as modes of situated knowledge (Haraway, 1988; hooks, 1991) are quite common in some fields—namely, gender studies, queer studies, critical race studies, and critical disability studies. Yet, for the most part, they have been excluded from the field of design (and related fields such as human–computer interaction), which has, in the past several decades, clung tightly to notions of objective, universal, and rational truth in order to garner respect, power, and resources, as illustrated by recent feminist design scholarship (Ahmed & Irani, 2020; Bardzell, 2010; Costanza-Chock, 2020; D'Ignazio & Klein, 2020; Forlano, Ståhl, Lindström, Jönsson, & Mazé, 2016; Irani, 2018; Light, 2018; Mazé, 2019; Rosner, 2018). A deeper cultivation of design's intimacies with our own lived experiences of the natural and artificial worlds, embracing an orientation to "design in use" (Björgvinsson, Ehn, & Hillgren, 2012), can introduce necessary reflection on many questions that design researchers face, including for whom is this a "good" design, what do we mean by "good," for whom is this a failure, how might this go wrong and how might we design otherwise?

Posthumanism and its discontents

For me, theories of the cyborg, the posthuman, and the more-than-human offer interesting ways of thinking about my own experiences in navigating the everyday dilemmas of living with an algorithm. These concepts are intended to offer alternatives to the individualistic, human-centred worlds of binary oppositions inherited from much of Western European thinking. Yet, for the most part, these often-abstracted theoretical arguments have excluded disabled bodies (such as myself) as well as Black, Indigenous, and people of colour (BIPOC), women and many others who have never fit into existing categories of the human. As such, without being grounded in situated experiences, the posthuman risks becoming another colonizing, universalizing, totalizing, hegemonic, and exclusionary discourse as anthropologist Zoe Todd argues (2015).

While these concepts have been in circulation in some fields for several decades, they are only more recently beginning to make inroads in the field of design. One of the first scholars to engage the more-than-human in the field of design is Anne Galloway with her More-Than-Human Lab, which was founded in 2010 (Galloway & Caudwell, 2018).[2] The lab is full of lovely humans and sheep engaged in questions about what it means to live and die together. Since that time, there has been a growing conversation, discussion, and debate at this intersection, with articles, workshops, and even entire conferences devoted to the topic. To name just a few projects at this intersection, design scholars have recently engaged with topics including "coperformance" with algorithms (Giaccardi & Redström, 2020), "designing with" technology such as the internet of things (Wakkary, 2021), for example, nonanthropocentrism and the ways in which drones and robots "see" and act in urban spaces (DiSalvo, 2016; DiSalvo & Lukens, 2011). Similarly, design scholars engaged with environmental questions have developed approaches for co-designing textiles and living with plants (Keune, 2017, 2021); prototyping with chimpanzees at the zoo as a cosmopolitical encounter (Tironi & Hermansen, 2018), design events, experiments, and prototypes with urban animals (Jönsson, 2014; Jönsson & Lenskjold, 2014; Lenskjold & Jönsson, 2017); and walking tours about plastiglomerates (Lindström & Ståhl, 2017).

Yet, if we are to engage with these ideas at all, we must do so critically and with deep reflection around the implications of our choices as well as for who is included in our new categories and who is once again excluded, ignored, erased, and harmed. As a starting point, it is important to note that, unlike human-centred design, there is no such thing as "posthuman design," or if there is, I would very much argue against it. This is because "posthuman design" risks becoming another universalizing paradigm—and, thus, committing many of the same errors as human-centred design. Instead, in keeping with the relationality and multiplicity intended in the philosophical discussions of these terms, there are multiple varied ways in which these ideas might come together with design practices. This is why I prefer to think of the intersection between posthumanism and design (Forlano, 2017b), specifically of new questions that can be posed in design projects, programs, and practices (Redström, 2017). I think of this as using *theory as a design material*, an approach that I am not able to expand on in this chapter. In brief, ideas become more malleable, existing categories are transcended, and concepts are refracted through design processes.

Depending on which strand of theory one follows, these concepts and ideas have very different associations, meanings, and trajectories that are often oversimplified, misinterpreted, or confused. For example, Haraway's figure of the cyborg is frequently (and I believe incorrectly) conflated primarily with techno-utopian imaginations that extend and exceed the human body through technology. Similarly, the "post" in posthuman often gets interpreted as a temporal shift to a future state of humanity akin to transhumanism. While on the other hand the "more than" in more-than-human might signify a quantitative expansion, an excess or scalar dimension (though

66   Laura Forlano

this meaning is not common in the anthropological texts that take up this concept). And "other than" human seems to emphasize notions of difference. My own approach is to read both alongside and against these various associations in order to embrace aspects of the conversation that offer new questions and politics for the field of design. At the same time, rather than abstract notions, I seek to find and invent more specific concepts to explain my own experience as a disabled person living with technological systems.

One thing that these varied approaches seem to have in common is their emphasis on relationality, multiplicity, and transgressing the categories of liberal humanism that have been foundational to the cultivation of Western knowledge since the Enlightenment. This boundary crossing is potentially transformative for the field of human-centred design, which has been predicated on an understanding of the human based on the notion of a universal subject—usually white, male, Western, privileged, well-off, able-bodied, and young—that does not exist in reality or that does not represent the vast majority of people.

In *Feminist, Queer, Crip*, Alison Kafer provides a critical analysis of Haraway's figure of the cyborg from a disability studies perspective. She writes:

> The blurring of boundaries, the permeability of bodies, the porousness of skin—all take on different meanings depending on whether they are viewed through the prism of institutionalization or as part of a strategy of feminist analysis. Arguing for the breakdown between self and other, body and machine, takes on a different hue in the context of coercive medical experimentation and confinement. The cyborg, in other words, can be used to map many futures, not all of them feminist, crip, or queer.
>
> (Kafer, 2013)

However, drawing on Indigenous thought and practice, Todd argues that the rush to engage with the Anthropocene is a way of "gentrifying our discourses" with abstracted notions. Instead, she argues for a "radically decolonising praxis":

> a praxis that dismantles and re-orients not only the academy's and the art world's presuppositions about themselves, but also dismantles the heteropatriarchy, racism, and whiteness that continue to permeate political and intellectual systems in North America and Europe.
>
> (2015)

Such critique is not isolated but often they are taking place in very different conversations, fields, and subdisciplines. For example, communication scholar Julia DeCook's recent article, "A [White] Cyborg Manifesto," argues that such concepts are limited because they "exacerbate categories of

Design's intimacies   67

difference" and are embedded with white, patriarchal violence, emphasizing the point that our theoretical constructs do not exist outside of our politics (DeCook, 2020).

In her book, *Becoming Human*, Zekkiyah Iman Jackson takes a different approach to critiquing notions of the human. By analysing literary and visual texts by Black women, she uncovers alternative modes of being "in a manner that neither relies on animal abjection nor reestablishes liberal humanism as the authority on being (human)" (Jackson, 2020). Instead, she captures "an unruly sense of being/knowing/feeling existence, one that necessarily disrupts the foundations of the current hegemonic mode of 'the human'" (Jackson, 2020).

As these critiques of the cyborg, the posthuman, the more-than-human, the other-than-human, and the Anthropocene illustrate, experiences of human difference based on gender, race, and ability both challenge and expand our notions of who/what counts as human. In particular, these authors engage with the ways in which female, Black, queer, and disabled bodies reconfigure and reorient our lived experiences towards other realities and futures.

Is a pluriversal posthuman possible?

Taking these broader experiences of the human into account, we might work towards a more pluriversal (Escobar, 2018) notion of the posthuman or, as Escobar writes quoting the Zapatistas, a "world where many worlds fit." This might also require that we create design practices that are explicitly oriented towards justice (Costanza-Chock, 2020). Building on these turning points in the field, in this chapter, I ask how might these indeterminacies, intimacies, and posthumanism(s) come to shape new conversations in the field of design? Can the posthuman enthusiasm for technology be reconciled with its engagement with biology and the natural environment? What futures are possible/impossible in these times of technological and ecological indeterminacy? As we search for alternatives to the white, male, able-bodied, and Western conception of the posthuman, we must acknowledge that it is exactly in our design criteria and engineering principles that the politics of design play out. What are control, freedom, and autonomy and to whom, how, and why are highly contextual questions!

For me, the more-than-human suggests an alternative set of concepts to motivate design practice, which includes a shift from:

- experiment to *experimental*
- optimization to *imagination*
- prediction to *possibility*
- persuasion to *speculation*
- control to *indeterminacy*
- perfection to *fissures*
- universals to *differences*

68   Laura Forlano

- solutions to *questions*
- exploitation to *symbiosis*
- transmissions to *translations*
- nodes to *relations*

I offer this set of concepts, which are drawn from a wide set of literatures in order to open up new avenues for design research and practice.

As we can see, there is a growing conversation on the ways in which notions of the posthuman can be both problematically totalizing and universalizing as well as nuanced and critical. In the field of design in particular, the posthuman has the potential to shift the conversation away from the discrete individual subject that is centred in "human-centred design." So, is a pluriversal posthuman possible in indeterminate times? I'd better check with my sensor system and get back to you.

Acknowledgements

I would like to thank Celso Carnos Scaletsky and Ana Maria Copetti Maccagnan at UNISINOS in Brazil for their invitation to give a keynote talk, "Making Critical More-Than-Human Futures," as part of the Design Culture Symposium on November 23–24, 2020, where I presented an early version of this piece and benefited from the lively discussion and questions. My sincere thanks also go to Colbey Reid and Dennis Weiss for inviting me as a respondent in their session on the "Domestic Posthuman" at the Philosophy of Human-Technology Relations conference on November 6, 2020, where I presented "Is a Pluriversal Posthuman Possible???" Anne Galloway, Ann Light, Daniela Rosner, and Andrew Schrock also offered kind and generous feedback on this piece and allowed me to refine some of the arguments.

Notes

1 See https://www.nytimes.com/interactive/2020/12/02/magazine/tree-communication-mycorrhiza.html. Accessed on December 23, 2020.
2 See http://www.morethanhumanlab.nz. Accessed on December 23, 2020.

Bibliography

Ahmed, Alex, & Irani, Lilly. (2020). Feminism as a Design Methodology. *Interactions*, 27(6), 42–45.

Amoore, Louise. (2020). *Cloud Ethics: Algorithms and the Attributes of Ourselves and Others*. Durham, NC: Duke University Press.

Bardzell, Shaowen. (2010). *Feminist HCI: Taking Stock and Outlining an Agenda for Design*. Paper presented at the Proceedings of the SIGCHI Conference on Human Factors in Computing Systems, Atlanta, GA.

Björgvinsson, Erling, Ehn, Pelle, & Hillgren, Per-Anders. (2012). Design Things and Design Thinking: Contemporary Participatory Design Challenges. *Design Issues*, *28*(3), 101–116.

Bleecker, Julian. (2009). Design Fiction: A Short Essay on Design, Science, Fact and Fiction. https://blog.nearfuturelaboratory.com/2009/03/17/design-fiction-a-short-essay-on-design-science-fact-and-fiction/

Candy, Stuart, & Dunagan, Jake. (2017). Designing an Experiential Scenario: The People Who Vanished. *Futures*, *86*, 136–153.

Chin, Elizabeth. (2016). *My Life with Things*. Durham, NC: Duke University Press.

Choi, Jaz Hee-jeong, Forlano, Laura, & Kera, Denisa. (2020). *Situated Automation: Algorithmic Creatures in Participatory Design*. Paper presented at the Participatory Design Conference, Manizales, Colombia.

Costanza-Chock, Sasha. (2020). *Design Justice*. Cambridge: MIT Press.

Cottom, Tressie McMillan. (2018). *Thick: And Other Essays*. New York: The New Press.

D'Ignazio, Catherine, & Klein, Lauren F. (2020). *Data Feminism*. Cambridge: MIT Press.

DeCook, Julia R. (2020). A [White] Cyborg's Manifesto: The Overwhelmingly Western Ideology Driving Technofeminist Theory. *Media, Culture & Society*, *43*(6), 1158–1167. https://doi.org/10.1177/0163443720957891

Dilnot, Clive. (2020). Tony Fry's Defuturing: A New Design Philosophy. In T. Fry (Ed.), *Defuturing (Radical Thinking in Design)* (pp. 9–10). *Bloomsbury Publishing. Kindle Edition. Defuturing: A New Design Philosophy*. London: Bloomsbury Publishing.

DiSalvo, Carl. (2012). Spectacles and Tropes: Speculative Design and Contemporary Food Cultures. *Fibreculture 20*(20), 109–122.

DiSalvo, Carl. (2016). The Irony of Drones for Foraging: Exploring the Work of Speculative Interventions. In J. H. Rachel Clark & Kapser Tang Vangkilde (Ed.), *Design Anthropological Futures* (pp. 139–154). New York: Bloomsbury Press.

DiSalvo, Carl, Jenkins, Tom, & Lodato, Thomas. (2016). Designing Speculative Civics. In *Proceedings of the 2016 CHI Conference on Human Factors in Computing Systems (CHI '16)* (pp. 4979–4990). New York: Association for Computing Machinery. https://doi.org/10.1145/2858036.2858505.

DiSalvo, Carl, & Lukens, Jonathan. (2011). Nonathropocentrism and the Nonhuman in Design: Possibilities for Designing New Forms of Engagement with and through Technology. In M. Foth, L. Forlano, M. Gibbs, & C. Satchell (Eds.), *From Social Butterfly to Engaged Citizen: Urban Informatics, Social Media, Ubiquitous Computing, and Mobile Technology to Support Citizen Engagement* (pp. 421–435). Cambridge: MIT Press.

Dunne, Anthony, & Raby, Fiona. (2013). *Speculative Everything: Design, Fiction, and Social Dreaming*. Cambridge: MIT Press.

Escobar, Arturo. (2018). *Designs for the Pluriverse: Radical Interdependence, Autonomy, and the Making of Worlds*. Durham: Duke University Press.

Forlano, Laura. (2017a). Data Rituals in Intimate Infrastructures: Crip Time and the Disabled Cyborg Body as an Epistemic Site of Feminist Science. *Catalyst: Feminism, Theory, Technoscience*, *3*(2), 1–28.

Forlano, Laura. (2017b). Posthumanism and Design. *She Ji: The Journal of Design, Economics, and Innovation*, *3*(1), 16–29.

Forlano, Laura. (2019). Stabilizing/Destabilizing the Driverless City: Speculative Futures and Autonomous Vehicles. *International Journal of Communication*, *13*, 2811–2838.

Forlano, Laura. (2020, April 13). *The Danger of Intimate Algorithms*. New York: NYU Institute for Public Knowledge.

Forlano, Laura, & Mathew, Anijo. (2014). From Design Fiction to Design Friction: Speculative and Participatory Design of Values-Embedded Urban Technology. *Journal of Urban Technology*, *21*(4), 7–24.

Forlano, Laura, Ståhl, Åsa, Lindström, Kristina, Jönsson, Li, & Mazé, Ramia. (2016). *Making, Mending and Growing in Feminist Speculative Fabulations: Design's Unfaithful Daughters*. Paper presented at the Design Research Society, Brighton, England.

Fournier, Lauren. (2021). *Autotheory as Feminist Practice in Art, Writing, and Criticism*. Cambridge: MIT Press.

Fry, Tony. (2020). *Defuturing: A New Design Philosophy*. New York: Bloomsbury.

Galloway, Anne, & Caudwell, Catherine. (2018). Speculative Design as Research Method: From Answers to Questions and "Staying with the Trouble." In G. Coombs, A. McNamara, & G. Sade (Eds.), *Undesign: Critical Practices at the Intersection of Art and Design* (pp. 85–96). London: Routledge.

Giaccardi, Elisa, & Redström, Johan. (2020). Technology and More-Than-Human Design. *Design Issues*, *36*(4), 33–44. Doi: 10.1162/desi_a_00612

Haraway, Donna. (1988). Situated Knowledges: The Science Question in Feminism and the Privilege of Partial Perspective. *Feminist Studies*, *14*(3), 575–599.

Harrington, Christina, Erete, Sheena, & Piper, Anne Marie. (2019). Deconstructing Community-Based Collaborative Design: Towards More Equitable Participatory Design Engagements. *Proc. ACM Hum.-Comput. Interact*, *3*(CSCW), Article 216. Doi: 10.1145/3359318

Höök, Kristina. (2018). *Designing with the Body: Somaesthetic Interaction Design*. Cambridge: MIT Press.

Hooks, bell. (1991). Theory as Liberatory Practice. *Yale JL & Feminism*, *4*, 1.

Huerta, Monica. (2021). *Magical Habits*. Durham, NC: Duke University Press.

Ingold, Tim. (2010). Bringing Things to Life: Creative Entanglements in a World of Materials. *World*, *44*, 1–25.

Irani, Lilly. (2018). "Design Thinking": Defending Silicon Valley at the Apex of Global Labor Hierarchies. *Catalyst: Feminism, Theory, Technoscience*, *4*(1), 1–19.

Jackson, Zakiyyah Iman. (2020). *Becoming Human: Matter and Meaning in an Antiblack World*. New York: New York University Press.

Jain, S. Lochlann. (2013). *Malignant: How Cancer Becomes Us*. Berkeley: University of California Press.

Jönsson, Li. (2014). *Design Events: On Explorations of a Non-Anthropocentric Framework in Design*. Copenhagen, DK: The Royal Danish Academy of Fine Arts.

Jönsson, Li, & Lenskjold, Tau Ulv. (2014). A Foray into Not-Quite Companion Species: Design Experiments with Urban Animals as Significant Others. *Artifact: Journal of Design Practice*, *3*(2), 7.1–7.13.

Kafer, Alison. (2013). *Feminist, Queer, Crip*. Bloomington: Indiana University Press.

Keune, Svenja. (2017). Co–designing with Plants: Degrading as an Overlooked Potential for Interior Aesthetics Based on Textile Structures. *The Design Journal*, *20*(supp1), S4742–S4744.

Design's intimacies 71

Keune, Svenja. (2021). Designing and Living with Organisms Weaving Entangled Worlds as Doing Multispecies Philosophy. *Journal of Textile Design Research and Practice*, 9(1), 1–22. https://doi.org/10.1080/20511787.2021.1912897.

Lenskjold, Tau Ulv, & Jönsson, Li. (2017). Speculative Prototypes and Alien Ethnographies: Experimenting with Relations beyond the Human. *Diseña 11*, 134–147. https://doi.org/10.7764/disena.11.134-147.

Light, Ann. (2018). *Writing PD: Accounting for Socially-Engaged Research*. Paper presented at the Proceedings of the 15th Participatory Design Conference: Short Papers, Situated Actions, Workshops and Tutorial-Volume 2 (August 2018), Hasselt and Genk, Belgium.

Lindström, Kristina, & Ståhl, Åsa. (2017). Plastic Imaginaries. *Continent*, 6(1), 62–67.

Lucero, Andrés, Desjardins, Audrey, Neustaedter, Carman, Höök, Kristina, Hassenzahl, Marc, & Cecchinato, Marta E. (2019). *A Sample of One: First-Person Research Methods in HCI*. Paper presented at the Companion Publication of the 2019 on Designing Interactive Systems Conference 2019 Companion (DIS '19 Companion) (pp. 385–388). New York: Association for Computing Machinery. https://doi.org/10.1145/3301019.3319996.

Mazé, Ramia. (2019). Design Educational Practice: Reflections on Feminist Modes and Politics. In L. Forlano, M. W. Steenson, & M. Ananny (Eds.), *Bauhaus Futures* (pp. 3–23). Cambridge: MIT Press.

Parisi, Luciana. (2013). *Contagious Architecture: Computation, Aesthetics, and Space*. Cambridge: MIT Press.

Prado de O. Martins, Luiza (2014). *Privilege and Oppression: Towards a Feminist Speculative Design*. Paper presented at the Design Research Society, Umea, Sweden.

Redström, Johan. (2017). *Making Design Theory*. Cambridge: MIT Press.

Rosner, Daniela K. (2018). *Critical Fabulations: Reworking the Methods and Margins of Design*. Cambridge: MIT Press.

Stengers, Isabelle. (2005). The Cosmopolitical Proposal. In B. Latour & P. Weibel (Eds.), *Making Things Public: Atmospheres of Democracy* (pp. 994–1003). Cambridge: MIT Press.

Tironi, Martín, & Hermansen, Pablo. (2018). Cosmopolitical Encounters: Prototyping at the National Zoo in Santiago, Chile. *Journal of Cultural Economy*, 11(4), 330–347.

Todd, Zoe. (2015). Indigenizing the Anthropocene. In H. Davis & E. Turpin (Eds.), *Art in the Anthropocene: Encounters among Aesthetics, Politics, Environments and Epistemologies* (pp. 241–254). London: Open Humanities Press.

Tsing, Anna Lowenhaupt. (2015). *The Mushroom at the End of the World: On the Possibility of Life in Capitalist Ruins*. Princeton, NJ: Princeton University Press.

Wakkary, Ron. (2021). *Things We Could Design: For More Than Human-Centered Worlds*. Cambridge: MIT Press.

Wark, McKenzie. (2020). *Reverse Cowgirl*. New York: Autonomedia.

Wilde, Danielle, Vallgårda, Anna, & Tomico, Oscar. (2017). *Embodied Design Ideation Methods: Analysing the Power of Estrangement*. Paper presented at the Proceedings of the 2017 CHI Conference on Human Factors in Computing Systems, Denver, CO, May 6–11. https://doi.org/10.1145/3025453.3025873.

4 Growing materials
Technical and caring processes as rooted design practices

Nicole Cristi

In this chapter, I explore the experience of "growing materials" as a more-than-human and rooted design practice based on caring. The research is grounded on a 16-month collaborative ethnography on biofabrication practices in Chile during 2020–2021. I deployed a mixed-method approach consisting of both remote/digital and in-person participant observations with makers from different laboratories working towards new materiality integrating organic sources, living organisms, and biological and biochemical processes.[1] These labs are more-than-disciplinary spaces, where different skills and knowledge bodies from cooking, design, and architecture to biology and biochemistry are mixed and intermingled together. By combining them, makers are *cooking materials* with agar agar, pectin, and starch, among other sources, and *growing materials* with fungi and bacteria. I base this text on the experience with the *Laboratorio de Biomateriales de Valdivia* (henceforth, LABVA), growing maqui-biomaterial through and with bacteria and yeast in Valdivia, southern Chile.[2]

For that, I am working with processes of fermentation, seen as techniques to co-produce new materials: these techniques are analysed here as founded upon the entanglement and continuities between human makers, bacteria, yeast, the territory, tools, machines, and institutions. Through such an approach, I explore the possibilities to stretch design towards a less anthropocentric and more situated discipline through the expansion of its technical structures; that is, challenging a universal "technology" to welcome a technodiversity (CATT, 2022; Hui, 2019), i.e., integrating "specific technical relations with their local, social, cultural and natural environments" (CATT, 2022). Towards such an aim, I interweave perspectives from the anthropology of technics, material culture studies, design theory, and feminist care studies.

In this study, I seek to examine what often remains behind the scenes of design results, the very technical activities, the experience of production, and the micropolitics of making. I understood them as a key element in design's ontological capacity-making worlds (Escobar, 2018; Tlostanova, 2017; Willis, 2006) and for the reconfiguration of the design discipline. Following Marcel Mauss (1979 [1935]) and the French tradition of the study of technical

DOI: 10.4324/9781003319689-5

Growing materials   73

activities as social, I focus on the process of production and the interlacement and relationality of agents, materials, and scales throughout biofabrication. Borrowing from recent discussions about cosmotechnics, defined as the "unification between the cosmic order and the moral order through technical activities" (Hui, 2017, 4), I describe and analyse how care *for* and *with* more-than-human agents takes place growing a material as a part of vital and technical processes (Coupaye and Pitrou, 2018), and how an ontological continuity with the territory as a cosmic order converges with this.

This chapter starts with the discussion of the categories of growing and making. Then, I introduce an ethnographic approach to growing materials, in which I present the main points of the analysis through the notions of scales, "hidden" makings, and care. Finally, I will address how, from the reconfiguration and expansion of the technical apparatus, it is possible to explore beyond hegemonic design practices, cultivating critical makings based on the relationality and continuity with more-than-human agents towards post-anthropocentric and rooted design practices and futurities.

Grow as a technical activity

In Valdivia, it seems that everything is growing, even during a lockdown where many things seem to me stuck and paralysed by the pandemic. I appreciated from the flight how the landscape was becoming greener as I moved deeper into the south. From the airport to the centre of Valdivia, I could feel the abundance of life in the water lands and in the "Valdivian rainforest." Life appears everywhere in those wet places, everything seems to be growing.

From the beginning of my fieldwork, I realised the relevance of the *emic* perspective on "growing" as a production process.[3] It started when we were working together on an application form for a public funding competition. The project was around one of the biomaterials created by the laboratory from maqui (*Aristotelia chilensis*). I was editing the Gantt chart of the form when I read one of the stages described as *"crecer la pieza de exposición"* [to grow the exhibition piece]. I re-read it to verify whether I was reading it correctly. I checked the steps before, but I still could not make sense of the sentence. I thought it was a mistake, and rather than growing, they mean building or making the piece, so I wrote a note to share at our next meeting: "correct or clarify this." A day later, during the meeting, I asked María Jose and Valentina, two of the makers, to fix that point. Responding to my puzzled face, they answered me with naturality, *"¡vamos a crecerlo, nosotros crecemos cosas!"* [we will grow it, we grow things!]. There, I realised how limited my vision around making was and how, through my confusion, two different onto-epistemic formations (Escobar, 2018) around making and design practice manifested and clashed against one another.

The design discipline has been strongly built supporting capitalist and patriarchal schemes (Buckley, 1986, 2020). Critical design studies further qualify said schemes also as modern, colonial, and anthropocentric (Escobar,

74 *Nicole Cristi*

2018; Forlano, 2016, 2017; Fry, 2020; Gutiérrez, 2018, 2022; Irwin, 2015; Mareis and Paim, 2021; Tlostanova, 2017; Tonkinwise, 2015; Willis, 2006). My perspective in this encounter was precisely this—I was looking at those practices of biofabrication from a modern lens when I realised this was too limited a way to understand them. As Claudia Mareis and Nina Paim stages, design's practice, discourses, and pedagogy should be reconfigured under the recognition that "design and its thinking is deeply complicit in many structural systems of oppression, serving to concretise, perpetuate, and disseminate power and privilege" (2021, 11). The design discipline has been reproducing a hegemonic configuration and an onto-epistemic formation and, with that, reinforcing its power.

This modern configuration is, in the technical domain, embodied by the category of "technology" as vernacular from modernity (Coupaye, 2022; Hui, 2017, 2019). Following Yuk Hui's critique of the synchronisation of the modern world under the universality of "technology" (Hui, 2019), the study of "growing" in Chilean laboratories challenges the synchronisation of the design discipline under a limited and limiting technical structure. As David Edgerton observes:

> When thinking about "the material" and techniques in design, and indeed about the product of design, we need much richer and variegated concepts. We also need a much more substantial understanding of the modern world that we get through thinking about the concept of 'technology'. It is a master concept only for a very poor account of our world.
>
> (Edgerton et al., 2021, 3)

Instead, the experience of growing maqui-biomaterial allows us to see and reconfigure technical relations from a pluralistic perspective which eschews the dominant modern mode of reticulation. Following this, an exploration of growing as a technical activity could contribute to bifurcate the homogenisation of design disciplinary practices towards a more plural schema and, considering the design ontological capacity, diverge the worlds and futurities co-constructed there.

The relations between "growing" and "making" have been discussed inside the anthropological field. Elizabeth Hallam and Tim Ingold (2014) have proposed the study of "making" as "growing" (or making in growing), questioning an artefactual end's focus and the hylomorphic model that, for the authors, "making" involves. In their view, many handicraft processes, such as making pottery, weaving, or carpentry, cannot be understood from the focus on the result or on the prescriptive form: rather, their value lies in the very processes of constant becoming. Authors understand this condition as growing rather than making, following Heidegger's distinction between dwelling and building (1971). Differently, Ludovic Coupaye (2009, 2013,

2022) and Perig Pitrou (2015, 2017) have proposed the study of growing (from the study of yams and life) from a pragmatic approach based on the anthropology of technics. This is the study of "growing" as "making." In this case, "making" responds to a methodological and analytical apparatus to the study of growth, from an ecological and ontogenetic perspective as the result of the entanglement of technical and vital processes, where both come together (Coupaye, 2022).

In this sense, my research looks at growing not as a conceptual, super-imposed category. Rather, growing is a vernacular element emerging from the *emic* dimension of the production processes of biomaterials in Chile, which invites me to study it from its technical dimension. Consequently, I am approaching "growing" methodologically and analytically as "making," through the use of the chaîne opératoire (Coupaye, 2013; Lemonnier, 1992; Martinón-Torres, 2002; Schlanger, 2005) and the French anthropological tra-dition for the study of technics (Coupaye, 2013; Haudricourt, 1987 [1968]; Lemonnier, 1992, 1993; Leroi-Gourhan, 1964 [1999]; Mauss, 1979 [1935]). In this frame, I am using the same limitations of the analytical apparatus to challenge and expand it towards a technodiversity that welcomes growing and making not separately but as structurally joined. In the following sec-tions, I will examine the production process of the maqui-biomaterial based on the ethnographic observation of multiple sessions of making and the oral accounts of human makers, interwoven with the analytical dimensions of scales and care.

On scales of growing: "invisibles" and tangled technical activities

The anthropology of technics has been historically driven by Sigaut's argu-ment (1994) that we cannot *see* techniques but only people doing actions. Consequently, we can only study techniques following the technical activities people perform. While this idea also guided my research, integrating other, more-than-human communities and processes pertaining to the making became necessary to open the field. This movement welcomes processes that we cannot see in terms of human performance, but the results of which bring about real, human, non-human, and material transformations and conse-quences (see, for example: Coupaye and Pitrou, 2018). In this sense, growing materials is a practice that needs to be understood from the entanglement of different scales of (technically) making and doing; some of these scales remain "invisible" to human-centred perception, scales, and temporalities. I take the notion of "scale" from the vernacular understanding of human makers of their practice, and at the same time, I use scale as a methodological tool to approach those "hidden" makings. Despite its division by scales, the accounts make clear that growing material is a practice based on the entan-glement, mutual transformation, and continuity of these scales. This section focuses on the micro and macro scales of making and its agents, describing

76   Nicole Cristi

their technical activities and agencies while interweaving them with the scale of human making and technical objects.

Everything starts on the scale of the territory. Maqui is an endemic tree from the south zone of Chile, especially from the Valdivian temperate rainforest, which human makers from LABVA use to create a maqui-biomaterial.[4] It is harvested once a year, between the spring and summer months in the Global South (November, December, January). The fruit is small but abundant in these months, and its intense purple colour makes it easy to recognise. Before human makers collect the maqui, they know it has already grown, sometimes wildly, helped by the abundant rain and the sun in the area, and sometimes cared for by humans that water and collect them. Although we cannot see the performative impact of the activities of the Valdivian rainforest on growing, we can see the material transformation produced through the presence or colours of the fruit, which indicates to us when it is ready to be harvested by birds or humans.

Human makers of the laboratory mostly understand their practice as indivisible with their territory, criticising other un-situated approaches to biofabrication, where materials and processes are seen as universal, without any correlation between the territory and the making. Differently, in the laboratory, the materials they grow as well as their practices start (analytically defining a point to start) and end (analytically defining an end, despite its continuity in a cycle) in the territory. In their oral accounts, human makers present the laboratory within the Valdivian rainforest, the coast, and the wetlands, which are all part of the laboratory *milieu*; similarly, they define their practice as *"modelar la abundancia natural de nuestro territorio"* [shaping the natural abundance of their territory]. Consequently, similarly to what Jaqueline Field proposes concerning its study of silk production, questioning what we often understand as "raw material" (2014), growing maqui-biomaterial there is not raw material, nor separations between the "natural" and the human, but a continuity of transformations where there is a key agency attributed to the territory and its cycles, conceiving their practice as a continuum of it.

However, territory for my informants (and for many Chileans) does not equate with geography. Rather, *territorio* [territory] comes to encompass knowledge, histories, struggles, identities, and day-to-day lives profoundly situated and entangled in a given geographical space. Territory acts here as a dynamic *emic* category that by itself challenges the great modern divisions between culture and nature (Descola, 2013 [2005]; Viveiros de Castro, 2012) and society and nature (Latour, 1993), which are also profoundly contained in the division between growing and making, where growing becomes nature and making part of the domain of culture and society.

Talking about the territory, makers often bring another macro scale into the conversation: it is not a scale of making per se, but one concerning technical knowledge expressed in a given process, for example, that of maqui and fermentation. This knowledge is historically built, transferred, and modified.

Maqui is a sacred tree for the Mapuche people, the original community of the area. One of the first times we talked about maqui, María José told me that Mapuche communities have ancestrally used it as food, a natural pigment, and a medicine because of its antioxidant properties. She added that it is a very powerful fruit and full of local meanings, especially because of its colour, which they work to keep in the material. For human makers, their use of the maqui in biomaterials is also part of this tradition, transferring and preserving that knowledge and identity. Similarly, fermentation is a long-standing technique; it has been transferred through multiple generations as a popular way to conserve food. The knowledge and techniques associated with it are open, collaborative, and dynamic, while traditional: they are continually becoming and are continually transformed in new applications but are always part of a historical, situated, and rooted continuum. This historical "invisible" macro scale of technical knowledge also takes part in growing materials, that is, in their techniques and understanding of their territory and their practice.

Other "hidden" technical agencies appear on a micro-timescale. The micro-community drives the process of production. After collecting maqui in their neighbourhood, human makers *cook* the infusion at the *kitchen-laboratory*, as they call it. They grind fruits and leaves, where the microorganisms are, with a wooden spoon, then boil water in an electric kettle and wait ten minutes for it to cool. Then, human makers add maqui leaves and fruits into the water, and with that, bacteria and yeasts dive into it. Human makers wait for five minutes more, add sugar, pour the infusion into a jar, and wait again for a couple of days. We can see how the infusion takes on the unique bright purple colour of maqui fruits. This infusion is the nourishment of the crops (their communities of bacteria and yeasts); human makers pour the infusion slowly into them, which are waiting in the incubator they have built.

Human makers have been testing different times and temperatures to *feed* and *shelter* bacteria and yeast. Alejandro, one of the makers, who is often in charge of these activities, *shelters* bacteria and yeast, keeping the incubator around 28 degree Celsius and leaving the crops there for weeks or months, depending on the bacteria and yeast's production needs and the kind of fermentation required.[5] As they say, they leave the infusion *resting* and they wait; however, while in human terms, it is *resting* (and they are waiting), fermentation is happening, and bacteria and yeasts are producing cellulose. Waiting is a crucial technical activity during the process. Human makers wait for the harvest of maqui fruit, for the temperature of the infusion, for fermentation, which shows how other more-than-human agents guide the process of making and how makers incorporate their rhythms into the process, which I will deepen in the next section.

Gabriela, also a maker, performed the exercise to explain in simple words what is happening in the micro-community while it is *resting* in the incubator. She says it is necessary to "immerse" oneself in the infusion, using different

78 Nicole Cristi

scales to visualise from our human world what is happening there. To explain it, she introduces an imaginative exercise. She starts introducing a rule of 20 centimetres. Then, she proposes zooming in on one centimetre, focusing now on the millimetres (amplifying the initial view ten times). Now, she introduces what happens if we amplify it again 10,000 times. Now we are on the scale of micrometres: "We now can see that the initial infusion has many live organisms on that scale. We call these organisms a SCOBY (symbiotic culture/colony of bacteria and yeast), a living being made by thousands of microscopic organisms." Gabriela comes back to the scale of technical objects (the rule), and from there, she proposes to zoom in 100,000 times. Now we are on the scale of nanometres. On this scale, she says, bacteria become visible. Based on the information that is today available but not yet confirmed, one of them is the *Komagataeibacter sp.*[6] These bacteria have the capacity to *produce* cellulose, which Gabriela describe as an amazing capacity that she compares with a printer: "*Komagataeibacter* is printing fibre, it is a live printer," she adds. Here, Gabriela assigns a technical and productive capacity to the bacteria. She uses a comparison with a technical object to imagine and make sense of it from her technical world, entangling the scales and giving a vernacular technical quality, to microorganisms through their biological processes.

Gabriela continues describing the process. The *printer fibre* made by the bacteria then generates a kind of *ribbon* and, finally, forms a kind of *textile*, which is the bacterial cellulose, later, the biomaterial. After explaining the technical activity of the bacteria, she goes to one of the yeasts. She explains that yeast has a relevant role because they live in a *community* with the bacteria. With their enzymes, they divide the sucrose molecule into fructose and glucose, making it available for themselves and for the bacteria.[7] Gabriela explains that yeasts also benefit from being *friendly* to their *neighbouring* bacteria. As the bacteria are *fed*, they produce the cellulose and make the weave, which she compares with a *raft,* because it goes to the top of the infusion to *protect* them from invasive species. Yeast and bacteria *take care and protect each other,* having not only a vernacular technicity but also performing activities of care.

In the oral accounts, as in the very practice of growth, the "invisible" making of the micro-community and the territory are crucial: they guide making. However, making happens in the entanglement of the different scales. To finish the oral accounts, human makers continue attributing technical dimensions from technical objects and human scale to the process. This time they use *tejido ecosistémico [ecosystem weave]* to explain that this process works with multiple relations and agents, where the Valdivian rainforest and maqui trees, bacteria and yeast, the same kitchen-laboratory with its technical objects and human makers constitute an ecosystem. María José adds that we are, all together, interweaved with this material.

Growing materials 79

The use of scales to approach the process is a methodological tool to registry the making identifying the different technical activities and agents involved in it, and it follows the vernacular strategy of human makers to make sense of their practice and understand other technical worlds. However, all scales work together interrelatedly and as a vernacular continuity of processes. What happens on one scale is transforming the realm of the others. Human makers are aware of this relationality, driving their technical activities towards care, as I will explain in the next section.

Caring, technical, and vital processes

It is the consciousness of this relationality and the understanding of processes from continuity by human makers that put the logic of care at the forefront. Many scholars agree that care starts in the recognition of the other (Hamington, 2004; Philip, 2016; Price and Shildrick, 2002). While it is involved in the growth of individuals, it is, at the same time, committed and aware of the interconnectedness between them (Hamington 2004, 3; Phillip, 2016). As Mary Philip observes, "an ethics of care begins from an understanding of human interaction such that people are constantly enmeshed in relationships and not seen primarily as rational actors pursuing their own goals and maximising their own interests" (2016, 475). As I will show here, on growing materials, the consciousness of the tangled activities involves respect and care for and with more-than-human agents, because the process depends on the interconnection of different agents and biological processes of bacteria and yeast, territory, technical objects, and human makers. Consequently, here, the technical processes are vital processes (Coupaye and Pitrou, 2018) but also processes of care.

Additionally, care has been widely studied by feminist scholars as to the sustainability of life (Carrasco, 2001), directly linked with domestic activities to ensure human life. Consequently, care processes are vital processes that keep humanity alive. However, care also goes beyond domestic space, human social relations, or mothering logic (Curtin, 1991; Gaard, 1993; Kheel, 1993; Plumwood, 1993; Warren, 2000). It can also sustain other more-than-human lives. Donna Haraway has shown (2003, 2008) that in the interspecies relationship with animals, care has a central role as an everyday logic, where both species train each other to co-exist. Ecofeminist or environmental feminist accounts offer an interesting frame for this (Alaimo, 2008; Bauhardt and Harcourt, 2019; Mies and Shiva, 1993; Phillip, 2016; Shiva, 1997, 2010; Van Den Berg, 2019). Ecofeminism has been criticised for maintaining nature in a passive position, as well as for maintaining an essentialist relationship between woman and nature (Van Den Berg, 2019); however, there are critical positions within the field (Alaimo, 2008; Bauhardt and Harcourt, 2019; Phillip, 2016; Van Den Berg, 2019) which mark an essential starting point for the study of more-than-human care. As M. Phillip observes, it "provides

80   *Nicole Cristi*

a jumping-off point for re-envisioning relations within the more-than-human in a way that values care, emotion and embodiment" (2016, 472). Ecofeminism starts from the consciousness of relationality described above, but this time around human and non-human lives, "for ecofeminism, caring is grounded in an ability to see connections to others who are different from us" (2016, 476).

In growing materials, the imbrication and relationality from logics of care with the territory and the micro-community are crucial. By the human maker's accounts, the use of any sources or technical activities in their production process is driven by what they call *capacidades ecosistémicas [ecosystem capacities]*; that is, using sources or transforming them while keeping an equilibrium in their milieu, what they are constantly exploring with the local communities, specialists, and in their daily practice. Consequently, the lab's productive capacities are driven by ecosystem ones. As Gabriela says, "one of the beautiful things maqui teach us it is how to increase our production without overgrowing the ecosystem capacities," putting in the centre a logic of care in terms of relationality and sustainability of life.

In more pragmatic accounts, this is clear in maqui's fermentation, where *ecosystem capacities* affect the most evident layers, such as the availability of local maqui to make the infusion and find a shared rhythm of production. This coordinates their technical activities, integrating the different technical worlds' rhythms taking part in the process. This is firstly manifested in the *waiting*, as described above, but in a more systemic view, in creating a cycle based on a mutual relationship between the SCOBY and humans, through the repetition and coordination of the technical activities of *feeding, sheltering*, producing cellulose, *harvesting, and waiting*. The creation of bacterial cellulose (after harvest, the maqui-biomaterial) by the bacteria and yeast demonstrates that the infusion is already colonised; it is a new symbiotic colony, an SCOBY. While the colony is *fed* and *sheltered* over time, it constantly becomes stronger, and as a consequence, it creates cellulose faster. This cellulose *protects* the colony of bacteria and yeast of external agents. When the SCOBY is strong enough (thanks to care and time), human makers start to *harvest it*, collecting the cellulose with disinfected tweezers to process it as the biomaterial. After some weeks, the production of bacteria cellulose starts to be slower, but after harvest, it starts to be fluid and active again. Consequently, human makers have been searching for a rhythm that does not entail a risk to bacteria and yeast and keeping a good production for them. This means approximately harvesting every two weeks and feeding the crops after that, while they are in the incubator under controlled conditions. As María José comments, we were exploited in our last jobs, and now, we are searching not to exploit ourselves, neither other humans, nor non-humans; we are searching for our *welfare*, that of the crops and that of the territory.

However, in this coordination, they also should negotiate their rhythm with another technical world, this time, an institutional one which supports

Growing materials 81

them economically. While these activities and agents are not very present in human makers' oral accounts, they are crucial in the ethnographic observation. This brings their rhythms into the process, precisely the deadlines of their funding, often public awards to promote industry or arts or innovation accelerators from universities, which often do not work on the slow rhythms of fermentation. In contrast, as the very name implies, they often search to speed up projects based on market logic, where "growing" becomes, this time, an economic imperative. The search for balance with this technical world is manifested in experimentation to speed up the process facing deadlines, such as the mix of tea fermentation with maqui fruits. However, this always takes care of the welfare of the crops, which is an ethical position for the makers but also a pragmatic need; the very crops decelerate the process, while they only work in certain times and conditions. Consequently, the current coordination of their technical activities results from the negotiation of different technical worlds, including the institutional one, giving place to each rhythm until a shared one is reached, based on their relationality and mutual transformation. Consequently, this shared rhythm is, by itself, a rhythm of care, which, at the same time, involves actions of care.

The association of the technical activities with care not only comes from its analytical relation with the sustainability of life and the study of relationality, but it also first comes from a vernacular understanding of the processes by the human makers. The *emic* categories of *feeding* and *sheltering* (their micro-community) are manifested in their oral accounts of how they understand and feel their practice as activities of care, which are both technical and vital. At the same time, human makers describe some activities performed by more-than-human agents as *caring, feeding*, and *protecting*, such as the function of the bacterial cellulose against external agents and the relationship between bacteria and yeast. As I described above, human makers described more-than-human actions in analogy with technical objects, attributing to their biological process a technicity but also a logic of care based on their relationality. They attribute technical, vital, and care processes to them. Consequently, care relations are not one way (from humans to non-humans) but are also performed by and between humans and non-humans, all contributing to the ecosystem's equilibrium. Therefore, growing materials is not only about caring *for* but also about caring *with* the micro-community, the territory, and the technical objects.

Finally, Puig de la Bellacasa proposes that to take "care" means knowledge politics. Following Latourian "matters of concern," she proposes "matters of care," challenging STS directly from a feminist frame. In her view, science and technology studies must pay attention to devalued or neglected assemblages; that is, they must concern themselves with gender relations but also question knowledge production in a broader sense. That is from the feminist call to rethink power positions at different levels. Following Puig de la Bellacasa's proposal, to pay attention to a humanly "invisible" making, integrating more-than-human technicity and care to understand the complexity

82 Nicole Cristi

of growing materials is also an act of care by itself, while it is questioning the hegemonic technical structure of design through focusing on hidden technical assemblages. Similarly, the study of what is often obscured under design results, or I could say relegated to the domestic domain, follows this call too, while it pushes, from a feminist perspective, the micropolitics of design practices into the front of design studies. Consequently, different dimensions of how to care for and with design can be traced from growing materials and the associated technical, vital, and caring activities.

Challenging design from technodiversity

The study of growing materials on the experience of maqui as a cosmotechnic based on caring relations and vernacular continuities from the territory contributes to exploring and cultivating a technodiversity inside of design practice, expanding its technical structures towards more sustainable, less anthropocentric, and situated ones. The ethnographic accounts of growing material show how the territory, microorganisms, humans, technical objects, and institutions co-act (Pitrou, 2016) and become having at its centre logics of care, expressed in the technical activities, in the rhythm of production and in the ecosystem view of their making. Facing the crisis of the Anthropocene and the massive demand for social and political changes in recent years in Chile and Latin America (where this research is conducted), it has become vital for the design discipline to expand its technical domain towards becoming a more plural one, both welcoming and caring. This approach puts relationality in the centre of its practice and opens a more comprehensive understanding of its processes and agents from the territory to support more-than-human forms of life and the *capacidades ecosistémicas* [*ecosystem capacities*].

Studying technical, vital, and caring activities based on relationality and an ontology of making based on the continuity with the territory challenges a capitalist/neoliberal/modern patriarchal/anthropocentric understanding of making and design practices. As Carrasco states, capitalism and patriarchy have neglected care and the domestic sphere under the discourse of the self-autonomy of workers, as neoliberalism has fragmented the relationality by the individualism. In contrast, growing materials questions extractive logic and the self-autonomy discourses through a radical relationality. At the same time, integrating more-than-human life rhythms in the production questions anthropocentric ways of conceiving of the practice of design and its modern-industrial hegemony. In this criticism, care is far from a romantic, naive, or abstract proposal but a pragmatic, embodied, and needed one.

Following Silvia Rivera Cusicanqui's *"teoría enrazaida"* [rooted theory] (2018), in which theory and knowledge are becoming from experience, that is, without "deny[ing] its own history or its own genealogy for understanding the world" (187), I understand growing materials as a *práctica de diseño enraizado* [rooted design practice]. That is a design practice that is constantly becoming from a situated experience and genealogy, creating worlds from its roots. It is a practice that could not be understood without its *milieu* and its trajectory of becoming with it. A rooted design practice could contribute to embracing a technodiversity inside of design discipline, expanding it not from a speculative frame but from the very recognition of its plurality on the existence of situated practices which are already challenging the hegemonic universal and modern structure of design. As Cheryl Buckley states, "thinking about the innumerable ways in which design is produced, where it is produced and by and for whom it is produced has the potential to prompt a changed understanding of design" (2020, 19). This duty implies reconfiguring from situated experiences some technical relations that have been reproduced under the hegemonic/modern domain of design practice, such as the dualisms between nature and culture, human and non-human, practice, and knowledge, "low tech" and "high tech," design and craft, among others, in which the experience of growing materials contributes to thinking critically around them.

Finally, the study of growing material from the design frame and the anthropology of technics is opening other relevant dimensions which are not developed in this chapter because of its extension and scope. This is the case of the reconfiguration of the creative processes in co-activity with the micro-community and the territory, or a detailed study of gender relations inside of the practice, among others. However, as the very practice of growing materials and other "critical makings" (Hertz, 2012) continue growing, they will carry on challenging and expanding hegemonic disciplinary frontiers of design from diverse dimensions, constantly surpassing them while they grow.

Acknowledgement

I would like to thank LABVA for opening to me their kitchen-laboratory, for sharing with me fruitful conversations for the development of this ongoing research, and for their valuable comments for this text. I would like to thank Ludovic Coupaye and Raffaele Buono for their extremely helpful comments and suggestions to this chapter. Finally, I would like to thank the Centre for the Anthropology of Technics and Technodiversity (CATT) for the conversations and interchanges from which this text was built.

Notes

1 This chapter does not seek to approach biofabrication in general terms or as an international trend. Instead, it focuses on a very situated production experience, particularly growing with bacteria and yeast in the south of Chile.
2 LABVA was founded in 2018 by María José Besoain, Alejandro Weiss, and Valentina Aliaga in Valdivia. Today, it is also integrated by Gabriela Carrasco, Esteban Osses, and Valentina Ehrenfeld and a constellation of collaborators from different areas and skills.

84 *Nicole Cristi*

3 While working with design practices in Chile, I am doing anthropology at home in two senses, first, as a Chilean and, second, as a designer. Consequently, I share with the human makers a cultural and technical background. Despite this, I identified the emic dimension in my research: how the community of biofabrication in Chile refers, categorises, organises, understands, and makes sense of their practice and existence.
4 While human participants on the process identified their practice as *growing*, they do not call themselves growers. Because analytically I am using the frame of "making" to study "growing," I call the human participants in the process "makers." Considering the more-than-human agency in the process, I use the category of human makers to identify them.
5 It depends on whether the process is started from scratch (where it could take months) or if a fully colonised culture is fed (where it takes weeks). In the case of the maqui material, it was started from scratch as a wild culture (wild fermentation); that is, without prior inoculum.
6 There are multiple types of bacteria, but this species is the one that produces the most cellulose in acetic acid fermentations.
7 Bacteria cannot digest the sucrose molecule, but they can digest smaller versions like glucose and fructose, thanks to the help of yeasts with their enzymatic scissors. Through this process, yeasts generate ethanol and CO_2. Acetic acid bacteria also transform this ethanol into acetic acid, making the culture acid enough to avoid intruders.

Bibliography

Alaimo, S. (2008). Ecofeminism without Nature? Questioning the Relation between Feminism and Environmentalism. *International Feminist Journal of Politics*, 10(3), 299–304. https://doi.org/10.1080/14616740802185551.

Bauhardt, C., & Harcourt, W. (2019). *Feminist Political Ecology and the Economics of Care*. New York: Routledge.

Buckley, C. (1986). Made in Patriarchy: Toward a Feminist Analysis of Women and Design. *Design Issues*, 3(2), 3–14. https://doi.org/10.2307/1511480.

Buckley, C. (2020). Made in Patriarchy II: Researching (or Re-Searching) Women and Design. *Design Issues*, 36(1), 19–29. https://doi.org/10.1162/desi_a_00572.

Cacopardo, A. (2018). "Nada sería posible si la gente no deseara lo imposible". Entrevista a Silvia Rivera Cusicanqui. *Andamios*, 15(37), 179–193.

Carrasco, C. (2001). La sostenibilidad de la vida humana: ¿Un asunto de mujeres? *Mientras tanto*, 82, 43–70. http://www.jstor.org/stable/27820584.

Centre for the Anthropology of Technics and Technodiversity (2022), University College of London. https://www.ucl.ac.uk/anthropology/research/centre-anthropology-technics-and-technodiversity-catt.

Coupaye, L. (2009). What's the Matter with Technology? Long (and short) Yams, Materialisation and Technology in Nyamikum Village, Maprik district, Papua New Guinea. *Australian Journal of Anthropology*, 20(1), 93–111.

Coupaye, L. (2013). *Growing Artefacts, Displaying Relationships: Yam technology in Nyamikum Abelam*. Oxford and New York: Berghahn Books.

Coupaye, L. (2018). 'Yams Have No Ears!': Tekhne, Life and Images in Oceania. *Oceania Publications*, 88(1), 13–30. https://doi.org/10.1002/ocea.5177.

Coupaye, L. (2022). Making "Technology" Visible: Technical Activities and the Chaîne Opératoire: Technique. In Maja Hojer Bruun, Ayo Wahlberg, Rachel Douglas-Jones, Cathrine Hasse, Klaus Hoeyer, Dorthe Brogård Kristensen, Brit Ross

Growing materials 85

Winthereik (Eds.), *The Palgrave Handbook of the Anthropology of Technology* (pp. 37–60). [Online]. Singapore: Springer Nature Singapore.

Coupaye, L., & Pitrou, P. (2018). Introduction. The Interweaving of Vital and Technical Processes in Oceania. *Oceania*, 88(1), 2–12. https://doi.org/10.1002/ocea.5178.

Curtin, D. (1991). Toward an Ecological Ethic of Care. *Hypatia*, 6(1), 60–74. https://doi.org/10.1111/j.1527-2001.1991.tb00209.x.

de la Bellacasa, M. (2011). Matters of Care in Technoscience: Assembling Neglected Things. *Social Studies of Science*, 41(1), 85–106. https://doi.org/10.1177/0306312710380301.

Descola, P. (2013 [2005]). *Beyond Nature and Culture*; translated by Janet Lloyd; foreword by Marshall Sahlins. (Lloyd, Trans.). Chicago, IL: University of Chicago Press.

Edgerton, D., Palmarola, H., & Álvarez Caselli, P. (2021). Some Problems with the Concept of 'Technology' in Design: Interview with David Edgerton. *Diseña*, (Num. 18), Interview.2. https://doi.org/10.7764/disena.18.Interview.2.

Escobar, A. (2018). *Designs for the Pluriverse: Radical Interdependence, Autonomy, and the Making of Worlds*. Durham, NC: Duke University Press.

Field, J. (2014). Silk Production: Moths, Mulberry and Metamorphosis. In E. Hallam & T. Ingold (Eds.), *Making and Growing: Anthropological Studies of Organisms and Artefacts* (1st ed.). London: Routledge, pp. 25–43. https://doi.org/10.4324/9781315593258.

Forlano, L. (2016). Decentering the Human in the Design of Collaborative Cities. *Design Issues*, 32(3), 42–54. https://doi.org/10.1162/DESI_a_0039.

Forlano, L. (2017). Posthumanism and Design. *She Ji: The Journal of Design, Economics, and Innovation*. Special Issue on Transforming Design Matters, 3(1) 16–29.

Fry, T. (2020). Defuturing a New Design Philosophy (1st ed.). London: Bloomsbury Visual Arts. https://doi.org/10.5040/9781350089563.

Gaard, G. (1993). *Ecofeminism: Women, Animals, Nature*. Philadelphia, PA: Temple University Press.

Gutiérrez, A. (2018). De Diseños Otros: La Vuelta De Las Canoas Polinesias, Ponencia presentada en 17 Festival Internacional de la Imagen, Diseño y Creación y Foro Académico Internacional, Colombia.

Gutiérrez, A. (2022). DISSOCONS, Diseños del sur, de los sures, otros, con otros nombres. Tesis Doctoral, Universidad de Caldas Doctorado en Diseño y Creación Manizales, Colombia.

Hallam, E., & Ingold, T. (2014). *Making and Growing: Anthropological Studies of Organisms and Artefacts* (1st ed.). London: Routledge. https://doi.org/10.4324/9781315593258.

Hamington, M. (2004). Embodied Care: Jane Addams, Maurice Merleau-Ponty, and Feminist Ethics. In *Embodied Care: Jane Addams, Maurice Merleau-Ponty, and Feminist Ethics*. Champaign, IL: University of Illinois Press, pp. 1–8.

Haraway, D. (2003). *The Companion Species Manifesto: Dogs, People, and Significant Otherness*. Chicago, IL: Prickly Paradigm.

Haraway, D. (2008). *When Species Meet*. Minneapolis: University of Minnesota Press.

Haudricourt, A. G. (1987 [1968]). *La Technologie, science humaine: Recherche d'histoire et d'ethnologie des techniques. Editions de la Maison des sciences de l'homme*, Paris.

86 Nicole Cristi

Heidegger, M. (1971). Building Dwelling Thinking. In *Poetry, Language, Thought*, by M. Heidegger, translated by A. Hofstadter. New York: Harper and Row, pp. 143–161.

Hertz, G. (2012). *Critical Making*. Hollywood, CA: Telharmonium Press.

Hui, Y. (2017). On Cosmotechnics, for a Renewed Relation between Technology and Nature in the Anthropocene. *Techné: Research in Philosophy and Technology*, 21(2/3), 319–341. Special Issue on the Anthropocene, https://doi.org/10.5840/techne201711876.

Hui, Y. (2019). What Begins after the End of the Enlightenment? *e-flux Journal*, (96), 1–10.

Irwin, T. (2015). Transition Design: A Proposal for a New Area of Design Practice, Study, and Research. *Design and Culture*, 7(2), 229–246. https://doi.org/10.1080/17547075.2015.1051829.

Kheel, M. (1993). From Heroic to Holistic Ethics: The Ecofeminist Challenge. In Greta Gaard (Ed.), *Ecofeminism: Women, Animals, Nature*. Philadelphia, PA: Temple University Press, pp. 243–271.

Latour, B. (1993). *We Have Never Been Modern*, translated by Catherine Porter. Cambridge, MA: Harvard University Press.

Lemonnier, P. (1992). From Field to Files: Description and Analysis of Technical Phenomena. In Pierre Lemonnier (Ed.), *Elements for an Anthropology of Technology*. Ann Arbor: Museum of Anthropology, University of Michigan, pp. 25–50.

Lemonnier, P. (1993). Technological Choices : Transformation. In Pierre Lemonnier (Ed.), *Material Cultures Since the Neolithic*. London: Routledge.

Leroi-Gourhan, A. (1964 [1999]). *Le geste et la parole I- Technique et langage*. Paris: Albin Michel.

Leroi-Gourhan, A. (1971 [1943]). *Evolution et Techniques I: L'Homme et la Matière*. Paris: Albin Michel.

Leroi-Gourhan, A. (1973 [1945]). *Evolution et Techniques II: Milieu et techniques*. Paris: Albin Michel.

Leroi-Gourhan, A. (1993). *Gesture and Speech*. Cambridge and London: MIT Press.

Mareis, C., & Paim, N. (Eds.) (2021). *Design Struggles: Intersecting Histories, Pedagogies, and Perspectives*. Amsterdam: Valiz.

Martinón-Torres, M. (2002). Chaîne opératoire: The Concept and Its Applications within the Study of Technology. *Gallaecia*, 21, 29–43.

Mauss, Marcel. (1979 [1935]). Body Techniques, Part IV. In *Sociology and Psychology: Essays by Marcel Mauss*. London: Routledge and Kegan Paul, pp. 95–123.

Mies, M., & Shiva, V. (1993). *Ecofeminism*. London: Zed Books.

Phillips, M. (2016). Embodied Care and Planet Earth: Ecofeminism, Maternalism and Postmaternalism. *Australian Feminist Studies*, 31(90), 468–485. https://doi.org/10.1080/08164649.2016.1278153.

Pitrou, P. (2015). Life as a Process of Making in the Mixe Highlands (Oaxaca, Mexico): Towards a "General Pragmatics" of Life. *The Journal of the Royal Anthropological Institute*, 21(1), 86–105. https://doi.org/10.1111/1467-9655.12143.

Pitrou, P. (2016). Co-Activity in Mesoamerica and in the Andes. *Journal of Anthropological Research*, 72(4), 465–482. https://doi.org/10.1086/689295

Pitrou, P. (2017). Life as a Making. *Nature*, 4, 1–37.

Plumwood, V. (1993). *Feminism and the Mastery of Nature*. London: Routledge.

Price, J., & Shildrick, M. (2002). Bodies Together: Touch, Ethics and Disability. In Mairian Corker & Tom Shakespeare (Eds.), *Disability/Postmodernity: Embodying Disability Theory*. London: Continuum, pp. 62–75.

Schlanger, N. (2005). The chaîne opératoire. In C. Renfrew & P. Bahn (Eds.), *Archaeology: The Key Concepts*. London: Routledge, pp. 25–31.

Shiva, V. (1997). Economic Globalization, Ecological Feminism, and Sustainable Development. *Canadian Woman Studies*, 17(2), 22–27.

Shiva, V. (2010) *Staying Alive: Women, Ecology and Development*. London: Zed Books.

Sigaut, F. (1994). Technology. In Ingold (Ed.), *Companion Encyclopedia of Anthropology: Humanity, Culture and Social Life*. London: Routledge, pp. 420–459.

Tlostanova. M. (2017). On Decolonizing Design. *Design Philosophy Papers*, 15(1), 51–61. https://doi.org/10.1080/14487136.2017.1301017.

Tonkinwise, C. (2015). Design for Transitions – From and To What? Design Philosophy Papers, 13(1), 85–92. https://doi.org/10.1080/14487136.2015.1085686

Van den Berg, K. (2019). Environmental Feminisms: A story of different encounters. In C. Bauhardt & W. Harcourt (Eds.), *Feminist Political Ecology and the Economics of Care*. New York: Routledge, pp. 55–69.

Viveiros de Castro, E. (2012). *Cosmological Perspectivism in Amazonia and Elsewhere*. Manchester: HAU Network of Ethnographic Theory.

Warren, K. (2000). *Ecofeminist Philosophy: A Western Perspective on What It Is and Why It Matters*. Lanham, MD: Rowman and Littlefield.

Willis, A. M. (2006). Ontological Designing. *Design Philosophy Papers*, 4(2), 69–92. https://doi.org/10.2752/144871306X13966268131514.

5 Learning from accidental abundance

Carl DiSalvo

As designers, we seem compelled to make anew. Much of this impulse comes from the relation of design to industry in the West, and the predominance of Northern and Western perspectives in design. Whether manufacturing desire or innovation, the techniques of design are regularly put towards creating novelty. But it's also worthwhile to recognise and appreciate what exists already. This seems particularly important as so many of the ideas that have been foundational to design are being called into question, ideas such as growth, progress, and human-centredness. More and more in contemporary discussions of design, we hear of the need to de-centre and unlearn. But how? Can design teach itself how to design differently? That seems a tall order. One way to learn otherwise is to look to different exemplars, different conditions and practices that offer different perspectives on how we are and might be in the world together. Foraging—the gathering of fruits, nuts, herbs, and yes mushrooms, growing wild—is one such practice. As Anna Tsing states: "It is time to pay attention to mushroom picking. Not that this will save us—but it might open our imaginations" (2015, 19).

For a decade now I've collaborated with a foraging collective in Atlanta, Georgia. This collective—Concrete Jungle—gathers fruit from trees growing wild in the city and near-suburbs and then gives that food to people in need: homeless shelters, food pantries, and other social service providers. Over time, the collective has expanded to gleaning dormant orchards in rural Georgia and tending a small farm in the city, but foraging remains central to the collective. And it is foraging that has affected me most, shaping how I think about and do design in the world.

Like any practice, as you begin performing its habits and customs, your perception and actions change. Once you begin foraging, you start looking for fruit everywhere and you start seeing it. Sometimes you've known a fruit tree was there all along, but for whatever reason, you never thought about eating that fruit. There's a peach tree on Dekalb Avenue, just outside of a bakery I frequent. It's crammed into a patch of dirt, where sidewalks awkwardly meet at the corner of two streets. I suppose the dirt is soil, but somehow it seems more like dirt as it's certainly not tended to. The tree has been there longer than I've lived here. Taking in its life and rhythms becomes

DOI: 10.4324/9781003319689-6

Learning from accidental abundance   89

a point of reflection and transforms how I understand and appreciate living in Atlanta. Once you've seen the peaches it stands out, and for a few weeks early every summer, it's glorious. And yet, it wasn't until I began foraging that it registered, I could eat those peaches, or I could give them to someone else to eat. That peach tree isn't the only fruit growing wild nearby. Within walking distance of where I live, there are plum and persimmon trees at the edge of a park I pass daily, there are mulberries and figs along the block where I walk my dog in the morning, and there's an abundance of serviceberries at the end of my street. This isn't unusual for Atlanta. Many, perhaps even most neighbourhoods can boast the same. Throughout much of the year, the city is lush and full of fruit.

Foraging, however, isn't a romantic affair. It isn't a return to nature amid the city. Foraging is a negotiation with automobiles and pedestrians, with the traffic of streets and sidewalks, with the crowds of parks. Standing in Dekalb Avenue to pick peaches isn't safe. Gathering persimmons from a tree next to the playground in the park can bring unwanted attention from children and their parents: "*What are you doing? Are you allowed to eat those? It is safe to eat those? Please don't let the children see you doing that.*" Foraging is also a negotiation with the policies and regulations of a municipality, with the boundaries of the public and private. There are rules that determine what plants (and by extension what fruits) you can pick from where. In some cases, some of those rules can be broken or bent without much thought, and in other cases, doing so is risky. No one really cares if you gather mulberries because they are considered a nuisance, mucking up the sidewalk every summer. But taking apples from Piedmont Park could result in ticket costing much more than the apples are worth. Such negotiations are part of what I find so compelling about foraging. Experiencing and appreciating such negotiations shape practices of living, doing, and making in the world that are different from what we've become accustomed to.

What seems to ultimately characterise foraging is that it's opportunistic, or to use terminology suggested by Michel De Certeau, it's a practice of tactics, of "making do" (1984). Foraging abandons the idea that there is a proper place for agriculture and instead finds the bounty of fruit whenever we come across it. The peach tree that grows along Dekalb Avenue, the plums and persimmons in Candler Park, the fig trees and mulberries in the front yard, and the serviceberries at the end of my street were likely planted on purpose. But they were not likely planted with the intention that someone would gather their fruits and eat them or share them with others. And yet the fruit is there to be gathered and to be shared. Foraging attunes us to a world of accidental abundance.

And through this attunement, foraging calls into question design. At least it does so for me. Whatever design is, we tend to think of it as not accidental. To say that something happened by accident is antithetical to saying that something happened by design. But foraging is made possible by accident and by an awareness of the opportunity and excess that accident provides.

Furthermore, foraging was not invented or made, at least not in the usual ways we talk about invention and making in design. It's not innovative or strategic. It's simply fortuitous and resourceful. As foraging renders certain assumptions about food systems and social services askew, it also renders certain assumptions about design and designing askew. And it does so in ways that are particularly productive for considering how else we might live together and how else design might figure into those lives.

We tend to assume that systems should be efficient to be effective. And we tend to assume that for social systems to be effective, they should remedy a social condition. Such assumptions permeate both popular discourse and design. But foraging is not efficient. If we think of efficiency in relation to time and effort, foraging is grossly inefficient. Ironically, we might consider foraging as wasteful, at least from an efficiency perspective. And foraging is physically demanding, not all can engage in the labour of foraging. Nor is foraging is going to solve food insecurity. Foraging is not an effective way of addressing the conditions or consequences of need that manifests in hunger. Moreover, most of us want more than fruit to subsist on.

So many of these assumptions about efficiency and effectiveness, about making anew and novelty that characterise so much of design are driven by free-market ideologies and values run amok. These are the very ideologies and values that we need to unlearn to work towards other—more just and sustainable—ways of living together. And coupled with unlearning, we must also learn other practices and other ways of being and acting in the world. We also have to participate in ways of living together that indulge other worldviews that are already undertaking the work of making other worlds possible. Doing so is part of the work of offering alternatives to the dominant practices of design, which contribute to unjust and unstainable futures (Fry, 2020).

Participating in foraging is, for me, one such way of unlearning and learning. Foraging does not "make sense" within the familiar logics and purposes that drive contemporary design. This is precisely the reason to indulge it. It is an example of what Eric Gordon and Gabriel Mugar call a "meaningful inefficiency": situations and experiences that are not economical but are important for shaping relations towards care (2019). Underlying this extended and ongoing collaboration with Concrete Jungle and participation in foraging is the question "How might we design for foraging?" But this question alone is insufficient, indeed it's dangerous because too often the result of such a question is subsuming this or that practice into the dominant logics of design (see Irani, 2019). Instead, the question must be "How might we design foraging in ways that respects the ethics of this practice?" To derive answers to that question requires unlearning the familiar logics and purposes of design and learning how to participate in different logics and purposes (Lindström and Ståhl, 2020).

Perhaps it is obvious, but nonetheless, it seems important to say: to unlearn design, we have to step outside of design and let go of the impulse to make anew; an impulse born of the belief that design is necessary for invention and action. We have to step into practices of world-making that are already underway. When doing so, we will be confronted with conditions and ethics that are unfamiliar. Participation in those practices, and embrace of those conditions and ethics, as unfamiliar as they might be, begins the learning needed. Indeed, rather than consider the work of design as making anew, we might say that what's needed is for design to learn anew.

Bibliography

Certeau, M. De (1984). *The Practice of Everyday Life*. Berkeley: University of California Press.

Costanza-Chock, S. (2020). *Design Justice: Community-Led Practices to Build the Worlds We Need*. Cambridge: The MIT Press.

Fry, T. (2020). *Defuturing: A New Design Philosophy*. London: Bloomsbury Publishing.

Gordon, E., & Mugar, M. (2020). *Meaningful Inefficiencies: Civic Design in an Age of Digital Expediency*. Oxford: Oxford University Press.

Irani, L. (2019). *Chasing Innovation: Making Entrepreneurial Citizens in Modern India*. Princeton: Princeton University Press.

Lindström, K., & Ståhl, Å. (2020). "Un/making in the aftermath of design." In *Proceedings of the 16th Participatory Design Conference 2020-Participation (s) Otherwise-Volume 1*, pp. 12–21.

Tsing, A. L. (2015). *The Mushroom at the End of the World: On the Possibility of Life in Capitalist Ruins*. Princeton: Princeton University Press.

6 How would animals and architects co-design if we built the right contract?

Ignacio Farías, Tomás Sánchez Criado and Felix Remter

Design in crisis?

In the last decades, mounting evidence has put the harsh prospects of multifaceted environmental crises of anthropogenic origins on various activist and public agendas. In the fields of architecture and urbanism, cities and practitioners have responded to this challenge by searching for more sustainable materials, more effective technologies, and more sustainable business models. Yet, recent conversations in the field of architecture and urbanism, such as the ones around the "Critical Care" exhibition at the *Architekturzentrum Wien* (Fitz & Krasny, 2019), suggest a displacement of the conventional focus on mitigation and adaptation measures towards the question of "how architecture and urbanism can help to care for and repair a broken planet." The language of care and repair, as an alternative to that of adaptation and mitigation, has many important consequences for how design and architecture position themselves today.

One important lesson is that global climate or the planetary crisis might not be the right scales for care and repair practices. There is no universal unit of commensurability for ecological care, as the trading of CO_2 emissions demonstrates. There is not "one" planetary crisis, but a superposition of situated crises, each unfolding at different scales and speeds, affecting specific human and non-human bodies, and requiring different, often contradicting forms of care and repair. Another consequence is the need to ask about the role architecture or design itself has played in the production of a catastrophic present. This is not a matter of pure self-flagellation or public derision, but it entails asking how to readdress the practices of architecture.

Similarly, our starting point is that what needs to be put in crisis is the very practice of design. The key question designers and architects have to address is not simply how to design more sustainably or more ecologically or in a more participatory way, but how to imagine other ways of undertaking architecture and urbanism to take care of the entangled lives of many species they necessarily have an effect on. This goes well beyond Latour's 2011 dictum that design is always redesign – that is, critically engaging with previous orderings and arrangements and creatively developing new ones better

DOI: 10.4324/9781003319689-7

How would animals and architects co-design? 93

attuned to the present and the future. What seems to be at stake is not the redesign of architectural forms and urban landscapes, but the redesign of urban design and architectural practice themselves.

Accordingly, we approach this volume's exploration of "design for a more-than-human future" from the side, presenting a collective speculation about "futures enabled by more-than-human design." The more-than-human, we reckon, needs to be more than the content of a design brief. It is rather an opening to other-than-human capacities in co-design processes and, with that, to the unpredictabilities resulting from terrestrial and multispecies interdependencies. Yet, the task of "multispecies" care, repair, and maintenance of extremely fragile ecological dynamics is not devoid of ambivalences and problems. As Schroer, van Dooren, Münster and Reinert (2021) discuss, a "multispecies" approach to such care cannot fall back to a do-gooder attitude but needs to "interrogate the broader dynamics of power, understanding, and resource use that shape which modes of life and being are fostered, are rendered worthy of and legible to dominant regimes of care, and which are abandoned or disavowed." Such a concern also needs to include a decisive component of trust in and knowledge about non-human animals' own regimes of and abilities to care (Remter, 2021).

How to care, then, in architectural practice for terrestrial and multispecies entanglements? In this chapter, we provide no guidelines or general principles of practice to do so. Our offer is a story of collective experimenting and learning based on a question: what if we sought to relearn how to practise architecture from animals? By exploring this question and by telling this story, we aimed at circumventing two more conventional gestures: helping out animals survive in our contemporary urban environments – like advocates of *Animal-Aided Design* propose (Hauck & Weisser, 2015); or treating animals as "food for thought" about architectural practice, as Juhanni Pallasmaa (2002) has done in his groundbreaking *Animal Architecture*. Following STS and environmental humanities multispecies concerns, we pursued a different avenue: approaching urban animals as epistemic partners for rethinking architectural practice, thus engaging their capacities in attempts at *designing with* (rather than "for" or "from") them.

Beavering architecture?

In the winter of 2017–2018, we taught in the master's program in architecture at the Technical University of Munich the third installment of a series of studio courses called "Design in Crisis." Our main idea was creating conditions for "suspending" the practice of architectural design and pushing students to explore other ways of relating architecturally to issues, such as disasters and humanitarian crises, as well as bodily diversity and accessible infrastructures (Farías & Criado, 2018). The course "Design in Crisis 3: Sensing like an Animal" aimed to imagine a multispecies practice of transforming

94   *Ignacio Farías et al.*

urban landscapes. We were greatly inspired by Despret's question "What would animals say if we asked the right questions?" (2016), as well as by the answers she provides: stories of animal agency in a wide variety of situations, including experimental settings, thus disputing the machinic concepts with which they are treated in ecological and ethological thought.

The course began with four weeks of intense sensory experiments aimed at apprehending and interacting with the urban landscape "like an animal." The aim was not to simulate animal perception in order to substitute the experience of the architect – as though that would be possible – but rather to invent practices and artefacts that would challenge conventional sensory practices of architects, as well as better understand the speculative challenge of sensing like an animal. We took as our guides three animals – ants, dogs, and beavers – and we asked our students to thoroughly document their experiences (many times difficult to understand in the heat of the moment) through memos, videos, models, and other devices.[1]

In the case of ants, the sensory challenge was how they relate to space without visual perspective. For a whole rainy day in Munich's Maßmannpark, blindfolded students had to learn to act and survive as an ant colony of sorts: launching expeditions and learning to orient themselves without getting lost, finding items in the landscape they required to build a shelter, moving collectively, and learning to build a safe shelter under a playground's slide. All with the sole help of their bodies, their voices, and some umbrellas (bodily extensions and building material at once), we had placed them randomly in their surroundings. Their subsequent task was to create a how-to guide for exploring space and building like an ant so that other architects could also experiment how to move beyond the ocularcentrism of architectural knowledge and practice.

Another day we sought to learn how dogs practise and know urban space by means of two exercises. Firstly, we walked and were walked by two of them in a stroll in Munich's Hirschgarten. After this, we used a furniture roller (aptly called in German *Hundt*, a homophone of the word for dog), in order to move around urban space in quick abrupt movements, sniffing and observing the city from a dog's point of view. After a long day of moving around with and like dogs, we asked students to build a model or a device that would document and translate how dogs experience space.

After four weeks, we developed the brief that would guide the rest of the course. For this, we took as a starting point the third animal we also had been investigating: the beaver. We undertook a day-long site visit to a hotspot area of conflicts with beavers in the North of Munich. There we met the *Biberbeauftragter* (literally, the beaver representative) of Bavaria, who explained that beavers had historically lived in the basin of the river Isar before they had been hunted down to the last in the 1860s. Later, the river was thoroughly channeled in a series of landmark modernist infrastructural interventions at the turn of the 20th century. Beavers were reintroduced in Bavaria in the 1960s, hailed as "biodiversity experts" capable of

How would animals and architects co-design? 95

intervening landscapes and creating ecological niches for large numbers of species. However, their return to Munich had not been devoid of conflicts with urban dwellers and those in charge of planning and maintaining the urban green infrastructure of Munich.

These frictions became stronger after the municipality engaged in a series of endeavors to "renaturalise" the Isar river basin. Ever since, the frictional encounters of humans and beavers have routinely featured in local media, displaying a wide variety of modernist approaches to said "renaturalisation": for instance, "conservationist" attitudes to beaver population management (Bayerisches Landesamt für Umwelt, 2009) but also enraged reactions in which beavers taking ornamentally placed trees or causing floods are conventionally framed as "destructive behavior" or as a problem, leading urban authorities to protect trees with mesh wire or other lasting infrastructure.

This latter development was at the core of the brief: students should develop a "late entry" for the public competition that took place in 2003 for the renaturation of the Isar river basin in the city of Munich. However, and this was the only obstruction we put on their way, they needed to do it "like a beaver's contractor." With this brief, accompanied with a set of readings on more-than-human approaches to design and environmental humanities (Ingold, 2000; Rice, 2018; van Dooren and Rose, 2012), we wanted to push the students towards questioning the anthropocentric premises of their design practices. This seemed to us a relevant problem, because if the challenge is to undo the anthropocentric logic that has led us to the Anthropocene, and if architecture has had its part in it, then the question is: what elements of architectural and urban practice should be put on hold or in crisis – and what opportunities, visions, or inventions can emerge with such a crisis?

Yet, the first project ideas that emerged were not what we were expecting. After conducting a fairly detailed analysis of beaver presence in the river basin, as well as the forms of conflict and cohabitation associated with it, students had identified two sites that they intended to renaturalise, in order to ensure a peaceful co-existence between beavers and humans. After our criticism that such a proposal involved designing *for* the beavers, but not *with* them or even *authorised by* them, we reached a major moment of crisis:

> "If you don't like our solution, tell us how you would respond!"
> "The brief is an oxymoron: it is not possible to design like a beaver!"
> "What's the point of doing a design studio course, in which we can't design? What will I put into my portfolio?"

The crisis led to a potential solution:

> Since you have concluded that it is not possible to design like a beaver, perhaps one option to evaluate is to think about the beavers as your client. But if you opt for this option, what we will ask you is to first design a contract that authorizes you to design on behalf of the beaver.

96 *Ignacio Farías et al.*

But how to think of a contract by which the beavers would transfer to architects the right to speak and design on their behalf? The problem was just as complex, if not more so, than the initial one – and it was a problem we were all in: students and instructors.

The French philosopher Michel Serres came to our aid, and we devoted a session to a discussion of his premonitory book *The Natural Contract*: one of the first to address the philosophical–political implications of the ecological-planetary crisis. In it, Serres poses the question of how to establish a contract that would put an end to the relations of violence between a humanity turned into a geological force and the planet, that is, between humans and non-humans. In a crucial passage, Serres (1995: 51–55) explores the origins of contracts and the binding effects associated with them, by paying attention to the Egyptian figure of the *harpedonaptai*: the royal official who after the ascents of the Nile visited the flooded lands and, with some ropes of cord, marked the territory and re-established the relations of property. In its origin, Serres observes, the social contract was not a written document but a bond that binds: a material device that unites and separates, marking a territory in more permanent ways than words, capable of establishing more or less univocal relations between the land and humans, between territories and its owners. It was then clear for us that the contract we needed could well be an object or an artefact that establishes a material, physical, or bodily connection between the parties involved – the humans and the non-humans or, in our case, the students, the beavers, and the inner-city Isar.

To incite a conversation about how to create a physical bond with a non-human partner, we invited the designer Thomas Thwaites to give a public lecture and talk with us and our students in class. Thwaites (2016) had recently published an interesting speculative project called *Goat Man*: in an attempt at "taking a holiday from being human," he took a whole year to learn how goats move and eat; to that end, he designed an intricate exoskeleton with the help of natural scientists and engineers and, later, tested it for a week trying – and failing – to live among goats in the Swiss Alps.

The project sparked very relevant discussions with our students: rather than thinking of it as a "design solution" mimicking how to approach living like a goat, we foregrounded how it had helped Thwaites materialise an interesting design research question, learning about these animals' physiology and functionality through his own practice. Up to that moment, students had been learning about non-intrusive approaches to human–beaver communication commonly used in land management: electronic speakers or tubes creating sounds of water flows are used to incite beavers to build at particular locations, pipes that do not produce any noises are used to drain beaver dams, and scents emulating *Castoreum* are used to signal territories already occupied by other beavers. Thwaites' practice was critical for developing a more embodied approach to the contract with the beavers. The question now was not how to engage in a more embodied co-design practice.

How would animals and architects co-design? 97

Figure 6.1 Co-worker suit (left) and beaver experience suit (right). CC BY 2017 Katharina Meenenga, Laura Krohn, Marie Van Tricht, Pedro Racha-Pacheco, Seppe Verhaegen, and Victoria Schulz. Used with permission.
Source: https://thedesignincrisis.wixsite.com/designincrisis/submission.

The proposal developed by the students entailed equipping architects to create conditions for encountering and negotiating with beavers in a shared environment. The proposal consisted in two suits (Figure 6.1):

a A *beaver "experience" suit* (including gloves with claws, scissors and cutters instead of teeth, and dark glasses to simulate beavers' poor vision and stimulate the use of our other senses), designed for architects to de-learn the anthropocentric and ocularcentric approaches to design in experiencing other ways of relating to the environment;
b A *co-worker suit* (including a bottle with odors to negotiate in situ which trees not to cut, tubes that amplify the sound of the water and "ask" the beavers to intervene in a certain place, and other tools), designed to collaborate with beavers in the renaturalisation of the basin of the river Isar.

The suits-as-contracts made emerge manifold doubts and conversations: did this proposal imply that whoever wore these devices could – finally – feel authorised to start redesigning the Isar river basin on behalf of the beavers? Could it eventually lead to a renaturalisation project without the beavers' own expertise and knowledge in rewilding and fostering river biodiversity? The more we got involved in thinking about these suits, the more evident it became that for any design contract enabling beavers and architects to co-design, what had to be worked on were also the devices enabling those negotiations. So, what if such a co-design enabling suit and the material processes of *contracting* were turned into the very proposal for the "late entry" for the renaturalisation of the Isar river?

98   *Ignacio Farías et al.*

Understanding that the contracting process was the renaturalisation project led to a proposal that used the river basin as a space where to create a bond or, better, a binding co-design commitment between humans and beavers. Once this was established, students devoted themselves to prototyping the procedures and the institutional setting for such a project to continue developing in the future. This included a series of protocols on how to use each of the suits and tools (see Figure 6.2); protocols that were integrated in a *Plan of Diurnal and Nocturnal Action and Reaction* (see Figure 6.3); as well as the blueprint for a River Biodiversity Union, a river management institution created to ensure the implementation of the plan. These institutions were critical for how students imagined "the society of the future, in which different species work together and co-design in the city."[2]

Towards a multispecies architectural practice?

In closing, we would like to point out some lines of tension for a multispecies architectural practice that this experience helped us delineate. These involve three aspects that might need to be contrasted and further developed in the future.

1 *From design solutions to contracts as negotiation devices for joint problem-making*: Architects tend to express their expertise in designing objects proposed as solutions to well-articulated needs, wishes, or demands. This premise has no currency for more-than-human design: animals (and most humans too) are not capable of articulating problems in the language of architects. What is needed are modes of continuous joint problem-making. In this chapter, we introduced the notion of the contract to redefine the space in which architects might need to learn to correspond *in the present* with other human and non-human beings. What needs to be designed then is the very process of contractual negotiation: that is, the appropriateness and capability of designing with someone or in someone's name.

2 *From users to clients and co-designers:* Although approaches like Animal-Aided Design have considered animals as "end users" of architectural practice, what if this figure was not helpful to open up design to the non-human? In this chapter, we explore what it entails thinking of non-humans as "clients" and "co-designers." The client is a figure mostly invisibilised in architectural literature, even though it often acts as a full-blown co-designer intervening in all phases of design (see, e.g., Cuff, 1992). We think that by conceiving animals as powerful clients or as expert co-designers, rather than as subaltern users, a different architectural practice can be invented, engaging the beavers' abilities to make environments and hence develop more-than-human modes of co-design.

3 *From impartial arbiters to designers as committed partners*: Designers are often imagined as having to arbiter between (too) many incompossible requirements and demands, developing compromises between the

PROTOCOL N°6

ARTIFICIAL TREES

This document comprises the funtions, design and terms of use of Artificial Trees and becomes effective if signed by the River Biodiversity Union and approved by the beavers over a period of three months.

§1 Function
1) Providing sustainable dam material
2) Avoiding deforestation of a beaver active area

§2 Design
1) Sticks of 1-5 m length
2) Material: reused/recycled timber or organic, compostable material
3) All components need to be robust and ment to last over and under water for a minimum period of one year
4) No sharp or hard materials such as glass or metal
5) Max. weigth of one object: 10 kg

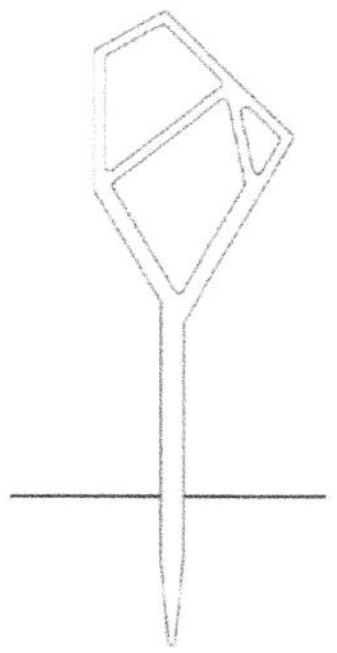

§3 Terms of Use
1) Distributed and fixed by employees of the River Biodiversity Union
3) Location:
  a) In areas with beaver action or possible future beaver action
3) Instructions:
  a) Use Co-Worker-Suit according to PROTOCOL N°3
  b) Implant objects in a maximum distance of 10 m to the river
  c) Work during the day and remove all signs of a building site (f.e. trucks, not yet implanted trees or tools) before dawn

Agreed and accepted:
River Biodiversity Union

By: _____
    An Authorized Signer

Federal I.D.
Number: _____

Date: _____

Beavers **agree** legally by:

Integrating at least 30% of the Artificial Trees in their territory into the dam or lodge within three months

stamp here

Beavers **disagree** legally by:

Integrating less than 30% of the Artificial Trees in their territory into the dam or lodge over a period of three months

stamp here

Figure 6.2 The last protocol.[3] CC BY 2017 Katharina Meenenga, Laura Krohn, Marie Van Tricht, Pedro Racha-Pacheco, Seppe Verhaegen, and Victoria Schulz. Used with permission.

Source: https://thedesignincrisis.wixsite.com/designincrisis/5-weeks.

100 Ignacio Farías et al.

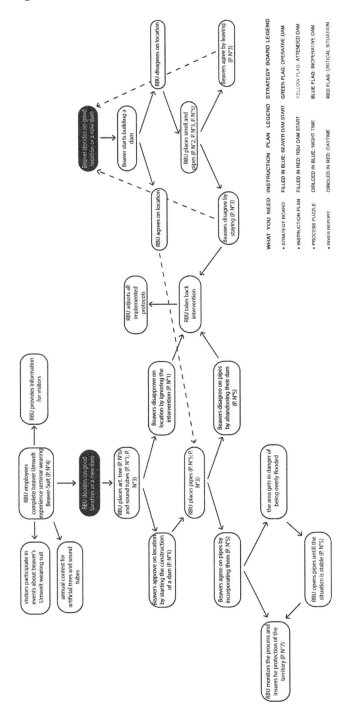

Figure 6.3 Action and reaction plan. CC BY 2017 Katharina Meenenga, Laura Krohn, Marie Van Tricht, Pedro Racha-Pacheco, Seppe Verhaegen, and Victoria Schulz. Used with permission.

Source: https://thedesignincrisis.wixsite.com/designincrisis/5-weeks.

How would animals and architects co-design? 101

technical and the political, the social and the economic, and the ecological and the aesthetic dimensions of a project. A multispecies architectural practice requires radically overcoming that figure: no longer an impartial arbiter but a partner committed to creating conditions for more-than-human co-design. Indeed, if the great challenge that the Anthropocene imposes on architecture is precisely the need to incorporate non-human animals, their capabilities, expertise, and perspectives, this entails transforming architectural practice: becoming sensitive to the practices and perspectives of other-than-human life and non-human animals, in particular, exploring how to engage with their issues and, more importantly, learning to take their side.

Notes

1 As a result, students Katharina Meenenga, Laura Krohn, Marie Van Tricht, Pedro Racha-Pacheco, Seppe Verhaegen, and Victoria Schulz created this blog: https://thedesignincrisis.wixsite.com/designincrisis.
2 For which they created a corporate identity and a website of its own: https://riverbiodiversity.wixsite.com/union.
3 A complete guide including all protocols and designs can be found here: https://45d6c820-55c0-421b-8a7f-2b58f56d5dac.filesusr.com/ugd/091edb_876526354dbd4f4faa38b7eac2e02129.pdf.

Bibliography

Bayerisches Landesamt für Umwelt. (2009). *Biber in Bayern – Biologie und Management*. Augsburg: LfU.

Cuff, D. (1992). *Architecture: The Story of Practice*. Cambridge: MIT Press.

Despret, V. (2016). *What Would Animals Say If We Asked the Right Questions?* Minneapolis: Minnesota University Press.

Farías, I., & Sánchez Criado, T. (2018). "Co-Laborations, Entrapments, Intraventions: Pedagogical Approaches to Technical Democracy in Architectural Design." *Diseña*, 12, pp. 228–255.

Fitz, A., & Krasny, E. (2019). *Critical Care: Architecture and Urbanism for a Broken Planet*. Cambridge: MIT Press.

Hauck, T. E., & Weisser, W. (2015). *Animal-Aided Design: Bauen für Mensch und Tier*. Freising: Lehrstuhl für Terrestrische Ökologie, Technische Universität München.

Ingold, T. (2000). "Building, Dwelling, Living: How Animals and People Make Themselves at Home in the World." In *The Perception of the Environment: Essays on Livelihood, Dwelling and Skill*, edited by Tim Ingold. London: Routledge, pp. 172–188.

Latour, B. (2011). "A Cautious Prometheus? A Few Steps Toward a Philosophy of Design (With Special Attention to Peter Sloterdijk)." In *In Media Res. Peter's Sloterdijk's Spherological Poetics of Being*, edited by Willem Schinkel Liesbeth Noordegraaf-Eelens. Amsterdam: Amsterdam University Press, pp. 151–165.

Pallasmaa, J. (2002). *Eläinten Arkkitehtuuri / Animal Architecture*. Helsinki: Museum of Finnish Architecture.

Remter, F. (2021). "Ecologizing Honeybee Care: Multispecies Bodies and Trust in the Varroa Pandemic". Cultural Anthropology, Theorizing the

102 *Ignacio Farías et al.*

Contemporary, *Fieldsights*, January 26. https://culanth.org/fieldsights/ecologizing-honeybee-care-multi-species-bodies-and-trust-in-the-varroa-pandemic

Rice, L. (2018). "Nonhumans in Participatory Design." *CoDesign*, 14(3): 238–257.

Schroer, S., Thom van Dooren, A., Münster, U., & Reinert, H. (2021). "Introduction: Multispecies Care in the Sixth Extinction." Cultural Anthropology, Theorizing the Contemporary, *Fieldsights*, January 26. https://culanth.org/fieldsights/introduction-multispecies-care-in-the-sixth-extinction

Serres, M. (1995). *The Natural Contract*. Edited by Elizabeth MacArthur and William Paulson. Ann Arbor: University of Michigan Press.

Thwaites, T. (2016). *Goat Man: How I Took a Holiday from Being Human*. Princeton, NJ: Princeton University Press.

Van Dooren, T., & Bird Rose, D. (2012). "Storied-Places in a Multispecies City". *Humanimalia: A Journal of Human/Animal Interface Studies*, 3(2), pp. 1–27.

7 Before the idiot, the poet?
Aesthetic figures and design

Alex Wilkie and Mike Michael

Introduction

In a number of recent writings, the conceptual persona of the idiot has been held up as means for opening up the meanings of practices and knowledges presupposed by various practitioners, notably academics and designers (e.g., Michael, 2012b; Wilkie et al., 2015; Tironi, 2018). However, for the idiot to operate in this way, we argue, it requires certain qualities and capacities, not least those that modulate or mitigate its more extreme or disruptive guises. In what follows, we explore one particular means to such modulation, namely the figure of the poet. This figure, we shall argue, allows us to think how the idiot can be productive in terms of resourcing the design process, both at the level of designing artefacts and methods and at the level of engaging with participants. Central here is the idea that the poet enables a "possession by the richness of the world"—that is to say, a capacity to become attuned to the world in its complexity and becoming. In what follows, we begin with an account of the idiot and the design used to which it has been put. But we also document a number of the ways in which the idiot has had to be modulated in order to function as a figure that slows down thought and opens up potentiality. In this regard, we consider how the conceptual persona and aesthetic figure can be combined to enhance the speculative in design processes.

The idiot: tool or tool?

In Stengers' (2005) *Cosmopolitical Proposal*, the figure of the idiot, drawn from Deleuze and Guattari's (1994) discussion of conceptual personae, is assigned the role of slowing down the thinking of practitioners who are involved in composing common worlds. As such, the idiot prompts practitioners to resist consensual ways in which circumstances and emergencies present themselves, mobilising reasoning and action. However, rather than offer a solution or explanation, the idiot merely invites those involved in modern science and its attendant politics to pause and reappraise the common worlds in whose construction they are participating: "the idiot demands

DOI: 10.4324/9781003319689-8

that we slow down, that we don't consider ourselves authorized to believe we possess the meaning of what we know" (Stengers, 2005: 995). In design, this means that the idiot, embodied in, for example, cultural probes (Gaver et al., 1999) or speculative devices (Wilkie et al., 2015; Wilkie and Michael, 2018) that are playful, non-functional, open-ended, obscure, and so on, can encourage research participants to re-think their usual ways of thinking and to question standard forms of practice (e.g., Michael, 2012a). However, these idiotic artefacts don't always perform in this way. They often misbehave.

If the idiot is a tool in relation to design, let us reflect on the dual meaning of "tool." On the one hand, it is an object that allows certain tasks to be accomplished. On the other hand, in a different colloquial idiom, a tool is a derogatory term that points to someone who overestimates their talent, cleverness, or amiability and behaves in ways that they think make them appear talented, clever, or likable but ironically have the opposite effect of making them appear ridiculous and less congenial. Synonyms include "prick," "dick," or "schmuck," where schmuck can also be a synonym for idiot.[1,2] The point here is that the idiot is not straightforwardly an asset to the speculative design process. To be sure, the obscurity of an idiotic research device might prompt less speculation and more rejection. For instance, let us consider the Home Health Monitor (Gaver et al., 2009): in brief, this entailed a series of sensors installed throughout a home that detected a range of physical conditions and their frequency of occurrence (e.g., whether a door was opened or shut over a period of time, whether a sofa was used, etc.). These measures served as indices of particular domestic situations such as privacy, social intimacy, and cleaning. The sensor data was translated into a range of aphorisms, photographs, and depictions of daily metrics. Rather than engage playfully with these obscure "products" of the sensor measures to re-think the "health" of the home, the participants focused on the accuracy of the outputs. In essence, the participants did not really see the point of the project. For Gaver et al. (2009), this lack of engagement could be attributed to a range of factors which can be boiled down to the sense that the system afforded few meaningful experiences within a particular domestic setting (see Michael, 2016).

Here, we see how an idiotic design was tool-like, meaning that it was too "clever"—too opaque—for its users and tended to push them towards a reaction against it. After all, we should not forget that even the idiocy of the naïve Prince Myshkin in Dostoyevsky's *The Idiot* (2004 [1868]) rarely precipitated an "appropriate" engagement but served to re-trench the prejudices and status seeking of his various interlocutors. The question that follows, then, is what is "required" to render the idiot a tool of speculative intervention?

In their final adventure in thought, *What Is Philosophy?* Deleuze and Guattari (1994: 65) draw a sharp distinction between *conceptual personae* and *aesthetic figures*. Where conceptual personae refer to the capacity of concepts to elicit beings into thought, as it were, providing what they call a

Before the idiot, the poet? Aesthetic figures and design 105

"Thought-being" and, as such, play a key role in the philosopher's repertoire of creative reasoning, aesthetic figures designate processes of experience that operate on and in (political) compositions. If conceptual personae exceed commonsensical understanding, then aesthetic figures have the power to go beyond customary or mundane experience, affect, and objects of perception. In accordance with this contrast between conceptual personae and aesthetic figures, we can see how Stengers' version of the conceptual persona of the idiot has its impact on thought—rendering a greater ideational creativity through its non-sensicalness that prompts both a slowing down and a questioning of the thinker's (or the practitioner's) authority to believe they "possess the meaning of what they know" (Stengers, 2005: 995).

This is depicted as primarily an epistemic process. The idiot is predisposed to questions of knowledge, of what "we" know. But as we have seen, the idiot can disable this creative and questioning thought because it is the wrong sort of tool. This should come as no surprise. The idiot—in its murmuring—can be hugely threatening, not only to one's commonsensical thoughts or habitual ways of thinking but to thinking per se. The idiot can be dangerous as well as intriguing, threatening as well as promising. Here, we glimpse the essentially affective dimensions of the idiot: it has in operate at a particular affective register in order to function as the right sort of (speculative) tool.

The poet's feeling

There are numerous ways in which the affective underpinnings of the idiot's functionality can be entertained. Consider the case of the Energy Babble, a research device designed to broadcast more or less nonsensical talk about matters concerning energy demand and its reduction (see Boucher et al., 2018, for details about its design and implementation). The purpose here was to encourage in its various users and audiences speculations about the nature of energy-related information, the parameters of community, the delineations of the future, and the complex and unfolding meanings and practices around energy and energy-demand reduction. However, its idiotic "useability" had to be affectively shaped and designed. As part of making the Babble device feel less alien and more "relatable," it had to be instrumentalised. This meant downplaying its more speculative dimensions and emphasising its more utilitarian capacities. As Wilke and Michael (2018) document, this included portraying the Babble as, among other things, an energy saving appliance, as a means of solving problems, and as a marketing tool. In tempering the idiocy of the Energy Babble in these ways, rendering it more approachable, people could draw on what was left of that in-built idiocy, engage with it in a speculative fashion.

In partial contrast to this partial instrumentalisation of the speculative design device (see below), we can explore a different mode of affectively rendering a speculative intervention more accessible that focuses on aesthetics. Here, we take aesthetics as inviting us to ask different kinds of

106 Alex Wilkie and Mike Michael

questions, of what we "feel" and what is perceptible. As above, we assume that epistemic questions are prefaced by aesthetic questions: what we know is always preceded by what we feel, or at least, what we *can know* requires the semblance of what we feel. We have to *feel* something before we can *know* it.

In seeking a pertinent aesthetic figure that can "support" and make workable a conceptual persona, we turn to the poet. We ask how the poet and their poetry can set up the conditions that allow the idiot to do its idiotic work—to slow thought, to trouble the authority "to believe we possess the meaning of what we know." Heidegger (1971) sees poetry as a means to engaging with the complexities of dwelling, where dwelling entails the recovery of our "home"—our relation to the world—that has been corrupted by technologisation and instrumentalised as a "standing reserve," that is, a mere means (Heidegger, 1971). Of course, there is much to be critical about this schema: what world precisely are we talking about? Is technology not intrinsic to humans (see Michael and Gaver, 2009)? But in drawing upon poetry, Heidegger usefully suggests that by virtue of its unkempt relation to representation, its paucity of transparency, it affords possession by the richness of the world. But, if the poet's works provide affective access to the richness of the world, what does that richness consist of? In keeping with the speculative turn in philosophy and the social sciences (Halewood, 2011; Stengers, 2011; Savransky, 2016; de la Bellacasa, 2017; Debaise, 2017; Wilkie et al., 2017), we regard this richness as encompassing complexity, multiplicity, heterogeneity, becoming, and virtuality. If the poet and poetry can affectively convey sensibility towards this richness of the world evoking "a vivid feeling of what lies beyond words" (Whitehead, 1968 [1938]: 50), then this suggests that the idiot can operate more effectively.

In becoming sensitised to the figure of the poet, as an aesthetic persona, we can also begin to discern another, more thought-provoking, and for our purposes promising, understanding of aesthetics—a version that has been eclipsed since the success of Immanuel Kant and Alexander Gottlieb Baumgarten in establishing the foundations of modern aesthetic thought (Sehgal, 2018: 114). Here, we follow Sehgal's critical account of the bifurcation of aesthetic reasoning. This split is engendered by the bifurcation of nature (Whitehead, 2004 [1920]: 30), where aesthetics is designated a special domain and compartmentalised into the experiencing and expressive (human) subject and the aesthetic "art" object. By contrast, Whitehead provides a radically alternative and generalised version of aesthetics where aesthetic "values" are fundamental to the becoming of events and, as echoed in Guattari's "new aesthetic paradigm" (Guattari, 2006 [1992]: 91), in the very production of existence. The paragon of Whitehead's version of aesthetics can be found in the figure of the poet, more specifically the Romantic poet.[3] Wordsworth is particularly singled out, as it is he who bears "witness that nature cannot be divorced from its aesthetic values; and that these values arise from the cumulation, in some sense, of the brooding presence of the whole in its various parts" (Whitehead, 1997 [1925]: 87–88).[4]

Before the idiot, the poet? Aesthetic figures and design   107

For Whitehead, then, aesthetics is not predicated upon the experiencing and judging human subject nor a special category of objects imbued with beauty or the sublime but rather upon the generalised and "creative" production of existence where all entities have the capacity to feel and to be affected. In other words, aesthetic values are not conferred on the world but are immanent to its situated becomings as entities preferentially feel other entities and, in the process, concresce to generate new entities. Here lies the richness of the world, and the poet's role is partly to "protest" against the exclusion of such aesthetic values and the plethora of feelings from matters of fact (or, for that matter, matters of concern and care). More positively, the function of the poet is to invite a speculative sensibility towards the possibilities of the production of existence and the values and practices entailed therein. Put baldly, the poet evokes the richness of the world in its heterogeneous, unfolding, aesthetic complexity that lies at the heart of even the seemingly most straightforward observation.

We can unpack this further by drawing on Savransky's (2020) account of immanent aesthetic values. If, crudely, the poet more or less gently evokes the richness of the world, and the idiot confrontationally posits the possibility of that untapped richness, Savransky suggests a way of accessing that richness. By attending to aesthetic values, we can engage with that richness understood as "the plurality and manners of living and how these interoperate and interplay with other ways of being in … an 'ecology of values'" (ibid.: 7). From this, we can take it that aesthetic values—the feelings for, resonances with, relationalities to—are what the idiot gestures enigmatically and troublingly towards, and that the poet mitigates through evocation. But, of course, we are arguing for the idiot as a useable tool, one rendered useable through the poet, as it were. Savransky's suggestion is that this useability—the right sort of toolness—can be found in particular forms of experimentation. In other words, the task that incorporates both poet and idiot becomes one of experimenting *with* others' practices of existence, recognising the values at play and appreciating—as grasping and recognising the worth—of such values. But this is a proactive process precisely because experimental practices are engaging with aesthetic values as they are being concretely recomposed and redefined.

In the next section, we consider this nexus of figures and relations in more practical terms. Specifically, community engagement with, and involvement in, novel energy-demand reduction practices provides a case in which new aesthetic values and modes of living are being cultivated, tested, trialled, and negotiated. Can we find examples where before the idiot, the poet does their work? Or can we re-think cases where a poetical component might have allowed the speculative design's idiocy to have taken a more fruitful—that is, experimental—hold? Can we re-think aspects of the Energy Babble, as a "speculative design," in terms of its poetical components and content, that operate to allow the device to work "better" as a speculative device to engage aesthetic values?

108 *Alex Wilkie and Mike Michael*

Energy-demand reduction and aesthetic values

Let us take stock. We are suggesting that the poet mitigates the potential threats posed by the challenges of the idiot by hinting at the range of immanent aesthetic values (that together comprise the richness of the world). In the case of the Energy Babble, its idiocy was mitigated by a rather impoverished poet, as it were: an instrumentalised enactment of the Babble served only to point to a few, rather familiar aesthetic values. Specifically, these took the form of feelings for and resonances with relationalities to such elements as practical modes of energy-demand reduction, or commonsensical notions of "energy community" rather than the opening up to more inventive notions of energy-demand reduction, or more atypical conceptualisations of community. So, the poet was at work in rendering the Babble's idiocy palatable. However, our argument is that the poet can also support such idiocy to be exciting, promising, and expansive. Just as we discussed above in relation to the "tool," there are "bad" (debilitatingly threatening) idiots as well as "good" idiots, so there are "bad" as well as "good" poets.

In retrospect, and in light of the foregoing, the problem we faced is how practically to introduce the "good" poet and idiot so that speculative engagement with energy-demand reduction becomes a possibility. Drawing on Savransky's suggestion of a particular version of "experimentation," the Babble might have been, for example, accompanied by a more proactive presence of the researchers in the energy communities: their (poetical) co-presence and (poetical) articulation of the Babble might have served to generate discussion about the participants' aesthetic values while at the same time directing them towards the aesthetic values enabled by the Babble, in the process concretely recomposing and redefining them.

But this should give us pause. As Savransky hints, there is an ecology of values at play. The experimental interventions of the poetic–idiotic Babble must locate themselves within, and to some extent reconfigure, this ecology. The issue, as we have written elsewhere (Wilkie and Michael, 2018), is that this ecology entails aesthetic values that are shaped by such factors as, for instance, the need to compete against other energy communities (necessitated by the structure of the energy-reduction funding process). In some respects, it is difficult to imagine how our speculative design intervention can have purchase in such an ecology in which long-standing values seem paramount. And yet, the very fact that our project was invited into energy communities suggests that perhaps the poetic–idiotic Energy Babble did offer attractive aesthetic values or engender the reappraisal of existing values. Most obviously, participation in our project offered a reframing of the energy community as one especially willing to innovate and collaborate in pursuit of energy-demand reduction—to re-situate itself within the ecology of values (including advantageously within the competitive landscape of energy communities). Perhaps less obviously, our speculative research project offered another aesthetic value—one of simply doing "something different" from the usual social scientific participation (energy communities have been some of

Before the idiot, the poet? Aesthetic figures and design 109

most studied groups in the UK—Clark, 2008). It was its very otherness that was attractive.

But again, we should proceed cautiously. The term aesthetic values connotes something tangible in the sense that "the feeling for, the resonance with, the relationality to" has a substantive degree of discreteness, demarcation. What the poet–idiot does is not so much identify, indicate, or even implicate an aesthetic value so much as hint, suggest, insinuate. It plants a seed of a value, occasioning the (com)possibility of crystalising new experiences, feelings, practices, and knowledge. New aesthetic values might not have been apparent in the responses we received when we returned to talk to those participants who had lived with the Energy Babble, but perhaps down the line—in the absence of the stream of barely intelligible talk—an aesthetic value takes shape, a feeling for a feeling emerges as it were. The experiment yields not a result but the prospect of a result.

Concluding remarks

What we hope has become clear, in the above, is that idiotic design, as a tool in staging and engaging in epistemic practices, affords practitioners the prospect of experimentally accessing the complex ecologies of aesthetic values immanent to practices of existence—in this case communities engaged in novel forms of energy-demand reduction. The relevance of this lies not merely in the production of knowledge of and about others' knowledge, so to speak, but in how the interplay of values undergirds what we know and can know as well as the possibility of bearing witness to or seeding new modes of valuation. Indeed, our case suggests that those involved in experiments in living with the environment—of actively reconfiguring the relationships between nature, energy technology, and practices of living—where established ecologies of aesthetic values are *in* play and undergoing processes of re-evaluation are precisely the settings where the figure of the poet aids the appraisal of more-than-human possibilities begotten by the idiot.

Notes

1 https://www.urbandictionary.com/define.php?term=Tool.
2 https://www.urbandictionary.com/define.php?term=Schmuck.
3 It goes without saying that we are keenly aware that Whitehead, as a person of his times, draws upon the figure of the Romantic poet that is embodied as white, western, and male and oftentimes practically enabled by the female (Day, 1996). There are, of course, "other great figures of aesthetic thought" (Deleuze and Guattari, 1994: 65) that make perceptible new compositions and formations of existence, be they witches (Pignarre and Stengers, 2011: xviii) or fugitives (Moten, 2018) for instance.
4 It is not without quite some irony that Whitehead (1997 [1925]: 54), lamenting on the "practical outcome" of modern scientific reasoning based on the bifurcation of nature, exhorts poets to "address their lyrics to themselves ..." to "... turn them into odes of self-congratulation on the excellency of the human mind."

Bibliography

Boucher, A., Gaver, B., Kerridge, T., Michael, M., Ovalle, L., and Wilkie, A. (2018). *Energy Babble*. Manchester: Mattering Press.

Boucher, A., Gaver, W., Kerridge, T., Michael, M., Ovalle, L., Plummer-Fernandez, M., and Wilkie, A. (2018). *Energy Babble: Entangling Design and STS*. Manchester: Mattering Press.

Clark, T. (2008). We're Over-Researched Here! Exploring Accounts of Research Fatigue within Qualitative Research Engagements. *Sociology*, 42(5), pp. 953–970. DOI: 10.1177/0038038508094573

Day, A. (1996). *Romanticism*. London; New York: Routledge.

de la Bellacasa, M. P. (2017). *Matters of Care: Speculative Ethics in More Than Human Worlds*. Minneapolis; London: University of Minnesota Press.

Debaise, D. (2017). *Speculative Empiricism: Revisiting Whitehead*. Edinburgh: Edinburgh University Press.

Deleuze, G., and Guattari, F. (1994). *What Is Philosophy?* London; New York: Verso.

Dostoyevsky, F. (2004 [1868]). *The Idiot*. New Edition ed. London: Penguin Classics.

Gaver, W., Bowers, J., Kerridge, T., Boucher, A., and Jarvis, N. (2009). Anatomy of a Failure: How We Knew When Our Design Went Wrong, and What We Learned from It. In *Proceedings of the SIGCHI Conference on Human Factors in Computing Systems*. New York: Association for Computing Machinery, pp. 2213–2222. https://doi.org/10.1145/1518701.1519040

Gaver, W., Dunne, T., and Pacenti, E. (1999). Design: Cultural Probes. *Interactions*, 6(1), pp. 21–29. DOI: 10.1145/291224.291235

Guattari, F. (2006 [1992]). *Chaosmosis: An Ethico-Aesthetic Paradigm*. Sydney, Australia: Power Publications; Powr Institute Foundation for Art & Visual Culture.

Halewood, M. (2011). *A. N. Whitehead and Social Theory: Tracing a Culture of Thought*. London; New York; Delhi: Anthem Press.

Heidegger, M. (1971). *Poetry, Language, Thought*. New York: Harper Colophon.

Michael, M. (2012a). Toward an Idiotic Methodology: De-Signing the Object of Sociology. *Sociological Review*, 60(s1), pp. 166–183. DOI: 10.1111/j.1467-954X.2012.02122.x

Michael, M. (2012b). "What Are We Busy Doing?": Engaging the Idiot. *Science, Technology & Human Values*, 37(5), pp. 528–554. DOI: 10.1177/0162243911428624

Michael, M. (2016). Engaging the Mundane: Complexity and Speculation in Everyday Technoscience. In J. Chilvers and M. Kearnes (Eds.), *Remaking Participation: Science, Environment and Emergent Publics*. Abingdon, Oxon; New York: Routledge, pp. 81–98.

Michael, M., and Gaver, W. (2009). Home beyond Home: Dwelling with Threshold Devices. *Space and Culture*, 12, pp. 359–370. DOI: 10.1177/1206331209337076

Moten, F. (2018). *Stolen Life*. Durham: Duke University Press.

Pignarre, P., and Stengers, I. (2011). *Capitalist Sorcery: Breaking the Spell*. London: Palgrave Macmillan.

Savransky, M. (2016). *The Adventure of Relevance: An Ethics of Social Inquiry*. London: Palgrave Macmillan.

Savransky, M. (2020). *A New Taste for Life: Value Ecologies and the Aesthetics of the Otherwise*. Adventures in aesthetics: Rethinking aesthetics beyond the bifurcation of nature. Goldsmiths, University of London.

Before the idiot, the poet? Aesthetic figures and design 111

Sehgal, M. (2018). Aesthetic Concerns, Philosophical Fabulations: The Importance of a 'New Aesthetic Paradigm.' *SubStance*, 47(1), pp. 112–129. DOI: 10.1353/sub.2018.0008

Stengers, I. (2005). The Cosmopolitical Proposal. In B. Latour and P. Weibel (Eds.), *Making Things Public*. Cambridge: MIT Press, pp. 994–1003.

Stengers, I. (2011). *Thinking with Whitehead: A Free and Wild Creation of Concepts*. Cambridge, MA; London: Harvard University Press.

Tironi, M. (2018). Speculative Prototyping, Frictions and Counter-Participation: A Civic Intervention with Homeless Individuals. *Design Studies*, 59, pp. 117–138. DOI: 10.1016/j.destud.2018.05.003

Whitehead, A. N. (1968 [1938]). *Modes of Thought*. New York: The Free Press.

Whitehead, A. N. (1997 [1925]). *Science and the Modern World*. New York: The Free Press.

Whitehead, A. N. (2004 [1920]). *The Concept of Nature*. Amherst, NY: Prometheus Books.

Wilkie, A., and Michael, M. (2018). Designing and Doing: Enacting Energy-and-Community. In N. Marres, M. Guggenheim and A. Wilkie (Eds.), *Inventing the Social*. Manchester: Mattering Press, pp. 125–147.

Wilkie, A., Michael, M., and Plummer-Fernandez, M. (2015). Speculative Method and Twitter: Bots, Energy and Three Conceptual Characters. *The Sociological Review*, 63(1), 79–101. DOI: 10.1111/1467-954X.12168

Wilkie, A., Savransky, M., and Rosengarten, M., eds. (2017). *Speculative Research: The Lure of Possible Futures*. Abingdon, Oxon; New York: Routledge.

Wilkie, A., and Michael, M. (2018). Designing and Doing: Enacting Energy-and-Community. In N. Marres et al. (eds), *Inventing the Social* (pp. 125–147). Manchester: Mattering Press.

8 Revisiting empathy by gentrifying our guts

Exploring design as a cosmopolitical diplomacy practice through microbial fruits of Istanbul

Uriel Fogué, Orkan Telhan, Eva Gil Lopesino and Carlos Palacios Rodríguez

A common narrative

Over the last two years, a multidisciplinary team led by an artist and researcher, Orkan Telhan, and an architecture office, Elii, developed a *design for more-than-human futures*, through a project entitled *Microbial Fruits of Istanbul* (MFoI).[1] Together with an extensive team of collaborators that includes cultural institutions, local collectives, university departments, artisans, laboratories, biotech companies, horticultural gardens, microorganisms, robots, and so on, they explored a particular understanding of design that questions some of the dominant definitions of the urban ecosystem.

As the project progressed, the design team realized that a *design for more-than-human futures* needed a shared narrative, not only to communicate the proposal to others but also to understand the project themselves among the team members. A shared imaginary helped the team share their knowledge and synchronize their skill-set to address different aspects of the project. In what follows, we—as authors and members of this team—try to summarize that narrative and collect some of the ideas, references, and learnings that were gathered by the team during the work.

Warning: what we discuss here is not a universal methodology to *design for and with more-than-human futures* but the way in which this particular team positioned itself in relation to this challenge. MFoI is the outcome of a design process in which a team of designers had the opportunity to think about the *future* and heritage along with other *more-than-humans*. Specifically, MFoI works *with* microorganisms. And after the global pandemic caused by COVID-19, this project will likely never be understood the same way.

Empathy revisited: designs for more than one

MFoI was developed at the invitation of the 5th Istanbul Design Biennial, entitled "Empathy Revisited. Designs For More Than One."[2] This edition

DOI: 10.4324/9781003319689-9

had a slightly different conceptualization from other encounters of this kind: instead of understanding the biennial as a *showcase* or the typical informative event featuring the latest trends in design, the curatorial team of this edition conceived the biennial as an opportunity to rethink design as empathy and vice versa.[3] To do this, they designed an ambitious program with several lines of work. MFoI was inscribed in one of those lines called "New Civic Rituals," a collection of tests developed in different public locations in the city of Istanbul to explore in situ within different forms of empathy. The "New Civic Rituals" were developed in collaboration with local actors. They became a network of dispersed events that tested new forms of "meeting," of "being together," of experiencing other ways of connecting with the city.[4]

MFoI was inaugurated in May 2021.[5] Throughout this long process, a multidisciplinary team was put together, incorporating, for example, the Department of Molecular Biology and Genetics at the University of Istanbul as well as local associations that work with soil, such as the Kokopelli Sehirde and Nadas collectives.[6]

An Istanbul of many Istanbuls

The millenary city of Istanbul is usually described by history books and tourist guides as "a historical place," as "an enclave for a multicultural encounter between Europe and Asia," as "a cradle of civilizations," as "a place full of monuments," as "the capital of a country where more than fifteen million people live," and nowadays also as one of the main destinations for health tourism, hair implants, and cosmetic surgery.

If we think about what is meant here by "historical," we realize that it is common to presuppose history as a collection of memorable human affairs. However, from an ecological perspective, Istanbul could be described in a different way: Istanbul is the product of an incessant work carried out by multiple generations of humans, animals, plants, and microorganisms who, for millennia, have collaborated with each other (consciously or unconsciously) to adapt and reconfigure the environment according to their interests. For Isabele Stengers, Gaia, the "living planet," is the product of a history of continuous coevolution, whose first artisans and true authors are the innumerable peoples of microorganisms (Stengers, 2008). Following Stengers's reflection, Istanbul may well be understood as the result of a series of co-evolutionary processes, as a shared place co-inhabited by multiple species. While humans transformed Istanbul with their architectures, infrastructures, gardens, ports, etc., other inhabitants such as microorganisms *built* other Istanbuls. Some of these other "neighbours" live *in* the earth, *under* the surface, *in* empty lots, *in* the water, *in* the mud, or *in* the sea. And slowly but surely, they have configured all those *other* Istanbuls. (Human) history tends to forget that Istanbul has many Istanbuls at the same time. Working with microorganisms, however, helped the team understand the city in a way that challenged some of its usual definitions and representations.

114 *Uriel Fogué et al.*

A few centimetres under our feet, *in* the earth that supports us, *in* the land that we cultivate, and *in* the plots where we walk, there are other worlds inhabited by other beings. Each of these species lives the city from its own perspective, from its own worldview, from its own cosmos (Viveiros de Castro, 2010). We usually give these other worlds different names, such as "earth," "terrain," and "dirt," depending on our interests, knowledge, fears, or beliefs. Other times, we do not even name them, and they go unnoticed by us. And even though for humans those strata often do not count, a single handful of soil contains billions of microorganisms. It may be said that there is more biodiversity *down* there, *within those* areas that generally count little or nothing for *us* (because they are not part of *our* history) than on *this* side: the human side, the one portrayed in history books and tourist guides.

Might we think of MFoI as a meeting point between those multiple Istanbuls, as a kind of infrastructure that puts those diverse worlds in contact, and that tells (not the history but) the other complex stories of Istanbul from the point of view of microorganisms? The next step, then, was to find a way to *invite* these special *neighbours* to take part in our project. We needed a location to *meet* with those ancestral local residents who have inhabited this land for centuries (Figure 8.1).

A green infrastructure of bostans

That place for the encounter with the microorganisms was a garden. In fact, it was a network of gardens called *bostans*. At the suggestion of the Biennale curators, the design team began to work on these local horticultural gardens, learning about their history and their urban condition.

Bostans are productive gardens and are steeped in Istanbul's history. For generations, they have provided food for their inhabitants, who had the right to plant their food in these public spaces distributed throughout the city. Distributed across Istanbul, each garden participates in the green infrastructure with their microclimate and unique urban conditions. Some are built adjacent to mosques, others along city walls built in the 500s.

Historically, Bostans have witnessed major transformations and have endured many migration patterns, accelerated urbanization, industrialization, and gentrification processes. Nowadays, as developable land is becoming scarcer in the metropolitan area, these gardens are under more political, productive, and commercial pressure, while also trying to cope with the ubiquitous effects of global warming on the soil, water, and vegetation in the city.

As public spaces, the bostans are important symbols in the political collective imaginary. Sometimes not for what they are but for what else they can be. They are often contested places—sites of conflict—claimed for vindication and demonstrations.[7]

After the city's growing population began to rely on industrial farming, bostans lost their role in the sustenance of the city and became unproductive agricultural fields that could be utilized in different ways (White, Shopov and

Revisiting empathy by gentrifying our guts 115

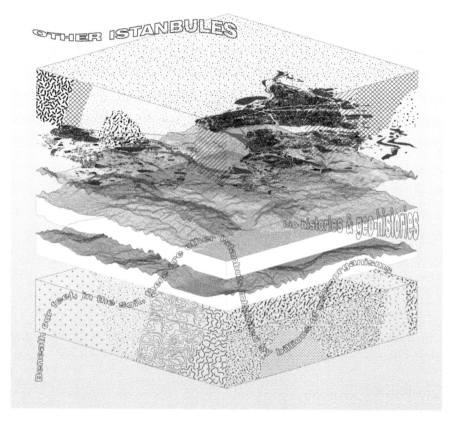

Figure 8.1 An Istanbul of many Istanbuls, 2021.
Source: Elii [architecture office].

Ostovich, 2015). As "empty plots," they have fallen prey to real estate and developer's imaginary, while some of them couldn't escape the fate of being turned into expensive private condos. Such controversial enclaves proved bostans to be ideal contexts to study human and microorganism coevolution.

Shared cosmos, common stories

The gardens, the air in the atmosphere, the food, and the water are all the result of a microbial work carried out over millions of years. Our bodies are as well. We tend to think that microorganisms live *in* our body. But we can also think of it the other way around: we are the architectures for the microorganisms. Maybe we humans are just *gardens* populated by microscopic beings that inhabit us and that populate us. We may not see them, and they tend to be left out of our daily conversations, but in fact, we are constantly

116 *Uriel Fogué et al.*

interacting with them as they shape our psyche, emotions, and decisions through the chemicals they produce. In general, they only become visible when something does not work as expected such as when we feel unwell or become concerned about a lack of hygiene. But the reality is that we share a cosmos with them.

Microorganisms are part of our everyday life. Artisans transform bacteria into pigments and fibres. Cooks *collaborate* with them on fermenting wine, cheese, beer, or yogurt. Designers prepare recipes to improve the strength and durability of bioplastics or make new types of packaging materials. Urban planners construct sophisticated sewage systems to decree a particular form of coexistence between humans and microorganisms, on an urban scale, by implementing sanitary and hygienic policies.

However, in general, this coexistence has favoured human interests and unfolded anthropocentric policies. At these times of the climate emergency, this form of coexistence today is strongly being questioned. History, that collection of human feats and events worth being remembered, does not allow us to face the complexity of these shared cosmos. We need to review what counts as historical, that is, to recognize those other bio-geo-stories that take place both on a micro and macro scale. Only in this way can we start to rethink our coexistence *with* microorganisms.

The MFoI project was conceived as an opportunity to tell the complex stories of Istanbul from the point of view of microorganisms and as a platform to rethink this shared cosmos. Designing an encounter to learn about these other micro and macro stories became a major goal for the project (Figure 8.2).

The encounter

The point of encounter had to be placed in a public space. For its design, the team investigated local traditions and specifically looked into a picturesque element that is ubiquitous among public spaces in Istanbul.

Istanbul is full of all kinds of kiosks. They organize the public space in different ways and have consolidated a particular urban landscape. Some of them have wheels and are mobile. Others are stationary and have retractable covers. A particular red kiosk, for example, is an important part of a city's heritage. There, one can buy food, souvenirs, newspapers, ask for directions, or pay for public transportation. They are places where many things change hands, including microorganisms (Figures 8.3 and 8.4).

MFoI was designed as a point of encounter based on a re-interpretation of the Turkish kiosk. But instead of reproducing its "postcard image," our design explored the ritual of kiosks in the ways citizens interact and build relationships with the vendors. Rather than mimicking the look of the kiosk, however, we designed it as a curious element, a strange totemic structure that would catch the attention of passers-by. As a contact zone, the structure was not only a place but also a platform of exchange between past, present, and future generations of species.

Revisiting empathy by gentrifying our guts 117

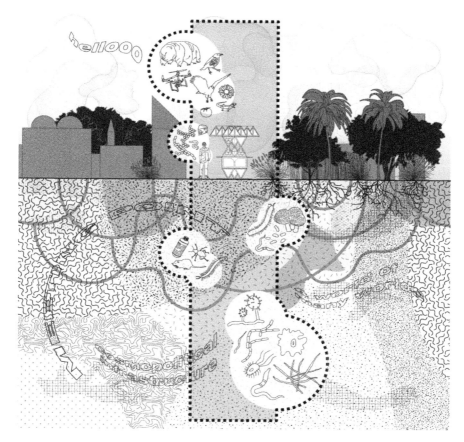

Figure 8.2 MFoI as a contact zone, 2021.
Source: Elii [architecture office].

The structure was equipped with a mechanical system that allowed its triangular roof to expand and retract in three directions. Once "activated," the kiosk can be equipped with side tables that would be ready to engage with the public.

The structure was installed at Özgürlük Park in Goztepe. When activated, it deployed its cover and opened its tables, as the kiosks of Istanbul do, to receive visitors and accompany the meeting ceremony (Figure 8.5).

MFoI hosted three kinds of encounters or ceremonies:

Encounter with the microworlds

The structure was made up of translucent pyramid-shaped elements. Placed on each face of these pyramids were three Petri dishes containing microbial cultures from each of seven bostans analysed during our initial studies.[8]

118 *Uriel Fogué et al.*

Figure 8.3 Kiosks as points of constant exchange of microorganisms, 2021.
Source: Elii [architecture office].

Thus, the platform in the park convened seven cultures from organisms who *belonged* to seven different locations in Istanbul.

Our main goal was to identify the local organisms living in each garden and see if we can show these microbial *locals* to the human *locals* through our platform. Using sterilized tubes, several soil samples were extracted from each bostan, at a depth of 20–30 cm. The samples were kept in refrigerators, becoming "circulating references" (Latour, 1999) that were later transferred to the university laboratory. The soil was then processed for DNA sequencing, in which the process reported the presence of all kinds of living and dead cells from bacteria to plants, animals, and humans. The sequence generated dozens of species names without being able to tell which sample belonged to whom or from when.[9]

We also decided to learn about who might be alive in the soil. Our scientific team began to culture the microorganisms from the soil samples inside the

Revisiting empathy by gentrifying our guts 119

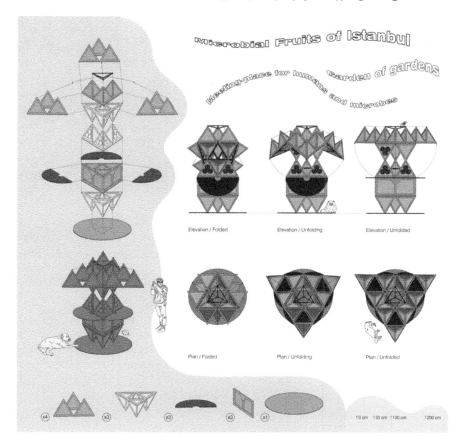

Figure 8.4 Kiosks as points of constant exchange of microorganisms, 2021.
Source: Elii [architecture office].

lab. This process required us to decide what type of organisms we are interested in cultivating as the growth conditions vary from species to species. We decided to use media that typically selects for non-pathogenic organisms used in food fermentation. The culturing process allowed us to reproduce several organisms from each bostan on Petri dishes. To be able to identify these species, we sequenced the cells again to be able to get a probabilistic verification of what they might be. This bioinformatic process relies on algorithmically searching patterns of DNA inside common public databases to see what species they might overlap with. Then, we were faced with a dilemma: if these organisms or their distant relatives have never been encountered and entered into a database before, we would never know if they existed or not. Luckily, the sequencing gave us some probabilistic matches (i.e., 95% *Weissella Paramesenteroides*), and we were able to match the names to what we see visibly on the Petri dishes.

120 *Uriel Fogué et al.*

Figure 8.5 The point of encounter as a strange totemic structure in Özgürlük Park, 2021.
Source: Engin Gerçek.

The microorganisms inside the Petri dishes were transferred to the MFoI platform to become representations of the microorganisms from the bostans, raising the question of how space can be represented from the point of view of microorganisms. Once installed on the platform, MFoI became a portal (Danowsky, 2021), a contact zone, a meeting point between the macro and micro worlds (Figure 8.6).

Encounter with the other stories

The platform hosted a robotic parrot ("the Diplomat") who told fables about different encounters among microorganisms, birds, adults, or children. As visitors approach the platform, The Diplomat would start telling stories about topics ranging from the gentrification of gardens to the impact of climate change and immigration to Istanbul. The genre of the fable made it possible to explain inter-species controversies in a communicative way. The fables were told in Turkish by the parrot, who had his own tailor-made outfit for the diplomatic encounters. A famous professional voice actor known for voicing children's cartoons was hired for the recording. He brought the characters to life through the voice of the robot.

Encounter with the locals

We decided to disseminate a few organisms using a microbial kit. The kit consisted of a brochure that contained three sachets containing lyophilized

Figure 8.6 Structure for a point of encounter between the macro and micro worlds.
Source: Engin Gerçek.

(or freeze-dried) microorganisms which are known to have probiotic properties. The kit came with instructions to use the organisms to make a popsicle, which we called the "Impossible Fruit."[10] Thus, microorganisms were redistributed and disseminated through human and more-than-human bodies. This way, people were invited to experience a moment of empathy with those other unknown worlds, to explore new relationships with those special more-than-human residents. In a way, people were invited to become gardens, to *be-with* the gardens, to *be-with* the soil (De la Cadena, 2015).

The question then was transferred from the public space to our guts (Figure 8.7). What was going on in our intestines?

Re-naturalizing and re-gentrifying the intestines

Our intestines host millions of microorganisms. In a way, we share our body with different communities of bacteria. They determine our well-being, character, and health. They also witness other processes, such as the climate crisis and other urban phenomena. Due to different factors such as the presence of antibiotics in drinking water, the consumption of ultra-processed food, and the lack of contact with the soil, our intestines suffer from a severe loss of biodiversity, which we tend to compensate by taking medical or food supplements. Today, millions of intestines lose their biodiversity just as the bostans of Istanbul do.

122 *Uriel Fogué et al.*

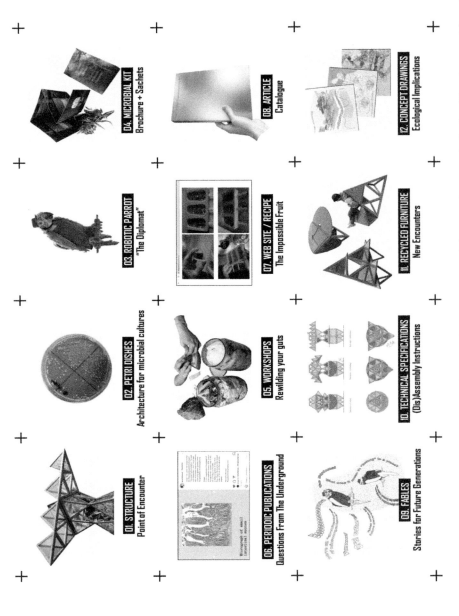

Figure 8.7 Multiple formats: platform, Petri dishes, fables, robotic parrot, workshops, website, periodical publications, articles, plans, and drawings.

Source: Elii [architecture office].

Revisiting empathy by gentrifying our guts   123

By ingesting the microorganisms supplied by MFoI, people incorporated "wild type microorganisms" that had evolved within Istanbul.

MFoI offers a different perspective on what "place" and "belonging" to a place means. By introducing these "local" actors into our bodies, something technically called "rewilding your gut" takes place. With the ingestion, citizens experience an intimate relationship, a special form of empathy with these new species for your body that have lived many other Istanbuls, for countless generations in evolution. When they become part of people's bodies, the possibility of *being-with-others* opens up to them.

Furthermore, ingesting the microorganisms implies the initiation of a gentrification process in their intestines. Gentrification is an urban phenomenon in which some local neighbours are displaced by other, newer inhabitants. Gentrification yields undesirable consequences, such as damage to the local social fabric, disruption of community processes, and displacement of the weakest and economically less well-off. A similar process happens on a microbial scale in the body: when people ingest MFoI's microorganisms, the local organisms are also displaced by the new ones. The result will depend on how the locals react to the newcomers.

It was concluded that many of the processes that occur in urban ecosystems take place across different scales. That is to say, some of these processes, such as the loss of biodiversity or gentrification, take place in parallel and at the same time within the city, the gardens, and our intestines. Although this was a discovery for the team of architects, it was not so surprising to those familiar with microbiological processes. The microbiologists on our team stated that "it's not that strange; after all, we are all architectures for microorganisms," they declared. Indeed, from an ecological and microbiological approach, the difference between a garden and a human is not so vast.

The organisms were ready to be alive again. After removing them from their sachet, one can rehydrate them by mixing them with other foods. This will end their state of "suspended animation," so they can come back into circulation by entering our bodies. Once inside us, they may stick around or leave immediately if they cannot get along with the current locals of our guts. If they stay, they may have beneficial probiotic capacities for our bodies; they can make us feel better or shape our thoughts. But this project is not about "saving" microorganisms. Microorganisms are not "in danger." They are simply mutating due to the change in the climate regime. The goal was not to preserve them from extinction (which makes no sense on a microbial scale) but to activate different ecological relationships with the microbial ecosystem of Istanbul, to put these microorganisms into circulation, in other ways. If climate change continues the way it is going, it may come to pass that, in the future, humans will have to "beg" these kinds of microorganisms to "colonize" them for health reasons.

MFoI asked the citizens to become just another of Istanbul's gardens. What if the answer to loss of biodiversity were to become a garden (of gardens)?

124 *Uriel Fogué et al.*

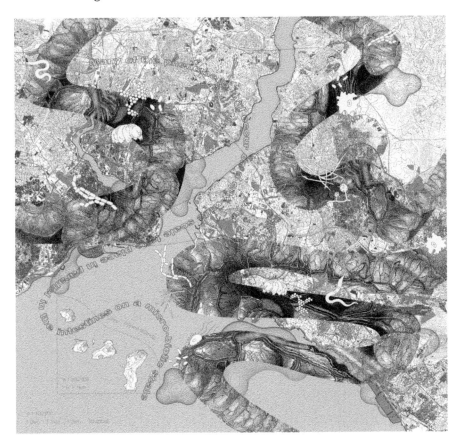

Figure 8.8 From the city to the guts: Transcalar condition of urban phenomena, 2021.
Source: Elii [architecture office].

Thousands of people becoming thousands of bostans. This answer to the Biennial's question was to rethink empathy as a way of *living together*, of *making place* together, of *being-with-the place* (De la Cadena and Blaser, 2018), or maybe just *becoming the place* (Figure 8.8).

Future lives

After the biennial closed, the platform was reused. The design team prepared a catalogue of possibilities that allowed the piece to be reassembled in different ways.

Thanks to the work of some of the biennial production team, different workers at some bostans were contacted.[11] Together with them, they

Revisiting empathy by gentrifying our guts 125

brainstormed about the possibilities of the fragments of the platform, their programs, and locations. The components were reassembled, reconfiguring the piece into work and storage furniture for workers at different bostans in Istanbul.

MFoI went back to the bostans, finding new life and participating in new encounters with other local inhabitants of Istanbul: rabbits, dogs, cats, insects, plants, citizens, and, of course, microorganisms (Figure 8.9).

Figure 8.9 MFoI recycled at Tarlataban and bostans.
Source: Eda Hisarlıoğlu.

126　*Uriel Fogué et al.*

Could design be a form of cosmopolitical diplomacy?

This project opened up an ongoing conversation about how more-than-human futures entail big challenges to the discipline of design. Here, we integrate some of the learnings and share some of the questions that were raised throughout the MFoI design:

- Do we need to update the narratives of design? Is (human) history enough to address ecological problems? If not, which other vocabularies, grammars, and genres of other bio-geo-histories should we explore?
- Do we need to work in multidisciplinary teams to face designs for more-than-human futures? Should complex problems be addressed by equally complex teams that favour a diverse composition of knowledge and skills?
- How are modern dichotomies such as subject/object, nature/culture, figure/background, or alive/inert challenged in these design processes? Who is the human and who is the garden, once we acknowledge that *we* are all "architectures of microorganisms?"
- How do we rethink from our individual worldviews, the idea of a shared cosmos in which we are co-involved with other species?
- How can designers experiment with different forms of empathy and build intimate relationships with more-than-humans? What are the sites of empathy? Our own bodies? Public space? Urban infrastructure?
- What do we learn when we pay attention to the non-visible? What can we learn if we can tune into microorganisms, knowing what they do to our bodies and what our bodies do to them?
- How can fields of design help us understand ecological processes across different scales? When climate crises, loss of biodiversity, or gentrification are all experienced at the same time whether it is in the macro scale of a city, or the micro scale of the guts, are traditional design disciplines still relevant?
- Can design pedagogy and practices for traditional fields of design such as architecture or urban planning be leveraged to ask questions, challenge assumptions, and critique ideologies, instead of focusing exclusively on solving problems?
- How should design acknowledge human fragility? Can we agree that modern Promethean views are being challenged? Can we think about frameworks of coexistence with more-than-humans in which humans have a more "modest" position? Can we reconsider *human* (so-called) *exceptionalism* in the world and learn to navigate the interdependence between things, materials, and microbial life better?
- Can design connect different time scales? Should design pay attention to the generations to come in parallel to ancestry, even to a time prior to human life? What different temporalities entangle these bio-geo-stories?

- How is the idea of heritage challenged from an ecological standpoint? Who is responsible for what should be preserved for future generations? How can design participate in its equitable distribution?
- Can we replace the traditional image of designers—the makers or creators—with mediators? Can the architect become a cosmopolitical diplomat who negotiates conditions or possibilities across different stakeholders (Stengers, 2020)? How would the cosmopolitical design process take into account different agencies, manage different priorities, arbitrate conflicts, and attend to conflicting matters of concern while acknowledging that there will never be a neutral or unbiased position?
- And finally, when we—as authors of the text—come back to soil and acknowledge our inherent material and cultural ties, how can we rethink our practices in relation to soil (Figure 8.10)?[12]

Figure 8.10 Could design be a form of cosmopolitical diplomacy?
Source: [architecture office].

128 *Uriel Fogué et al.*

Notes

1 Elii is an architecture office founded in Madrid in 2006 by Uriel Fogué, Eva Gil, and Carlos Palacios.
2 https://empathyrevisited.iksv.org/en/index.
3 Formed by Mariana Pestana (Curator of the 5th Istanbul Design Biennial), Sumitra Upham (Curator of Programmes), Billie Muraben (Assistant Curator and Deputy Editor), and Nur Horsanalı, Ulya Soley, and Eylül Şenses (curatorial group in Istanbul).
4 Early in 2020, the biennial team contacted the Mutant Institute of Environmental Narratives—IMNA, which belongs to the public centre for artistic creation Matadero Madrid, and invited them to undertake an investigation within the program of the biennial. For their part, IMNA and Matadero Madrid proposed Orkan Telhan (a Turkish/US artist based in Philadelphia) and Elii (an architecture studio based in Madrid with ties to IMNA) to work together on a project that explored a way to approach the city from the point of view of microorganisms. The Mutant Institute of Environmental Narratives (Instituto Mutante de Narrativas Ambientales—IMNA) is a space for research, interdisciplinary experimental creation, and learning "to adapt to uncertain futures" and test "new ways of approaching problems and telling." Matadero Madrid is a public centre for artistic creation promoted by the Government Area of Culture, Tourism and Sports of the Madrid City Council. See https://www.mataderomadrid.org/en/schedule/mutant-institute-environmental-narratives and https://www.mataderomadrid.org/en
The project was supported by the Spanish Agency for International Development Cooperation (AECID), the Weitzman School of Design, and the Municipality of Kadıköy.
5 Due to the pandemic, the biennial had to postpone the opening on several occasions, finally opting for an extended-in-time event that opened its doors in September 2020.
6 See https://www.kokopellisehirde.com/
7 In fact, the first place where MFoI was to be installed was a bostan, but due to the student demonstrations that took place during the opening days, at the very last moment, the installation had to be relocated to another park.
8 The number of bostans analysed is exclusively due to the budget limits of the project.
9 The soil extractions were carried out by the members of soil and compost collectives Kokopelli Istanbul and Nadas Istanbul, whereas the metagenomic analysis of the contents of the soil was done in collaboration with the Department of Molecular Biology and Genetics of Istanbul University.
10 The instructions on how to make the "Impossible Fruit" can be found here: https://www.design.bio/impossible-fruit
11 Specifically, Eda Hisarlıoğlu and Ra Yaviz, whom we thank for their hard work in this last phase of the project. Also, Mert Sarisu and Tarlataban Boğaziçi Team, for their help at Boğaziçi University.
12 While the authors were writing their catalogue entry text for the 5th Biennial with the title "We Are Soil" (Telhan and Elii, 2021), they were reminded that, in Turkish, when one meets an old acquaintance, friend, or colleague with whom they grew up together, they refer them as *topragim* (my soil) indicating a tie to the land. The phrase also has a double meaning that also literally translates as "I am soil." This popular expression reminded us that the kinship with soil has always already been present in language. Indeed, *we are all soil* the moment we (re)acknowledge it.

Bibliography

Danowsky, D. (2021). Lecture Presented at Encounters at The Edge. See: https://encountersattheedge.com/

De la Cadena, M. (2015). *Earth Beings: Ecologies of Practice across Andean Worlds.* Durham/London: Duke University Press. https://doi.org/10.1017/tam.2017.6

De la Cadena, M. (2022). "Listening in Pluriversal Contact Zones". Manuscript.

De la Cadena, M., and Blaser, M. (Eds.) (2018). *A World of Many Worlds.* Durham: Duke University Press. https://doi.org/10.1215/9781478004318.

Latour, B. (1999). *Pandora's Hope: Essays on the Reality of Science Studies.* Cambridge, MA: Harvard University Press.

Puig de la Bellacasa, M. (2017). *Matters of Care: Speculative Ethics in More Than Human Worlds.* Minneapolis: University of Minnesota Press.

Stengers, I. (2008). *Au temps des catastrophes. Résister à la barbarie qui vient.* París: La Découverte.

Stengers, I. (2020). "We Are Divided". Available at: https://www.e-flux.com/journal/114/366189/we-are-divided/

Telhan, O., and Elii. (2021). "We Are Soil", in Pestana, M. Upham, S. and Muraben, B. (Eds.) *Empathy Revisited: Designs for More Than One.* Istanbul: IKSV Tasarim, 301–307.

Viveiros de Castro, E. (2010). *Metafísicas caníbales.* Líneas de antropología estructural, Buenos Aires/Madrid: Katz Editores. https://doi.org/10.2307/j.ctvm7bdz4

White, C., Shopov, A., and Ostovich, M. (2015). "An Archaeology of Sustenance: The Endangered Market Gardens of Istanbul", in Cherry, J. and Rojas, F. (Eds.) *Archaeology for the People: Joukowsky Institute Perspectives.* Oxford: Oxbow, 29–38. https://doi.org/10.2307/j.ctvh1dmc4

9 Design beyond human concerns
A sancocho-style approach

Leonardo Parra-Agudelo and Edgard David Rincón Quijano

Introduction

In this chapter, we will expand, through a Colombian sancocho-style approach, the ongoing and designerly call to incorporate a relational and dialogical form of being, inter-being, and coexisting with the more-than-human.

> *Un sancocho de gallina es la comida sabrosa*
> *con buena yuca arenosa y con auyama y ñame espina*
> *así es como se cocina cuando llega el mediodía*
> *y escuchando una poesía se refrescan los caminos*
> *así como come el campesino en los Montes de María*
> - Rafael Pérez García, decimero (person that writes and recites poetry, typically associated with the Colombian sea shores)

> *A chicken sancocho is yummy food*
> *with good sandy cassava and pumpkin and spiny ñame*
> *that's how things are cooked when noon arrives*
> *and listening to poetry roads are renewed*
> *that's how the peasant eats in Montes de María*
> - Authors' rough, imprecise, but affectionate translation

The décima (poem) above was taken from a YouTube video entitled Cocinas Campesinas – Capítulo 6: sancocho de gallina criolla (Peasant Kitchens): Chapter 6: creole chicken sancocho (RadioTelevisión Nacional de Colombia, 2020). In the video, doña Cecilia Salgado, a local from Montes de María, explains how sancocho is made and shared.

By approaching design from a sancocho-style perspective, we aim to uncover entanglements that can provide avenues for making epistemological and ontological borders permeable to our kin and integrate ourselves in coexistence with the natural, abstract, spiritual, artificial worlds, and other forms of thinking, feeling, being, and doing, from a relational perspective. Which is what a sancocho does in the field.

DOI: 10.4324/9781003319689-10

Design beyond human concerns: a sancocho-style approach   131

Social transformation

Social transformation is a concept that explains the complex and fluctuating nature of society as it goes through searching for collective meaning. Society's own sense becomes evident in how people and their collective goals are related to each other. The form of this relationality is situated and is not indifferent to environmental conditions or natural, abstract, or artificial eventualities. An essential part of this transformation involves a relational and transformational shift to move out of a given situation, a pilgrimage.

This collective pilgrimage contains two components. The first one includes the mechanisms of social transformation, which prescribe how the process evolves, i.e., colonisation, innovation, métissage, etc. The second one refers to the level of uncertainty regarding the result of the transformation, its directionality, and its purpose, i.e., coexistence, governance, transmission of knowledge, etc. Each pilgrimage builds on these two components and constitutes a story, it is, for the pilgrim, the hero's journey, as Zerwas and von Anshelm (2015) describe it. The implementation of these components also defines and establishes an agenda.

The constitution and transformation of human societies focus on people and their relationships among them and the environment. This means that there's a dialectic opposition between the human journey, which could be perceived as unidirectional, and the multidirectional, and inherent, nature of the context in which these relationships and transformations take place. Taking on board the tensions between the human and more-than-human agendas (Ávila Gaitán, 2017; Pearson, 2015) means to understand the relational, multidirectional, and dynamic transformations that could come into being beyond the human.

What about beyond human concerns?

Our question is not new, Haraway (2016) opened the space for thinking beyond our own (Western) boundaries. Moving beyond human concerns means embracing difference through those things that make us intersect with other beings, and as Haraway (2016, 103) indicates "it is past time to practice better care of kinds-as-assemblages (not species one at a time)." In this plurality, the Zapatista path could take us to a world in which many worlds could fit (Shenker, 2012), where physical and otherworldly realities could also be entangled (Akama, Light and Kamihira, 2020) in an assemblage of kin beyond the flesh.

In this assemblage exists a tension for participation; otherwise, the human and beyond human co-exist, yet the mechanisms for relating to each other are limited by our own capacities. As a consequence, we're unable to acknowledge and engage *with* other purposes (whilst the notion of *other* distances from kin) and other minds, in the neurological, conscious, and creative sense

132 Leonardo Parra-Agudelo and Edgard David Rincón Quijano

(see Godfrey-Smith, 2016). Perhaps, what we need is to leverage and make use of the multispecies ethnography project that aims *"to understand the world as materially real, partially knowable, multicultured and multinatured, magical, and emergent through the contingent relations of multiple beings and entities. Accordingly, the nonhuman world of multispecies encounters has its own logic and rules of engagement that exist within the larger articulations of the human world, encompassing the flow of nutrients and matter, the liveliness of animals, plants, bacteria, and other beings"* (Ogden et al., 2013, p. 6). Yet, multispecies ethnography is limited in the sense that understanding alone does not provide a platform for action. However, we understand that action in a designerly way might also mean to stop action itself, where removal, replacement, restoration, and safeguarding may also take place (Pierce, 2012). Escobar (2018, p. 101) explains that we "inter-are with everything on the planet," and in that inter-being, the relational might provide an avenue for making epistemological and ontological borders permeable to our kin, so we can truly be a meaningful part of a dynamic assemblage.

Situated and boundless affectation

The expanding body of work related to understanding more-than-human relations presents philosophical, theoretical, and empirical challenges. We argue that inter-being, as a permeable membrane of, and for, kin, requires a suitable ecosystem in which to thrive and connect. In the following sections, we present a guiding lens that provides a platform to discuss how to engage inter-being through design. The lens is composed by Situated Lifeworlds, as an ecosystem, Boundless Connections, as connective tissue, and Relational Affectation as a dialogical milieu.

Situated lifeworlds

Engaging in a pluriversal manner requires embodying multiple worldviews and forge them into our thinking and practice (Akama, Light, and Kamihira, 2020). This engagement may only take place via the shaping of common lifeworlds (Ingold and Palsson, 2013) of becoming, where the intertwining between multiple entities takes place. In this collective coexistence, different states of matter, multiple life forms, the geological structures of earth, the spiritual, human, and more-than-human artefacts, and beyond (see, Akama, Light, and Kamihira, 2020; de La Bellacasa, 2017; Liu et al., 2018; Smith, et al., 2017) meet to engage each other in a dialogical ecosystem. These encounters, depending on the observer, take place in plain sight if acknowledged and backstage if not.

These lifeworlds provide a platform for the enactment of the multiple connections that occur. In a way, they are a more-than-human place in the sense that Augé conceives the anthropological place (1995). In this case, however, the more-than-human place isn't just a mechanism for human empowerment,

Design beyond human concerns: a sancocho-style approach 133

identity building, meeting other humans, and intelligibility for those outside such places. The more-than-human place can be conceived as a relational mechanism in which the constituents of a particular ecosystem can help us humans, not only to allow us to answer for what we are learning to see (Haraway, 1988) but also help us to engage and respond as species to the relational, and vital, call for survival. For instance, via a dialogue with unexpected participants such as fungi (Liu et al., 2018), in a sensible, respectful, care-full manner through, to, and via, these more-than-human lifeworlds that the planet supports (see de La Bellacasa, 2017).

Boundless connections

We argue that there's a need for an interweaving type of tissue, which can ontologically operate as an associative mechanism. We believe that there's a natural relationship that can illustrate what we mean: the mycorrhiza. This symbiotic association between plants and fungi helps "the host plants to thrive in adverse soil conditions and drought situations by increasing the root surface and mineral uptake efficiency" (Barman et al., 2016, p. 1093), whilst helping to mitigate environmental threats. Mycorrhizal associations provide mutual benefits to plants and fungi, in particular, the arbuscular-mycorrhizae type.

Plants provide carbon to their fungal counterparts, which can be easily transported through the fungal network. In turn, the surface area of roots is increased, improving the uptake of water and nutrients. For example, in nutrient-depleted regions, such as tropical areas with heavy rainfall where nutrients are washed away, the mycorrhizal fungi can extend themselves beyond depleted areas. This makes a larger volume of soil available to plant roots, and through various processing mechanisms, mycorrhizal fungi also help with the absorption of key minerals. The fungi structure grows into the soil and creates a sort-of skeletal structure that holds soil particles, helping to retain water during dry seasons, while helping plants increase hydraulic conductivity in roots, improving water absorption. Further, these fungi can also help with the production of plant defence mechanisms, such as the production of chemicals that protect plants from various diseases and provide defence mechanisms against metal toxicity, coming from a high concentration of heavy metals. As a whole, arbuscular-mycorrhizae also help to improve soil health (Barman et al., 2016).

As seen above, mycorrhizal associations act as (i) connective tissue, (ii) exchange mechanism, (iii) life-support extension, (iv) associative and protective structure, (v) detoxification system, and (vi) environmental medic of sorts. These benefits, as presented above, are better explained via a simple relationship between a plant and mycorrhizal fungi. However, the implications have a wide impact on whole ecosystems, such as forests, and the planet at large. Thus, this connective tissue that has multiple functions and serves multiple purposes, when scaled-up and understood as a global living matrix,

Relational affectation

The conflict involved in embodying our own discourses helps us reflect on what dialogue means and how it affects our relationships. We, as humans, can solve conflicts with other fellow humans and negotiate our differences. We can make use of our refined communication skills to engage each other, if all possibilities are present. Our limited capacities to engage and establish a coherent and meaningful dialogue with the more-than-human turn us into limited-hearing beings (see De Waal, 2016; Godfrey-Smith, 2016). Thus, constraining our abilities to listen and respond appropriately to the nuances of the more-than-human discourse.

The way in which the dialogue is affected is visible in its narrative qualities. If we were to consider this exchange as a simple story structure, composed by a beginning, a confrontation, and a denouement, there would be three key moments. The first one would deal with the current, and ongoing, relational conditions and make explicit the need that we have to understand that there are interests beyond ourselves. The second part of the confrontation is shaped by two conditions, the dialogical aspect itself and the emancipation of relational limits. The denouement brings about change and takes place once we acknowledge those other interests (which might not really be too far from our own) and transforms the dialogue into a web of exchanges. Thus, providing a platform to find ourselves as components of an extensive and situated relational fabric.

We understand this as a three-prong coexistence process of emancipation from representations that operate as accepted intelligibility mechanisms. The first stage challenges the subject/object dichotomy and transforms it into a relational strategy that acknowledges the possible subjectivity of the more-than-human (see Akama, Light, and Takihiro, 2020). The second part integrates feeling and thinking as something that could be beyond the human (see Escobar, 2018; Freire, 1974) and the integration of natural, artificial, abstract, and spiritual relationships (Akama, Light, and Takihiro, 2020; Escobar, 2018). In the third part, repair transformational mechanisms emerge from the previous two and aim to help reconstruct damaged relationships with the more-than-human, fostering new (or maybe old-forgotten) coexisting opportunities. We understand this process as a precursor for a holistic, situated, and boundless integration of human and more-than-human interests.

Relational design beyond human concerns

Human concerns find themselves at the centre of human life, that is no surprise, the vital aspect is undeniable. However, human life isn't at the centre of

Design beyond human concerns: a sancocho-style approach 135

life, we meet and engage other beings (Haraway, 2016), and life doesn't exist in a geological or spiritual vacuum (Akama, Light, and Kamihira, 2020), we exist and relate with, within, and beyond our senses.

Feelthinking in mycorrhiza

Relationship building is a process that contemplates acknowledging the other as a boundary for being. This principle allows us to understand dependence, interdependence, and other kinds of possible relationships among different entities, mostly coming from a human perspective. The act of designing as a transformational participation process moves the focus away from the human and centres on coexistence. Thus, we move towards a shift in how we relationally engage the more-than-human in a sensible, connected, and transformational manner through design. This relational process has three stages, depending on where the motivations and initiatives come from: (i) placing oneself in the lifeworld, (ii) boundless *feelthinking* (Aguilar, 2020), and (iii) emancipating oneself dialogically. The first stage refers to how a human entity situates, and places itself, in the lifeworld in relation to those other entities that exist in it, particularly, grounded in human interests. The access point rests in the initiative to try to transform society, which then transitions towards locating the human in the lifeworld in all its complexity. During the first stage, being in the lifeworld means becoming the lifeworld and acknowledging the more-than-human. It also means to acknowledge the tension between the human and more-than-human, as a matter of one's own affection (Duch, 2015) and the lifeworld.

The second stage refers to boundless *feelthinking* beyond the limitations of the human senses, which, clearly, constrain the possibilities. In this stage, interdependence acts as a conceptual entry point. It challenges the boundaries of the human, highlights the more-than-human, and transforms, firstly, the ideas of belonging to a place, from notions such as *territory* (i.e., Benach and Albet, 2010), and secondly, how these places are conceived and imagined (i.e., Silva, 2000). In turn, the result is an understanding about how relationships exist beyond one single place and can be found beyond specific locations. This means that lifeworld entanglements are weaved in a mycorrhizal manner, which dislocates hegemonic positions and braid relationships that stretch farther than what's perceived thereupon. The critical aspect is that *feelthinking* provides a platform for thinking while feeling and vice versa but also to acknowledge the spiral nature of the process.

The third stage refers to the dialogical emancipation of the self, where the emancipation is enacted through relationality in a boundless connectivity network. The entry point is the dialogical stance that aims to liberate, and thus, serves to break the ontological bonds of the human and transforms them to bind with the more-than-human through action. This results in a broader understanding of the rights that belong to all lifeworlds and their constituents. The rhizomatic organisation (Deleuze & Guattari, 1980) in

136 Leonardo Parra-Agudelo and Edgard David Rincón Quijano

which mycorrhizae weave coexistence(s) implies a relational and dialogical transformative practice. In turn, the dialogue is a mingling of worlds, an emancipation from the only-human, a dialogical entanglement with the more-than-human.

Coexistence: a sancocho-style approach

Design constitutes a coexistence act with the natural, abstract, spiritual and artificial worlds. It can make visible the multiple ways in which these worlds are interwoven and highlight the nuances of their connections. We approach the complexity and diversity of coexistence with the more-than-human as South Americans situated in the Caribbean shores, from the harmonic ways in which some of our food is cooked, shared, and eaten. We approach the problem in a sancocho-style. First, we're going to explain what a sancocho is and then will declare how the approach can be situated in design beyond human concerns.

The sancocho is a creole and mestizo stew that integrates meats, tubers, legumes, and other vegetables found for the occasion (de Castro and Gutiérrez de Piñeres, 2012). It's a dish that can be found in some areas of the Caribbean (Mangieri, 2006) and some parts of the Andean mountains. The ingredients and recipes vary depending on the occasion and the place, the shared spirit of cooks and diners is to facilitate and participate in an exchange ritual (Mangieri, 2006). This very particular meal relates diners with different interests and origins (Rosario, 2007) in a space that blurs the limits of the kitchen and the dining room space. This allows spontaneous communication and participation in the ritual of feeding (Mangieri, 2006). The understanding of sancocho is experiential. An example of this experience, a bone sancocho from the Montes de María region in Colombia, can be seen in Figure 9.1. This region is part of an isolated group of small mountains in the Caribbean region. The bone sancocho is served on the table, for all diners, with broth at the centre, and some of the ingredients for it, including corn, cassava, and ribs. Rice and avocado can also be seen, these are served as sides but can go into the broth or not, depending on the taste of the diner.

Figure 9.1 The dining experience changes depending on what each diner wants to include as part of their serving

This traditional sancocho is the result of the initiative to feed those at home and those who show up from the vicinity. As a broth-based meal, quantities can be quickly and easily adjusted by adding water and some additional cooking time, to accommodate moderate changes in the number of guests. The preparation of a sancocho begins by collecting some key ingredients, and some others that might change depending on the given conditions. In the picture above, corn, cassava, and ribs are central, and the spices used include garlic, chopped onion, and tomatoes, coriander, salt, and others. The cooking process aims to soften the available protein by submerging it for a few hours in a simple broth. Sometimes, the vegetables are added at the same time, sometimes they're added later on, or cooked beforehand in their

Design beyond human concerns: a sancocho-style approach 137

Figure 9.1 Bone Sancocho.
Source: DISCA Lab Archive.

own broth. Once protein and vegetables are mixed together, the sancocho is cooked until the soup is thick and ready to serve.

In the example of Figure 9.1, two banana leaves cover the table where all the ingredients are placed, including broth, vegetables, protein, and rice. Dried squash halves are used as spoons for serving broth and rice. They're also used as soup plates. The protein broth acts as a bonding mechanism, it's the joining component. The other ingredients make it thick and absorb the broth's substance, whilst the vegetables balance the flavour.

For the diner, the sancocho is an open platform with multiple access points. Eating can start with protein, broth, garnish, or any other ingredient. The non-defined structure allows people to follow their will, whilst negotiating quantities on-the-fly, and chatting, with others. In a sancocho, everything goes together. Everyone and everything are part of cooking and eating. The sancocho appears as a simple structure. At the end of the meal, leftovers are collected and wrapped in the banana leaves. These scraps are then taken, whenever possible, to the surrounding forests and are left to integrate back to the local ecosystem.

The complexity of the sancocho is evident when multiple interests appear on the table and are executed as different approaches to eating. This provides a relational authenticity to each situation; the boundaries exist only to be identified as possibilities rather than constraints. The diversity of

138   *Leonardo Parra-Agudelo and Edgard David Rincón Quijano*

experiences that a single sancocho can provide depend on how each participant approaches the meal. These do not separate but rather show how each
pathway evidences an inter-being state. The sancocho operates as a relational
platform to relate to others via multiple access points.

We propose a sancocho-style dual process for designing beyond human
concerns. The first process is a three-prong coexistence process of emancipation from representations that operate as accepted intelligibility mechanisms,
and it's listed in the section Relational Affectation. It is compound by (a) a
stage shaped by an acknowledgement of the possible subjectivity of the more-
than-human, (b) a stage where *feelthinking* can exist beyond the human, and
(c) a stage shaped by an integrative view of natural, artificial, abstract, and
spiritual relationships. The second one refers to designing as a transformational participation process that moves the focus away from the human, centres on coexistence, and is listed in the section *Feelthinking* in Mychorriza. Its
compound by (i) placing oneself in the lifeworld, (ii) boundless *feelthinking*,
and (iii) emancipating oneself dialogically.

As a sancocho, these stages can be understood as the ingredients, in this
case, allowing to access the process depending on where those who design are
situated. If questions about more-than-human subjectivity are at play, then
it's possible to access the dual-process from the possibilities of the situation.
If the human isn't at the centre, then enter from a place where *feelthinking*
isn't just part of the human domain. If the need is focused on relationships,
then consider how they could better integrate natural, artificial, abstract,
and spiritual aspects. If tensions between humans and more-than-human
are the initial emphasis, then access by placing those who design in the lifeworld so they can become the lifeworld. If the limitations of the human are
at the centre, then challenge human boundaries and enter via a boundless
feelthinking, focusing on interdependence. If questions about human and
more-than-human emancipation are emphasised, then enter via the dialogical emancipation of the self and inhabit a dialogical entanglement with the
more-than-human. Eat your design beyond human concerns with a relational
spoon, use your hands and get dirty (the leftovers will only make food for
others). This will bring you to a designerly, relational, mycorrhizal existence,
sancocho-style, which would give you, and others, access to realities beyond
the human, and, hopefully, insights about the more-than-human as well.

Conclusion

With this chapter, we'd like to contribute to the ongoing call for incorporating a relational and dialogical form of being, inter-being, and coexisting with
the more-than-human. We're after uncovering mycorrhizal entanglements
that can provide an avenue for making epistemological and ontological borders permeable to our kin, so we can truly be part of a dynamic assemblage.
This shift is grounded in an understanding of the potential of the dialogical
exchanges possible through a sancocho-style approach to designing, in which

Design beyond human concerns: a sancocho-style approach 139

emancipation rests not in the human, but in dialogical interactions with the more-than-human, whilst situated in a boundless network of connections.

This line of inquiry and integrative approach presents challenges for the future, including those associated with exploring epistemological and ontological borders. Further, the ongoing kin encounters that we're after, which may require new understandings of being, inter-being, and coexistence, require us to tune ourselves to our kin. How to do that in practical terms still needs to be explored in depth. However, we're not after a new methodology or a new agenda; rather, the sancocho-style approach that we propose could be understood to bring to the fore the multiple possibilities offered by staying with the trouble and becoming with each other (Haraway. D, 2016). In this sense, the work we have presented here is more about repositioning ourselves than a methodological proposition. Yet, we believe there is a need to acknowledge the effects that this repositioning might have on other methodologies, forms of thinking, feeling, being, and doing, aiming for a mycorrhizal coexistence. How to do this is an excellent question, for which we don't have an answer. However, we wanted to lay a transformative invitation to our kin and thus we say: we'll be waiting for you to make what Haraway (2016) has called oddkin.

Bibliography

Aguilar, L. F. B. (2020). Sentipensar el Pluriverso: Legado del maestro Orlando Fals Borda para la Sub-version, la utopía y el buen vivir. *Collectivus, Revista de Ciencias Sociales*, 7(1), pp. 63–74. https://doi.org/10.15648/Collectivus. vol7num1.2020.2532.

Akama, Y., Light, A., & Kamihira, T. (2020). "Expanding Participation to Design with More-Than-Human Concerns." In Proceedings of the 16th Participatory Design Conference 2020-Participation (s) Otherwise-Volume 1, pp. 1–11. https:// doi.org/10.1145/3385010.3385016.

Augé, M. (1995). *Non-places: Introduction to an Anthropology of Supermodernity*. London: Verso.

Ávila Gaitán, I. D. (2017). El Instituto latinoamericano de estudios críticos animales como proyecto decolonial. *Tabula Rasa*, (27), pp. 339–351. https://doi. org/10.25058/20112742.454.

Barman, J., Samanta, A., Saha, B., & Datta, S. (2016). "Mycorrhiza." *Resonance* 21(12), pp. 1093–1104. https://doi.org/10.1007/s12045-016-0421-6.

Benach, N., & Albet, A. (2010). *Edward W. Soja. La perspectiva postmoderna de un geógrafo radical*. Barcelona: Icaria.

De Castro, A., & Gutiérrez de Piñeres, V. (2012). Semiótica del sancocho: aglutinador social de la Costa Caribe colombiana. *Revista de la Universidad del Norte* (71), p. 72.

De La Bellacasa, M. P. (2017). *Matters of Care: Speculative Ethics in More Than Human Worlds*. Vol. 41. Minneapolis: University of Minnesota Press.

Deleuze, G., & Guattari, F. (1980). *Capitalisme et schizophrénie*. Paris: Les.

De Waal, F. (2016). *¿Tenemos suficiente inteligencia para entender la inteligencia de los animales?* Spain: Grupo Planeta.

Duch, L. (2015). Antropología de la ciudad. Mexico: Herder Editorial.

Escobar, A. (2018). *Designs for the Pluriverse: Radical Interdependence, Autonomy, and the Making of Worlds*. Durham: Duke University Press.

Forlano, L. (2016). "Decentering the Human in the Design of Collaborative Cities." *Design Issues* 32(3), pp. 42–54. https://doi.org/10.1162/DESI_a_00398.

Freire, P. (1974). "Conscientisation." *CrossCurrents* 24(1), pp. 23–31.

Godfrey-Smith, P. (2016). *Other Minds: The Octopus, the Sea, and the Deep Origins of Consciousness*. New York: Farrar, Straus and Giroux.

Haraway, D. (1988). "Situated Knowledges: The Science Question in Feminism and the Privilege of Partial Perspective." *Feminist Studies* 14(3), pp. 575–599. https://doi.org/10.2307/3178066.

Haraway, D. (2016). Staying *with the Trouble: Making Kin in the Chthulucene*. Durham: Duke University Press.

Ingold, T. (2007). "Materials against Materiality." *Archaeological Dialogues* 14(1), pp. 1–16. https://doi.org/10.1017/S1380203807002127.

Ingold, T., & Palsson, G. (Eds.). (2013). *Biosocial Becomings: Integrating Social and Biological Anthropology*. Cambridge: Cambridge University Press.

Ingold, T. (2015). *The Life of Lines*. London: Routledge.

Jonas, W., Zerwas, S., & von Anshelm, K. (2015). *Transformation Design: Perspectives on a New Design Attitude*. Berlin, München, Boston, MA: Birkhäuser. https://doi.org/10.1515/9783035606539.

Liu, J., Byrne, D., & Devendorf, L. (2018, April). Design for Collaborative Survival: An Inquiry into Human-Fungi Relationships. In Proceedings of the 2018 CHI Conference on Human Factors in Computing Systems, pp. 1–13. https://doi.org/10.1145/3173574.3173614.

Mangieri, R. (2006). Rituales de contacto a través de la cocina y las maneras de mesa: aproximación a una semiótica del sancocho. *designis* (9), pp. 21–32.

Ogden, L. A., Hall, B., & Tanita, K. (2013). "Animals, Plants, People, and Things: A Review of Multispecies Ethnography." *Environment and Society* 4(1), pp. 5–24. https://doi.org/10.3167/ares.2013.040102.

Pierce, J. (2012). "Undesigning Technology: Considering the Negation of Design by Design." In Proceedings of the SIGCHI Conference on Human Factors in Computing Systems, pp. 957–966. https://doi.org/10.1145/2207676.2208540.

Pearson, C. (2015). Beyond 'Resistance': Rethinking Nonhuman Agency for a 'More-Than-Human' World. *European Review of History: Revue européenne d'histoire* 22(5), pp. 709–725. https://doi.org/10.1080/13507486.2015.1070122.

Radio Televisión Nacional de Colombia. (2020). "Cocinas campesinas, sabores y saberes de Colombia". 22 de diciembre de 2020. Video, 11m37s. https://youtu.be/N1N7i68ZFu4 (Consulted on 20 February 2021).

Rosario, N. (2007). "Feasting on Sancocho before Night Falls: A Meditation." *Callaloo* 30(1), pp. 259–281.

Shenker, S. D. (2012). "Towards a World in WHICH MANY WORLDS FIT?: Zapatista AUTONOMOUS Education as an Alternative Means of Development." *International Journal of Educational Development* 32(3), pp. 432–443. https://doi.org/10.1016/j.ijedudev.2011.10.001.

Silva, A. (2000). *Imaginarios urbanos*. Bogotá: Tercer Mundo Editores.

Smith, N., Bardzell, S., & Bardzell, J. (2017). "Designing for Cohabitation: Naturecultures, Hybrids, and Decentering the Human in Design." Proceedings of the 2017 CHI Conference on Human Factors in Computing Systems. https://doi.org/10.1145/3025453.3025948.

10 Furrowing the *Maraña*

Designing to sail out of the Anthropocene

Pablo Hermansen and José Guerra Solano

Introduction

Reviewing the vast literature on the ecological crisis, we find narratives that are interwoven with million-dollar figures and well-known culprits, embarrassing events of the past and uncertainty about the future (Moore, 2020; Serratos, 2020). These elements, in addition to trying to convince us that we can understand the dimensions of the problem, often end up leaving us without alternatives; immobilising us. So, why write another well-documented text with conclusive fanaticism? Has it not been demonstrated that a wide and abstruse narrative lacks the necessary vigour to start moving tangible transformations? If it is, perhaps we have underestimated the value of a contour flying through broad, complex, more-than-human territories?

We write this reflection based on the conviction that creating from planetary narratives is as urgent as it is to delve into particular issues of our everyday experiences. As researchers from design, we have challenged ourselves to apprehend and materialise some of the most pressing concerns: (1) we are immersed in a multidimensional planetary ecosystemic crisis (ecological, military, epidemiological, political, technological, epistemological, and a long list of etceteras); (2) one of the likely consequences of this crisis is that, in a debatable but near term, large extensions of the planet will change their characteristics, becoming uninhabitable for the organisms that once no without effort, had prosper in them (including mammals like us); (3) this ecosystemic crisis is being precipitated by the constant expansion of the logics, ways of knowing and agencies of certain groups of humans and globalised non-human actors (psychopolitical algorithms, capital flows, production infrastructures, biopolitical devices...). We want to believe that the contour flying we develop in this text—emerged from readings and fieldwork, prototyping and speculations—contributes to the formulation of more creative, situated, and critical ways of worlding. That is, to resist the Western episteme that suppresses what exceeds it in order to reproduce itself, we will critically speculate on the myth of origin of modern hegemonic categories—*human-humanisable, civilised-civilisable, developed-savage*—and dualisms such as

DOI: 10.4324/9781003319689-11

142 *Pablo Hermansen and José Guerra Solano*

nature-culture (Latour, 1993), *subject-object* (Flusser, 1986), and *body-mind* (Tafalla, 2019).

Although the race of human development has been taken by modern science for centuries, the current uncertainty has brought with it the possibility of situating ourselves from other epistemes. As Stengers (2017) comments, it would be naïve to continue believing in the slogan "science at the service of all," since it is becoming increasingly difficult to hide the fact that modern science has succumbed at the delirium of a deadly and obscene abstraction that allows it to shamelessly propose "(...) The so-called rational calculations, which result in the conclusion that the only solution is to eradicate the vast majority of humans between now and the end of the century" (Stengers, 2017, p. 43). The truth is that science, complicit with capital, limits our horizon of possibilities, making it "easier to imagine the end of the world than the end of capitalism" (Fisher, 2016). Although this famous phrase—attributed to Fredric Jameson and popularised by Slavoj Žižek—has been installed as the univocal reflection of the current scenario, positioned from the design of the south we prefer to embrace the idea of Sousa Santos (2017), stating that although it is difficult to imagine the end of capitalism, it is also difficult to imagine that capitalism has no end. In order to expand the fertile grounds for speculation, we will descend to the *maraña*, a category that allows us to recognise the density of relationships in which we find ourselves and help design in its challenge to re-imagine our everyday life; our epistemological trench that gets tangled day by day. Considering the above it seems prudent to us to argue that, in part, it is in the hands of design to co-create the spaces of coexistence in which to intra-act (Barad, 2007) with "strange strangers" (Morton, 2018); refuges in which the lives of ignored and exiled can continue to reproduce themselves on the margins of the Western civilisational model.

As we will expose, researchers "from design" located in the south work "Staying with the Trouble," looking for new forms of navigation that take us out of the Euro-centric modernity, which insists on strategically forgetting the more-than-human and the other-than-Western.[1] This being so, it is our responsibility to set in motion an organic episteme through two urgent operations. The first is to apprehend (Butler, 2010) those entities and worlds exiled from modern morpho-immunological spheres (Sloterdijk, 2017). While the second, is to do so by means of the more-than-human prototyping, whose performativity has the power to make cosmopolitical moments emerge (Tironi, Hermansen & Neira, 2014; Tironi & Hermansen, 2018), intense and fleeting encounters between close ontologies that, however, usually exceed each other (de la Cadena, 2010).

The conqueror and the *maraña*

Into the more-than-human *maraña* that we usually call the Anthropocene, it seems that only *vulnerability* (Pick, 2011) and *precariousness* (Butler, 2010)

Furrowing the Maraña: *designing to sail out of the Anthropocene* **143**

hold us together. Although our fate seems to be tied—or tragically cast—we consider that questioning the obtuse naturalistic ontology (Descola & Pálsson, 2001) from a practical proposal could be an opportunity for the creatures and environments that thrived during the Holocene to have some chance of extending our survival.

According to the distinction made by Descola and Pálsson (2001) between the modes that define the frontier between the self and otherness, the naturalistic mode that prevails in Western society shapes cosmographies and topographies that manage to isolate nature, turning it into an entity independent of the human. In this way, an ontological domain has been formed whose expansive pace has been erasing all non-modern forms of coexistence, exiling the more-than-human not only from our ethical considerations but also from the political sphere in a practical sense. As we will try to defend in this chapter, the myth of origin of this epistemology can be located in the encounter of Alexander the Great with the Gordian Knot, an apparently distant and minuscule historical event that occurred 2,350 years ago but that allows us to trace links between the logics of production of *knowledge-power* (Foucault, 2001) that perpetuate our current planetary crisis.

In order to relate this mythologised moment and the current crisis, we will begin by delving into the black hole of notations, definitions and metaphors associated with the word *maraña*. Present in several regions of Europe and America, the word *maraña* has a deeply rich etymology, as promiscuous and inextricable as it is fertile, being attributed a great diversity of meanings that allow it to flourish in countless contexts. Just as Yakov Malkiel (1948) says, this word has found in Spanish language the place in which to deploy its richest range of meanings. According to Malkiel, the concept of *maraña* not only serves to designate a set of threads, hairs or similar things tangled and intertwined in such a way that they cannot be separated, but its meanings seem to share attributes with what it intends to name. The meaning of the word *maraña* is *enmarañado* which allows its metaphorical adoption in countless fields: in botany as "weed, bush, thicket," in music as "tangled mass of chords (of a musical instrument)," in logic as "difficult matter to resolve" or in morals as "deception, trick or cunning," complicating the task of finding a univocal meaning (Malkiel, 1948).[2]

Perhaps due to its broad spectrum of meaning or its indeterminate etymological origin, materialisation par excellence of its definition, we can affirm that the *maraña* contains intertwined elements that are very complex to understand individually, without this depending on the context in which it emerges or the type of elements it involves. At this point it is interesting to ask ourselves about its different meanings and uses according to the position or relation of the speaker with respect to the *maraña* in question: is the *maraña* enveloping or can it be observed from a distance? Are its scale and scope apprehensible, or do its boundaries exceed what we can comprehend? These questions raise epistemologically relevant and inspiring issues, allowing us to bring together in a single narrative event that are in principle

144 *Pablo Hermansen and José Guerra Solano*

independent, distant, and disparate—such as the myth of the Gordian Knot and the Anthropocene. With this new narrative we propose that the different appearances that the *maraña* has attained lack beginning and end, expressing itself as a simultaneous realisation which should not be segmented, a metabolism that suggests an underlying pattern in the planetary irruption of Western colonisation, whose modern epistemology acts by dissecting that entangled. As we will argue below, the recognition of the *maraña* and its ontological density succeeds in revealing the fact that the progress of the modern project is constituted by anthropocentric logics, strategies, and operations of objectification of the other-than-Western, attempts to control the more-than-human *marañas* through their reduction, dissection, and trivialisation. Although it is not reduced to this, the concept of maraña is related with what Morin (1990) calls the complex:

> At first glance, complexity is a fabric (*complexus*: that which is woven together) of heterogeneous constituents inseparably associated: it presents the paradox of the one and the multiple. On closer inspection, complexity is, in fact, the fabric of events, actions, interactions, retroactions, terminations, chances, that constitute our phenomenal world. Thus, complexity presents itself with the disturbing features of the entangled, the inextricable, disorder, ambiguity, uncertainty.
>
> (Morin, 1990, p. 32)

Morin's (1990) definition would not be able to grasp the *maraña* without being inoculated with the distinction offered by Barad (2007) between interaction and intra-action. In the *maraña*, the elements are so imbricated that it is not possible to recognise interactions exercised by individual or separate agencies, but only an intra-action in which the intertwined agencies do not pre-exist and only come to be constituted at the moment of the intra-action. As we will see in the following sections, all these features clustered around the *maraña* are arranged as keys that contribute to the interpretation of our convulsed present, encouraging researchers through design to navigate outside the Anthropocene (Haraway et al., 2016), from a present time and a particular territory that, as De la Cadena and Blaser (2018) put it, is the setting of political and economic forces that have perpetuated unprecedented destructive power.

Myth of origin: dissection of the pact-in-the-nude

Our journey to rediscover the *maraña* begins in the foundations of what is called Western culture. Robert Graves, in his book The Greek Myths 1 (2011), tells us about a curious enthronement that happened in the region of Anatolia[3], in which Gordius, a peasant, was blessed by the grace of Zeus:

> ...the King of Phrygia had died suddenly, without issue, and an oracle announced: 'Phrygians, your new king is approaching with his bride,

Furrowing the Maraña: *designing to sail out of the Anthropocene* 145

seated in an ox-cart!' When the ox-cart entered the market place of Telmissus, the eagle at once attracted popular attention, and Gordius was unanimously acclaimed king. In gratitude, he dedicated the cart to Zeus, together with its yoke, which he had knotted to the pole in a peculiar manner. An oracle then declared that whoever discovered how to untie the knot would become the lord of all Asia.

(Graves, 2011, p. 418)

The offering mentioned by Graves—later known as the Gordian Knot—grained an alliance with the divinity that materialised a dialogue between human and more-than-human forces. As far as we know, the object that Gordius offered to the gods was a knot made of "(...) dogwood strands, and it seemed to have no beginning and no end" (Arrian, 1982, p. 110). However, because of Gordius's origin, it is reasonable to suppose that the knot was a threshing knot commonly used to tie the tools used in agricultural work—two yokes, a stick and a cart—in order to prevent them from being stolen. This being so, the original interest of the knot technique made by Gordius lies nowhere else but in keeping safe what he seeks to guard, making it desirable that this predecessor of the modern padlock be as robust, intricate, and undecipherable as possible. After the theophany of Zeus, the knot ceased to only bind agricultural tools, *enmarañando* also the Gordius's transformation from farmer to prince of a new ruling lineage in Phrygia. In this case, when the law is revealed (Déotte, 2013), we see how the donation of meaning is materialised in an object, a knot that symbolises the alliance that gives order to the kingdom for about 15 centuries. Divinity, technique, and government are *enmarañados* in a pact between worlds.

Time passed and with it the Greek influence in Phrygia, due to the fact that in the middle of the 6th century BC this territory was annexed to the Persian Empire becoming one of its provinces. By then, the Gordian Knot *enmarañaba* not only the Greek world, its history and gods, but also the kingdom of Phrygia and its lineage, its political-cultural order, its status as a portal between Europe and Asia, and the Persian Empire, its culture and logic of government. All this took place without forgetting the declarations of the oracle and the promise to dominate Asia, so that the "(...) chariot and team were left in the acropolis of Gordium, a city founded by Gordius, where the priests of Zeus jealously guarded them for centuries (...)" (Graves, 2011, p. 418).

A few centuries later, in one of the most overshadowed city-states of the Hellenic world, Alexander the Great, who would be known as the most renowned conqueror of his time, would be born. Alexander III of Macedonia was trained to reign both militarily and intellectually, being entrusted with his education to Aristotle himself. As Sloterdijk (2010) comments, rage was for the Greeks the inspiration of their cosmology and the mobilising engine of their action. Situating himself from the rage, Alexander sought revenge for the damage that for centuries the Persians had caused to the Hellenes.[4]

146 *Pablo Hermansen and José Guerra Solano*

Achilles, the choleric conqueror drawn by Homer was always the model to follow for the Macedonian, who had the habit of always sleeping with his copy of the Iliad and a dagger under his pillow (Vallejo, 2019, p. 14). As far as we know his iron formation in the Hellenic world made Alexander a faithful believer in

> (...) legends of heroes; indeed, he lived and competed with them. He had an obsessive bond with the character of Achilles, the most powerful and feared warrior in Greek mythology. He had chosen him as a child, when his teacher Aristotle taught him the Homeric poems, and he dreamed of looking like him.
>
> (Vallejo, 2019, p. 14, our translation)

Echoing his personal history and the Greek epistemological substratum learned from Aristotle, Alexander's project mobilised an original mode of conquest. His strategy to colonise his adversaries achieved the Hellenic will of defeating the vast Persian Empire. Seeking to dominate the entire known world, Alexander arrived in Phrygia in 333 BC because at that time "Gordium was the key city for entering Asia (Asia Minor), because its citadel commanded the only practicable trade route from Troy and Antioch" (Graves, 2011, p. 421). After subduing the city and becoming the new king, the priest custodian of the Gordian Knot reminds Alexander of what the oracle had said centuries earlier, offering to take him to the oracle to try to resolve the challenge and thus possibly obtain confirmation of his desire. Convinced of the influence that overcoming this more-than-human problem would bring to his fate, he begins such an undertaking by playing the game as proposed by the gods—namely, trying to untie the knot. It is here that we see an Alexander intra-acting face to face with the knot that *enamaraña* (entangles) him. Enveloped by its atmosphere, Alexander surrenders himself by playing within its terms.

As was to be expected, untying the knot within the rules of the game proposed by the gods was a complex undertaking. To be sure, after 15 centuries, the knot was materially impossible to *desenmarañar*, or at least not within a time frame that suited the pace of conquest imposed by the influx of Greek rage on Alexander.[5] As the minutes ticked by, Alexander's impatience to untie the knot probably grew, as well as his imperial ambition for conquest, feeling increasingly pressured to reach a solution. Tired but frantic, encouraged by his own and his lineage's expectations, this young 23-year-old conqueror decides to break the more-than-human rules of the game. At that moment Alexander takes distance, looks at the knot from outside its atmosphere and ignores the legitimacy of the challenge with which the gods had put him to the test. By separating himself ontologically from the knot, Alexander realises that what stops his conquest is an insignificant *maraña*, namely, a thing, a banal problem that requires a practical and definitive solution. This simplification of the problem produces an epistemological revolution:

Furrowing the Maraña: *designing to sail out of the Anthropocene* 147

ontologically translocated, the Gordian Knot, now a foreign object, lacks the divine protection that, if it exists, must only be on the side of the conqueror:

> Alexander, in view of how difficult it was to find a way to untie it and as, on the other hand, he could not allow it to remain tied, lest it should influence the mood of his men, he cut—it is said—the knot with a blow of his sword and exclaimed: It is already untied!
>
> (…) he and his men left the chariot certain that the oracle about the untying of the knot had been fulfilled, for that night there was also thunder and lightning in the sky, as signs of something prodigious.
>
> (Arriano, 1982, p. 110)

Dissect to dominate

We will begin this section with a question: How was it that a Macedonian boy who grew up hearing about the need for the gods to bless any human enterprise was able to desecrate the Gordian knot by bypassing the sentence of the oracle?

Only by resorting to the wealth of meanings present in the concept of *maraña* will we be able to essay an answer to this complex question.[6] As we have already commented, after 15 centuries, it is only to be expected that the knot would have become an "intricate" obstacle, in the sense that, materially, its strings must have dried, hardened and stuck together, becoming practically a single entity. Confronted with this trap, composed of a divine dictate impossible to fulfil because of the material state of the ropes, the conqueror was plunged into the atmosphere of this "impassable" obstacle. Alexander could have described his situation using a Portuguese term related to *maraña,* namely *brenha.* In its connotations *brenha* agglutinates the ideas of "undergrowth" with those of "complication," "confusion" and, essential in this case, with those of "secret" and "arcane." Then, inscribed in this intra-action (Barad, 2007), the knot is a *maraña* that exceeds its control. Like an enveloping undergrowth, located at a point of obligatory passage, merging mystery and matter, intricate and impassable, this tangle stops, for an instant, its trajectory of conquest. Thus, while the Macedonian was trying to untie the knot, everything unfolded according to the epic of his Hellenic ontogeny, which intra-acted in a mutual constitution of intertwined agencies that did not precede but emerged as such by coexisting (Barad, 2007). However, when Alexander unsheathes his sword, the conqueror opens the way to interaction, performatively enacting those involved present as independent entities that can be subdued under the anthropocentric logics of functionalism and efficiency. Subject and object not only appear through interaction, but the separation of both is also its condition of possibility. Since then human subjects were able to design the laboratory exercise, and a plethora of new instruments of testing and observation that opened up the possibility of modifying the object at will. Alexander's interaction did

148 *Pablo Hermansen and José Guerra Solano*

nothing more than hide a maraña under rage, ontogeny, and the desire for power.

When Alexander "petulantly cut the knot with his sword" (Graves, 2011, p. 418), he not only flouted the imposed rules, but rendered ineffective the entire divine and political order of the world he inhabited. "Alexander's brutal cutting of the knot when he marshalled his army at Gordium for the invasion of Greater Asia, ended an ancient dispensation by placing the power of the sword above that of religious mystery" (Graves, 2011, p. 421). Regarding this act we can state that, unlike how a mere cheat who knows the rules and uses carelessness to his advantage would do it, Alexander acts as the killjoy (*Spielverderber*: "killjoy of games") described by Huizinga (2007). The cheater recognises the rules of the game and therefore tries to discreetly bend them in order to win, while the killjoy, on the other hand, withdraws from the game, thus revealing the relativity and fragility of the environment that until then he shared with his companions (Huizinga, 2007).

The Gordian Knot, before Alexander's arrival in Phrygia, already constituted a transcendental part of his conquest. It was an obstacle properly *marañoso*, in the sense that its scope and complexity more-than-human made it an enveloping challenge. The oracle of Phrygia enveloped him, making him part of the Hellenic world, despite being located beyond the territories dominated by the city-states. Thus, Alexander was involved by the prophecy in the Knot, since in it was inscribed the voice of Zeus, whose will permeated the fate of his army in its deployment in Asia. By cutting the knot, Alexander aggressively negotiates his fate with the gods, managing to impose his own will. Since his childhood he had listened to the myths and knew the rules of the knot that had been proposed by his own gods. However, he decided to consciously redefine the way of relating to the divine will: he innovated by imposing anthropocentric rules of the game. Alexander was not an outsider to the game, but a killjoy with the advantage of being able to change the rules, acting as a revolutionary leader who unites under himself a group willing to follow the new rules. Without stopping in the encircling exercise, Alexander overcomes the nonsense resulting from his act by recomposing the agencies that began to interact. Although Alexander had acted in the same way as a wagon thief trying to seize agricultural tools, he decides to thank the same gods he has defied, invoking them as divine witnesses by offering apotropaic sacrifices in his honour the next day, implying that the divinity was an accomplice of his act, celebrates his innovation and will favour him in his path of conquest (Arriano, 1982).

Our argument in principle coincides with Julieta Kirkwood's (2019) analysis of how Alexander in a rush of knives or swords [cuts the knot], to gain completely and immediately the empire of the things in dispute (Kirkwood, 2019, p. 195, our parentheses). Now, unlike the author, who stops to emphasise the brutality of this act, we prefer to place the attention on how Alexander's sword achieves the establishment not only of a new form of power but also of knowledge. When he renounces to solve the

Furrowing the Maraña: *designing to sail out of the Anthropocene* 149

riddle and takes distance, Alexander not only splits the knot in two, but separates from the divine challenge its inanimate materiality. In this way, the Alexandrian phylum initiates the Western project that, having become hegemonic, has translocated the ontological order of the world by means of a new epistemology.

The epistemology from which the conqueror positioned himself transformed the knot into a problem on whose solution depended the possibility of assuring the flow of his imperialist trajectory. In this area it is striking that the solution to Alexander's problem demanded that he break the rules of the game in order to be able to look *objectively* at the *maraña* from the outside. This new arrangement is particularly interesting because, according to Vilhem Flusser's (1986) exposition, the etymological origin of *object* can be homologated with that of *problem*, since both mean "thrown against," in this case, against a subject. In this way, the abysmal antagonistic dynamic that separates subject from object begins to be drawn, coupled with an epic that narrates a conqueror who must confront a universe of objects thrown against him.

After having taken the time to make all the above clarifications, it is possible to understand the importance of what happened with the Gordian knot. Although we must recognise Alexander's originality in using in his favour the epistemological criterion we have already described, the truth is that after giving his life in the field and adding up countless victories, it is still possible to affirm that Alexander's conquests were ephemeral, while those of Aristotle were long-lasting and extremely fruitful (Sarton, 1960, p. 17). The words of Sarton (1960) charge that the importance of Alexander the Great does not lie in the fact that he was the ruler of the First European World Empire on record, but in the fact that he set in motion a certain logic of knowledge inherited from Aristotle.

Located from the postulates of Ernst Cassirer retrieved by Rheinberger (2021), we recognise that behind the mythologised story of Alexander lies the basis on which Western science thrived. The amputation of the Gordian *maraña* was properly an innovative and disruptive design with ontological consequences, capable of founding the distinction between a subject that can be recognised, defined, thought and ultimately exist because it is confronted with an object that can be observed, isolated, defined and thought (Morin, 1990). According to Morin, this is the necessary condition for the birth of science in the modern sense, which operates by means of supralogical principles that separate, unite, hierarchise, and centralise significant data, diminishing complexity to produce knowledge that ends up governing "our vision of things and of the world without our being aware of it" (Morin, 1990, p. 28). The truth is that it is not possible to think of the sciences without mentioning the modern simplification and sanitisation of the *maraña*, since here is the root of the word Scire: to divide is the pleasure of the judge. Whoever engages in science incessantly adjusts, rules, guides, orients, corrects, and disciplines (Rheinberger, 2021, p. 35).

150 *Pablo Hermansen and José Guerra Solano*

As a modern entrepreneur, the Macedonian conqueror took distance from the pact to objectify it, dividing the continuous environment that the knot made tangible. By cutting the knot, Alexander creates a limit that allows him to position himself outside the pact and extract its narrative to use it as a resource. The dissection of the knot separates the matter from the divine design, the support from its meaning: on the one hand, the knot is reduced to an object and, on the other, the prophecy to a myth functional to its trajectory. From this interaction results in three distinct and independent entities: subject of power, object of domination and mythology. Applying the modern thought and technique, he isolates and reduces the prophecy of the oracle to myth—a merely cultural reality—and the offering to an object, constituting himself in the same operation the first modern subject of knowledge-power (Foucault, 2001). The offering, reduced to an object, split in two and split from its narrative, exhales its more-than-human vitality. The knot divided in two clears the way for its path of conquest.

The modern world is *enmarañado* and *enmarañándose*

Alexander's story not only ontologically transformed the Gordian *maraña* into a sum of independent entities available to be subdued by the modern subject of knowledge-power but also changed forever the European understanding of the world. Starting in 334 BC, Alexander's journey traversed the territories of Egypt and Asia Minor until he reached present-day India (Figure 10.1), tracing a trajectory of 25,000 kilometres that exceeds the distance between pole and pole. The ten years that followed the cutting of the knot ended with 750,000 lives of his own soldiers, blood with which 70 cities were founded—or rather refounded—of which 50 shared his name. Finally, after Alexander's body suffered the inclemency of disease and betrayal, he died in June 323 BC amid opaque circumstances (Heckel, 2008). Alexander's campaign is remembered as the inaugural milestone of the so-called Hellenistic Period, which after three centuries would end with the suicide of Cleopatra and Mark Antony in 31 BC. Although this period might pale in comparison to the later consolidation of the Roman Empire, the transformations imposed by Alexander in economy, culture, language, urbanism and religion inoculated with a renewed Hellenism all the territories reached, not only conquering, but colonising the entire known world to date with the hegemonic project that today we call *Western civilisation.*

Alexander's trajectory was not only a condition of possibility for the Hellenistic Period and what has been called as "classical culture." Alexander's rage, embodied in his founding epistemology of strategies, practices and logics of power, later inspired conquerors such as Julius Caesar and Napoleon, who each succeeded in consolidating their empires. Now, what we wish to emphasise is that Alexander's trajectory, seen with 23 centuries of distance, stands as a management model for the innumerable colonialist trajectories that seek to move away from the *maraña*, providing sustenance to

Furrowing the Maraña: *designing to sail out of the Anthropocene* 151

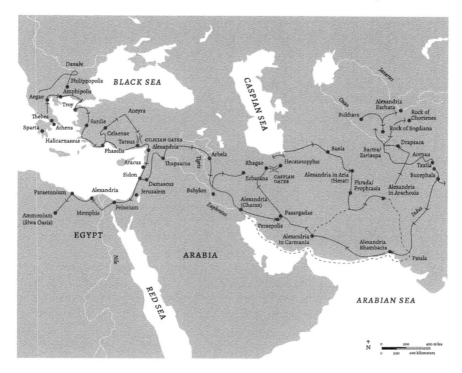

Figure 10.1 Alexander's campaign trail.
Source: Martín Pastenes.

the innumerable dimensions of the *Western civilising project*. Regardless of which colonising enterprise we refer to, the modern anthropocentric epistemology that allowed the dismemberment of the *maraña* continues to be the edge that reduces to an object-resource everything that exceeds its understanding (de la Cadena, 2010).

It is not difficult to see how the myth of the splitting of the *maraña* is repeated with percussive force, liberated from the military gesture to be ritualised in other areas of our spiral towards extinction. The elements of nature that are considered resources by capital, on many occasions still entail narratives of when we were *enmarañados*, as it happens for example in the case of cetaceans. By reviewing different works on the subject ("Ballenas: voces del mar de Chile," 2018; Capella & Giggons, 2019) we corroborated that the human groups that inhabited the territory of Chile before the arrival of the European colonisers maintained ways of relating with the whales that were far from the idea that these beings were resources available to be exploited, revealing themselves instead as entities entangled in our life and death. This can be seen in the Mapuche cosmovision, in which the wise old women are

152 Pablo Hermansen and José Guerra Solano

transformed into whales or *tempulaklwe*, beings in charge of transporting the souls of the deceased to the *wenumapu* located on the other side of the sea (Piña, 2021). On the other hand, the Yámana, the southernmost human group on the planet, called these beings *wapsa*, from whom they obtained much more than the elements necessary for sustenance (Barros, 1975). One of the myths of these *Yámanas* recorded by Sergio Lausic (1994), tells the story of Latchich:

> It was little Latchich who came up with the idea; the others answered him timidly; 'you can only try to jump into the whale's mouth, for you have courage for it.' He bravely replied, 'well, I will try,' and so too, back again went all the men to the shore where they had their camp. The men once more fetched all their weapons and went at once to replenish them. Little Latchich fashioned himself a sharp knife; the women arranged their canoes so that in this way they would again lunge at the whale.
>
> When they had all finished their work, they repeated the operation and left in their canoes, heading for the great round-headed whale. Once more they threw their men their heavy harpoons against this sturdy body, sticking into it very deeply, but they did not seem to have any effect on it.
>
> (Lausic, 1994, p. 161, our translation)

As the myth tells us, the human tools made by the *Yámanas* with the bones of other whales were not capable of breaking the tissue of the marine mammal. For this reason, Latchich decided to deep the *maraña* and from there to intra-act with the agencies of which he was also a part, and after much effort, he succeeded in killing the whale. After running aground, Latchich remained for several days inside the round-headed whale without the others suspecting that he was still alive. After some time, a couple of young men noticed his presence in the animal's entrails, finding him "pale and thin, without a hair on his head and almost faint" (Lausic, 1994, p. 166). Turner's (2007) postulates on the moments of the ritual process allow us to argue that the battered appearance with which Latchich emerges and his subsequent recovery in the communal space are a sign that the hunter was not only waiting inside the animal, but that this event triggered the liminal phase framed in a ritual of passage towards a transmutation of the subject. In this way, we understand that Latchich's search was not motivated by the obtaining of a resource, but that it concealed a process of transformation that can only take place in the more-than-human *maraña* that engulfs, in this case literally, human individuality in order to weave it back together with the things that exceed it.

The lives of humans and cetaceans have been *enmarañadas* since their beginnings not only in this part of the world. The relationship with whales

Furrowing the Maraña: designing to sail out of the Anthropocene 153

in Europe goes back a long way, with Norse myths telling of Lyngbakr, the giant whale. Monsters like this one are described in detail in 1555, when the work that later will be translated from Latin as *A brief history of the Goos, Swedes and Vendeans, as well as other Nordic peoples [Historia resumida de los goos, suecos y vendos, así como de otros pueblos nórdicos]* (Wendt, 1982) was published in Rome. Although whales and Vikings had a long history of relationship (Hennius, Gustavsson, Ljungkvist, & Spindler 2018), the 17th century marks the splitting of the *maraña* that involved us, being able to recognise a colonisation of Western epistemology on these beings. By this century, commercial hunting would begin, decimating the cetacean population at an unsuspected speed. Although the pioneers in the hunting of this animal were the Basques and the Vikings, the pressure to obtain oil and other raw materials led the island of Nantucket in Massachusetts to consolidate for a long time as the centre of a global market (Serratos, 2020). Increased demand and the low reproductive rate of these animals caused whales to cease to be sighted in the northern seas within a few years. This was resented mainly by the Netherlands, which depended on whaling for the manufacture of fuel, hygiene products and even textiles. This pressure caused ships to explore the southern Atlantic, later expanding to the Pacific and the Indian Ocean so as not to lose track of this animal that was considered deadly as an individual but inexhaustible as a species by the thinkers of the time (Serratos, 2020). As Serratos establishes, it is estimated that in the 1830s the hunting quota did not exceed 5,000 specimens per year. However, this figure would increase exponentially after steam-powered boats, and later those powered by internal combustion, were equipped with more and better hunting and capture tools.

As the 19th century progressed, whaling expeditions took longer and longer and reached farther and farther, managing to colonise the entire globe during this century. This not only caused certain species to disappear almost completely but also turned the cold coasts of Chile into a strategic place for the settlement of whaling groups. During November 20, 1820, the whaler Essex "was attacked and sunk by a sperm whale off the coast of South America. Eight people survived the shipwreck, with cannibalism included (...). After the media impact of the Essex, there are different sinkings due to the attack of one or several albino cetaceans" (Gracía-Reyes, 2018, p. 93). This event would later inspire Herman Melville to publish Moby Dick in 1851, a novel that encourages us to think that humans are lost if we do not use our strength to fight against fierce nature. It is difficult not to establish a correlation between Alexander and Captain Ahab, the protagonist of the work, who moved by rage ends up losing any bond or regard for his fellow men, sacrificing them to obtain his revenge of tearing apart the monster that mutilated him (Gracía-Reyes, 2018), becoming the most faithful representative of the need to subjugate Nature to the might of homo oeconomicus (Serratos, 2020, p. 63).

154 *Pablo Hermansen and José Guerra Solano*

Immersing us again into the *maraña* in the light of the background reviewed here, we can see interesting crossroads that show the worst face of colonialism. As is well known, much of the responsibility for the disappearance of the Yámana groups was due to the settlement of whalers and other extractivist groups whose economic interests took priority over possible measures to mitigate the disappearance of those who were sentenced as a people so pure and so primitive, had no defences to face "civilisation" (Barros, 1975, p. 25). On the other hand, despite the fact that Melville does not territorialise his work with such specificity, analyses of it usually place it on the coasts of Chile, precisely in the territory where Mapuche groups inhabit to this day (Gracía-Reyes, 2018). Melville's whale is a *tempulaklwe*, therefore, their death does not only mean revenge against nature, but an episticide directed at an element that is *enmarañado* and allows communities to construct meaning. It is possible to think that the struggle against nature is nothing other than the struggle against other ways of relating to the cosmos. This is what we see in General George W. Morgan who, in the same period in which Melville was writing his novel, came to the conclusion that the war against the American Indians would never be won until the last of the bison was wiped out.

> [T]he Indians will fade away like the grass of the buffalo or the berries of the antelope" and in their place will flourish "clover, timothy grass, apples and pears, wheat and corn, the cow and the horse, and the conqueror supreme, the dominating predestined white man will occupy his [the natives] fields, and then civilization will host its religious and scientific temples among the graves of those people who lived without purpose and died without history.
> (Serratos, 2020, pp. 96–97, our translation)

Despite the fact that General Morgan's plans counted on it, at that time there was a debate about the possibility of a species becoming extinct, as this contravened the prevailing idea at the time that nature was a divine cornucopia from which we should snatch its gifts in favour of human prosperity. Scientific developments during the 20th century settled this debate (Carroll, 2018), leading to the founding of the International Whaling Commission (IWC) in 1946 with the aim of regulating the hunting of cetaceans. Despite its intentions, the IWC would not prevent Russian whalers alone from hunting more than 150,000 whales between 1947 and 1972. In a way, the same is true of more recent initiatives promoted by new international organisations, which display information on the migratory routes of these animals in the hope of contributing to their protection. Notwithstanding the noble purposes of those who carry out these dissemination exercises, to unfold the *maraña* of cetacean routes that covers the globe and its subsequent exhibition only acknowledges the possibility that this information can also be obtained by those who try to hunt these animals.

Mutations in the *maraña*

Now, it is time to raise questions that we have already begun to answer a couple of pages earlier: how did we go from using *maraña* to describe the Gordian Knot to using it to describe the state of the planet in the Anthropocene? How did we transit through this term from a tangle of strings, threads, hairs or similar things that cannot be separated to an amalgam of trajectories of domination with planetary consequences? Our suspicion points to the fact that the division and objectification of the *maraña* still nestles in the spirit of modern science, exercising a dualistic materialism that transforms beings outside the spheres of power into inert matter that can be manipulated at will, constrained under the label of property (Plumwood, 2002). In this sense, the disposition of modern science when studying whales, larches, ecosystems, chickens, or pigs usually has no other motives than to turn them into increasingly profitable commodities and not for an objective eagerness that scientific rhetoric constantly tries to remind us of (Tafalla, 2019). Faced with this panorama, it is pressing to question whether there is any episteme that can construct an understanding of reality that does not reduce it to place it at the service of voracious neoliberalism that sacrifices the web of the *maraña* in its path.

The concept of cosmopolitics developed by Isabelle Stengers (2014) provides us with some possible tools to come out of this dilemma. It is useful not only to comprehend the onslaught of the maraña, but also to modify the material conditions that allow us to recognise its complex structure, which despite being gutted, still beats to entangle beings and agencies without distinction (Wilkie, 2016). Although *cosmopolitanism* and *cosmopolitics* converge in articulating the same concepts—cosmos and polis—they radically diverge in scope and meaning. While Kantian cosmopolitanism can be understood as a teleological exercise that envisions the universalisation of European culture and institutions (Derrida, 2000), cosmopolitics, as posited by Stengers (2014), refers to the more-than-human tangles that today burst and collapse our modern *immunological spheres* (Sloterdijk, 2017). The scale at which Stengers (2017) thinks his concept invokes planetary dimensions, alluding to the irruption of Gaia—a Greek mythical figure whose power predates the anthropomorphic gods that were born in the *polis*—to describe the planet as a living organism of a particular behaviour that demands our attention. Gaia's manifestations stress predictions, rationalities, and strategies. This entity disavows the modern concept of *nature*, an ontologically homogeneous and stable label, which pretends to separate itself sharply from humans and become a source of resources. Gaia bursts in to be heard without bothering to clarify the specificities of its message. Now, in the face of the impending crisis, misreading its signals could make us suffer the catastrophic consequences of its "unilateral intrusion, which imposes a question without being interested in the response" (Stengers, 2017, p. 42).

156 *Pablo Hermansen and José Guerra Solano*

Cosmopolitics, far from being a scientific proposal, suggests to us an *etho-ecological* mode of existence and political action (Stengers, 2004) that does not limit in advance the type or number of entities to participate in the composition of politics, extending this notion beyond the human. The cosmopolitical exercise invites us, therefore, to conceive concrete spaces where different entities, such as mammals and goddesses, algorithms, and viruses, reinvent polis and politics (Hermansen & Tironi, 2017), a world in common that is yet to be imagined and defined in intra-action. On the other hand, Ingold (2016) offers us the idea of "correspondence," which alludes to the permanent becoming or *joining with one another.* For those who carefully attend to this flow, the limits imposed on the world by modern science through classificatory categories, such as culture, subject, nature or object, are diluted. From the chorus of both authors and their references, an ethics of attention and correspondence arises that offers us the opportunity to apprehend the veiled background of the entangled ecosystemic crisis (Hermansen & Tironi, 2020).

Throwing ourselves into the task of working on codes that allow us to rewrite the aberrations proscribed by objectifying science implies suspending the understanding it has imposed on the other-than-human and beginning to recognise them for what they are, "strange stranger." This concept borrowed from Morton (2018) helps us to think ourselves together with everyone inside the *maraña* that composes us. Despite the fact that we think we can see them and define their boundaries, other species are *strange strangers* that will always be at the edge of our imagination. The closer we get to them and think we know them, the more evident becomes the abyss that separates us, which we usually try to bridge by introjecting a large part of ourselves into the idea we build about them. Cohabiting in the *maraña,* the strange strangers swarm "inside (and outside) each and every living thing" (Morton, 2019, p. 24), continually mutating, entangling, and surprising us at the moment of their appearance.

An interesting perspective on the strange can be illustrated with the short story *The Drowned Giant* written by James Graham Ballard. Originally published in 1964, it was adapted in short film format for the Streaming platform Netflix in 2019 as part of the second season of the *Love, Death & Robots* series under the direction of Tim Miller (2021). Both the adaptation and the story begin in the same place. After a stormy night the body of a giant has washed up on the beach. The narrator and protagonist who describes the scene plants in us the certainty that we are facing a fantastic event that has interrupted the usual chores. Without anyone knowing how to react to this "strange stranger," the inhabitants of the place form a circle around him. However, it will be enough that someone dares to take the first step to break the sacredness of the novelty that until that moment surrounded the discovery. As the days go by, the barrier of strangeness begins to descend more and more to the point of forgetting that it ever existed. And while a group of specialists sets out to gather information, the more

Furrowing the Maraña: *designing to sail out of the Anthropocene*   157

intrepid ones swing on their limbs or take a rest in the sinuosities of their bodies. Without ever wondering about the origin of the giant or the dangers it might pose, people seem to integrate it so confidently that if the story had been written in this century, it would be expected that the visit of the curious would allow them to reconstruct the evolution of the scene through selfies.

The story continues to show us how people begin to get rid of the corpse, metabolising it in a continuous appropriation of its parts in a scene covered with the most absolute ordinariness. Towards the end of the short film, we see that people gradually seem to have forgotten the extraordinary event. Only a few isolated material traces remember what happened, appearing without any scandal in different corners of the territory. However, no one seems to believe that the creature in question was a giant, but only a whale that, after running aground, allowed the locals to take advantage of its parts. Throughout the narration of the short film, the intrigue that this strange stranger causes in the protagonist is striking. Although his interest in the find was initially merely scientific, the sensation of being in front of something that is more than a sum of resources or an unusual spectacle pushes him to visit it periodically. The protagonist reflects on the sensations that this strange creature produces in him, confessing that he will never really be able to understand what has happened because the existence of the giant, despite being unquestionable, exceeds him.

As Rosa Luxemburg (1951, p. 416) states, "the ruins of (...) non-capitalist *milieu* is indispensable for accumulation" of capital. This premise can be verified in The Drowned Giant since the incommensurability of the stranded character in no case is a brake for the phagocytic action of extractivist operations, but a perverse condition of possibility. Capitalism and modern science decide to obscenely ignore gigantic and strange facts that exceed them, applying to them the "rule of the golden hammer."[7] By recognising that modern episteme takes the liberty to operate axiomatically in the face of any issue, we can homologate our concerns with the lucid argument expressed by Sousa Santos.

> The widespread crisis of the modern equation of modern solutions to modern problems is now so evident that we can safely state that, if we still choose to formulate our problems in the modern Western way, we must conclude that we are faced with modern problems for which there are no modern solutions.
>
> (de Sousa Santos, 2017, p. 14, our translation)

Reflecting on the golden hammer of capitalism allows us to question the content of the toolbox with which we design solutions to the immeasurable problems that constitute the Anthropocene. Faced with a golden hammer (capitalism/science) that transforms into nails all the problems in its path (entities in resources), tool, problem and subject converge to define each

158 *Pablo Hermansen and José Guerra Solano*

other, establishing together the range of what is possible to be designed. *Machines, machine-tools and designing subjects* do the designing, inscribe their praxis and constitute it ontologically, like the edge of the sword to the coloniser. Although this scenario amputates our capacity for action as designers, the incursion into radical thinking in and from design opens the opportunity to escape from the aporias caused by the use without discretion of the golden hammer of the modern episteme. Designing in the *maraña* becomes a way of being with the problem that, by arguing in favour of a new epistemic order, allows us to distrust the well-known resources, procedures and measures with which science and economics still defend their quality as saviours of the world.

In universities and companies, texts and exhibitions, seminars, and conversations, it is often uncritically assumed that design has its origins in the European industrial revolution. This inscription has several consequences. If we see the atmospheres of the Western civilisational project as native environments, we trivialise their constitutive qualities and modes of production. As fishes in water, we operate and interact confined to the interior flows and mutations imposed by modern design, naturalising the new agencies (capital, information, biopolitics, etc.), the modes of production of power, and the increasingly complex combinations between their components. Thus, the mutations of design practice have evaded the critical scrutiny of the epistemological program of the industrial revolution.

Anthropo- and Euro-centric design, today hegemonic, is the armed wing of the Western civilising project. Beyond the siren songs of green capitalism, in practice design assumes that, beyond the frontiers of its domain, there is a background landscape called *nature*, from which to obtain materials and where organic and inorganic resources abound. This background landscape is also inhabited by myths and gods, cultural practices and beliefs, pre-scientific stories, available to be extracted and turned into *design opportunities*. Our discipline, immersed in its shifting waters, occurs as a radical difference from that which *exceeds* (de la Cadena) its domain and the world in which it is inscribed.

The program of conquest and domination inaugurated by Alexander's interaction with the Knot presupposes that certain humans, convinced of their radical exceptionality, take control of the destiny of the world. However, the increasing metabolic autonomy and density of the anthropocentric tangle once again subjects the fate of this civilisational project to that of the exiled entities and environments of the West. Modern design as an enterprise of world control is today *enmarañado* and *enmarañándose* itself with that which exceeds it.[8] Today we are slowly realising that we inhabit a continuum densely populated by interdependent and ontologically diverse entities: animal, viral, vegetal, industrial, geological, algorithmic, narrative, political, religious, or financial.

For a long time, the practice of design did not hesitate to sacrifice whatever was needed in its creative trajectory. Now, following Escobar (2016),

Furrowing the Maraña: *designing to sail out of the Anthropocene* 159

the epistemological perspective in which designers inscribe themselves by recognising that they "articulate with the world by being immersed in it" (Escobar, 2016, p. 180) allows overcoming the dualistic existence in which our daily life is engrossed. In this regard, designing situated in the *maraña* can constitute an episteme to develop discourses that present alternatives that avoid linear narratives or narrow theologies, with a vocation for emergence and self-organisation. If science is nested in the will to isolate, characteristic of human beings, then we must find "the means to respond to the pathologies of isolation, to de-isolate in various ways" (Escobar, 2016, p. 119). Continuing the dialogue with Escobar (2016), we recognise that the discipline of design, being unable to separate itself from matter in its reflexive activity, is intrinsically qualified to mobilise politically in the widening of the range of possible ways of being through our bodies, places, flows and materialities, moving away from the usual deconstructive analysis to constitute itself in (pro)positive practice. The *maraña*, as an epistemic project, is empowered to amalgamate within itself—or entangle—diverse projects of speculative strands that emerge to collectively redefine reality and figure alternative ways of being (Dunne & Raby, 2013). To materialise the conceptual approach deployed in the present argument, we will end by reviewing *Material conditions for an enriched relational space with Huilo and Maqui: research through design*, developed by Marcela Mora (2020) under the guidance of Pablo Hermansen. After a year of empirical inquiry that ended in September 2020, this work demonstrates how "Among these valuable dispositions is the designer's acquired orientation to the pursuit of attentive and open-ended inquiry into the possibilities latent within lived material contexts" (Fry et al., 2015, p. 275).

Material conditions for an enriched relational space with Huilo and Maqui intended to contribute to the social and cognitive well-being of two male pumas (also known as cougars) (Puma *concolor*) in captivity and unable to be reinserted into the wild. Mora, through an exercise of iterative prototyping inspired by care (Puig de la Bellacasa, 2017) precipitated the conformation of an "us" that is more-than-human, designing the material conditions that allowed humans and non-humans to *enmarañarse*. As can be extracted from the work of Mora (2020), the beginning of the project was marked by an abysmal distance between the researcher and the animals that could not be resolved by resorting to secondary sources. This was due to the relative scarcity of systematised material on pumas. This deliberate oversight on the part of science should not surprise us: as we argued earlier, although pumas are distributed throughout most of the American continent, their presence is not of commercial interest, but on the contrary, they are often in dispute with livestock activity, as is the case in southern Chile (Franklin et al., 1999). At the same time, the limited material available describes pumas not as singular beings of situated behaviour, but as representatives of their species, an approach in friction with the epistemology in which this research was inscribed.

Figure 10.2 Huilo and Maqui meet through the fence, which is a point of encounter and separation.

Source: Mora (2020, p. 69). In "Condiciones materiales para un espacio relacional enriquecido con Huilo y Maqui." Investigación aplicada desde una perspectiva autoetnográfica en el recinto de dos Pumas con color. Pontificia Universidad Católica de Chile.

For Mora (2020), the lack of research precedents with puma subjects prompted experimental and empirical work that favoured an emerging singularisation of Huilo and Maqui, far from the *anthroponormative* criteria of truth imposed by modern episteme (Tironi & Hermansen, 2020). Through prolonged participant observation, Mora's findings corroborate that phenomena cannot be the mere translation of a laboratory exercise designed by human subjects, but differential patterns of matter or patterns of diffraction. These patterns emerge from complex intra-agential constants, multiple material-discursive practices or apparatuses of bodily production. These devices are not mere observation instruments but mapping and boundary marking practices—*specific material* (Barad, 2007). Mora's observations materialised Huilo and Maqui as entities with particular personalities. Evidence of the above is their enjoyment of meeting at the fence that separates their enclosures (Figure 10.2), contradicting the behaviour that is usually proscribed to this species by science of solitary animals that rarely meet without arousing conflict between them (Vidal, 2014). Huilo and Maqui do not have a parent-child relationship, nor a herd relationship, but they are certainly much more than neighbours, (their behaviour evidence) an affective bond and (that) they are companions (Mora, 2020, p. 68).

Claiming that animals possess their own desires, personalities, moods, and perform actions outside of their species' own behaviours challenges the

Furrowing the Maraña: *designing to sail out of the Anthropocene* 161

idea that these beings are organic machines or resources, which raises strong resistance and scepticism from the scientific community (Despret, 2018; Lestel, 2018; Tafalla, 2019). In Mora's work we see how design remarks the difference between *experientiality* and *experience*. For Rheinberger (2021) the former allows us to find alternatives to the debacle we have caused by following or allowing ourselves to be dragged along by myriad modern trajectories of conquest and colonisation.

> Experience makes it possible to evaluate and judge a work, an object or a situation. On the contrary, experientiality makes it possible to embody, so to speak, these same judgments and evaluations in the process of obtaining knowledge, that is to say, it makes it possible to think with tools and hands. Experientiality is an intellectual achievement. Experientiality, or in other words, acquired intuition, is a form of activity and life.
>
> (Rheinberger, 2021, p. 54, our translation)

Experientiality throughout Mora's work is a catalyst for cosmopolitical moments in which the ontologies represented by cougar-people and human-people become *enmarañados*, tangibilised through a cartographic exercise. Following David Rousell, we understand mapping as a practice that is not limited to recording extensive spatio-temporal relations (Figure 10.3), but incorporates intensive axes, "'affective constellations' comprised of intensive relations, events, and becomings" (Rousell, 2021, p. 5). As *mapping*, intensive cartographies are situated action, not thing or object. They become, that is, *they are made* in the encounters between multiple ontologies. To map intensities is to make available the intra-actions (Barad, 2007) that emerge in the more-than-human prototyping; it is to represent the traces and traces of the flows of entities that, entangled, are *apprehended* (Butler, 2010), coexist despite being mutually incommensurable.

> As Huilo and Maqui, I tried to hide when I heard tourists approaching to avoid being seen and thought that this area was also allowed for them. I walked stealthily so as not to disturb. I learned to tread softly, to breathe silently, to contemplate for hours. I missed the waterfall when it was dry, the noise and coolness of the water. I valued the trees as much as Huilo, taking refuge in them when the sun was exhausting.
>
> (Mora, 2020, p. 99, our translation)

Without losing sight of the material dimension of design, the result of the prototyping process carried out by Mora (2020) culminated in the development of an environmental enrichment device. As Martín Juez comments, Objects unite us and separate us from reality: they are a fundamental part of

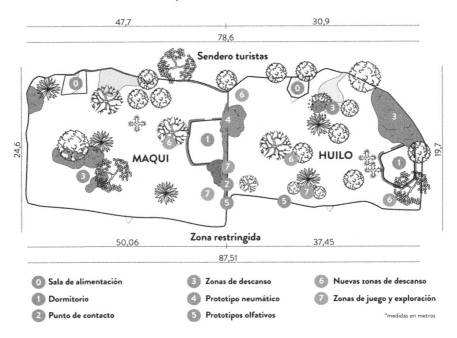

Figure 10.3 Planimetry of Huilo's and Maqui's enclosures, this was made during the research.

Source: Mora (2020, p. 77). In "Condiciones materiales para un espacio relacional enriquecido con Huilo y Maqui." Investigación aplicada desde una perspectiva autoetnográfica en el recinto de dos Pumas con color. Pontificia Universidad Católica de Chile.

the mortar with which a culture is built (Martín Juez, 2002, p. 15). Although at the beginning Mora's proximity to the Huilo and Maqui enclosures was considered by the pumas as that of just another visitor, the emergence of puma-human intra-actions achieve a broader material arrangement (i.e., a set of material practices) that challenges the Cartesian object-subject cut. In this sense, Mora iterates until she finds in olfactory perception a channel of interspecies communication that allows him to lay the foundations of a more-than-human conversation in order to singularise the agencies of those who take part in it (Figure 10.4). This conversation initiates by hanging a braid impregnated with herbal fragrances that intensifies its relationship with the pumas and between Huilo and Maqui, *enmarañando* a community composed of different ontologies. Prototype and prototyping are *marañas* in a material and conceptual sense, composing an ontological and epistemological territory that braids hair, fragrances, affects, agencies and community, expanding the understanding of the world and protecting a collective redefinition of reality and the possible ways of becoming.

Furrowing the Maraña: *designing to sail out of the Anthropocene* 163

Figure 10.4 Maqui played with the braids repeatedly. He rubbed himself with the parsley braid constantly, which was recorded with the hairs impregnated in it.

Source: Mora (2020, p. 86). In "Condiciones materiales para un espacio relacional enriquecido con Huilo y Maqui." Investigación aplicada desde una perspectiva autoetnográfica en el recinto de dos Pumas con color. Pontificia Universidad Católica de Chile.

Furrowing into the *maraña* to leave the Anthropocene behind

Without any certainty about our future, and in view of the events that will begin to unfold with the incessant crises that will come in our times, the title that heads this section suggests an aporia of similar calibre to that of having to write a conclusion to the present argument. We, as the authors of this article, have the strong conviction that science and the market are aware that cutting the *maraña* is the best way to suppress the agencies that hinder their pretensions; transforming a grandiose obstacle into a chronic sum of elements, arranged in such a way that they fail to intertwine under a narrative to resist the onslaught. Explicit and fully articulated knowledge, a pernicious illusion of analytical philosophy (Polanyi & Sen, 2009), has no problem in dissecting the more-than-human, echoing the Alexandrian cut to what it seeks to know and possess. In this way, as happened with the kingdoms confronted by Alexander, different groups with non-Western ways of imbricating the entities that populate their cosmoses are being decapitated, stripped of their lands, persuaded by developmentalist romances.

If we want to navigate into the *maraña* we need a post-Anthropocene horizon. Haraway (2015) had suggests the Chthulucene, a deep and intense moment where the "entangles myriad temporalities and spatialities and myriad intra-active entities-in assemblages—including the more-than-human,

164 *Pablo Hermansen and José Guerra Solano*

other-than-human, inhuman, and human-as humus" (Haraway, 2015 p. 160). In view of the above, as *designers-cyborgs-in-the-maraña*, we aim to contribute to the co-construction of new knowledges, capable of helping us navigate the tangle out of the Anthropocene to embrace, as soon as possible, *enmarañándonos* in coexistence without being conclusive, through these pages we have tried to surround the epistemology in which some design projects that do not seek to perpetuate the ambitions of voracious capitalism operate. Thus, despite the fact that modern design took an important role in the materialisation of the conditions of the imperialist lifestyle to which developing nations should aspire, design is a privileged field to divert our trajectory of infinite progress and production towards the *maraña* and subtle intra-actions that science is accustomed to neglect. If we set ourselves the task of recognising ourselves in the *maraña*, we will be closer to conceiving a cosmos in which the trajectories of power are slowed down, composing *enmarañadas* myriads of agencies, materialities and histories that, at the same time, coexist and exceed each other.

Notes

1 This phrase is a reference for the text: *Staying with the Trouble: Making Kin in the Chthulucene*, written by Donna Haraway and originally published by Duke University Press in 2016.
2 The word *enmarañado* is the action of *maraña*. These words are powerful and we think that they should remain in Spanish, if they are translated, they lose sense. *Enmarañado* can be understood as entangled, interwoven, enmeshed. Something that is hampered, chaotic, so tangled that it starts to feel fuzzy.
3 Today Antalya and Muğla, provinces on the Mediterranean coast of Turkey.
4 We take the concept of "rage" in the sense that Sloterdijk uses it: "At the beginning of the first sentence of the European tradition, in the first verse of the Iliad, the word "rage" occurs. It appears fatally and solemnly, like a plea, a plea that does not allow for any disagreement. As is fitting for a well-formed propositional object, this noun is in the accusative: "Of the rage of Achilles, son of Peleus, sing Goddess ..." That it appears at the very beginning loudly and unequivocally announces its heightened pathos" (Sloterdijk, 2010, p. 1).
5 *Desenmarañar* is the inverse act of *enmarañar*. It can be understood as something that is unraveled, untangled.
6 The meanings of the concept "maraña" retrieved from the work of Malkiel (1948) have been included throughout the text using low quotation marks to facilitate reading.
7 This aphorism, also called "law of the instrument" was popularized by Abraham Maslow, but we owe to him Abram Kaplan who originally stated "Give a small boy a hammer, and he will find that everything he encounters needs pounding" (Kaplan, 1998, p. 28).
8 *Enmarañado* is an adjective for when something is very tangled. *Enmarañándose* is the verb, the *maraña* in action, for when something is tangling.

Bibliography

Arriano. (1982). *Anábasis de Alejandro Magno. Libros I — III*. Madrid: Editorial Gredos.

Furrowing the Maraña: *designing to sail out of the Anthropocene* 165

Ballenas: voces del mar de Chile. (2018). In *Catálogo de la muestra "Ballenas Voces del mar de Chile,"* exhibited at Centro Cultural La Moneda, 2018.

Barad, K. (2007). *Meeting the Universe Halfway: Quantum Physics and the Entanglement of Matter and Meaning.* Durham: Duke University Press.

Barros, A. (1975). *Aborígenes Australes de América.* Santiago: Editorial Lord Cochrane.

Butler, J. (2010). *Frames of War: When is Life Grievable?* London: Verso.

Capella, J., & Gibbons, J. (2019). *Cetáceos y Hombres.* Ilustre Municipalidad de Punta Arenas, Universidad de Magallanes y La Prensa Austral. Punta Arenas, Chile: Universidad de Magallanes. pp. 262.

Carroll, S. (2018). *Las leyes del Serengeti. Como funciona la cida y por qué es importante saberlo.* Barcelona: Editorial Debate.

de la Cadena, M. (2010). Cosmopolítica indígena en los Andes: Reflexiones Conceptuales más allá de lo "Político." *Cultural Anthropology, 25*(2), pp. 334–370.

de la Cadena, M., & Blaser, M. (2018). *A World of Many Worlds.* Durham: Duke University Press.

de Sousa Santos, B. (2017). *Justicia entre Saberes: Epistemologías del Sur contra el epistemicidio.* Madrid: Ediciones Morata.

Déotte, J. L. (2013). *¿Qué es un aparato estético?: Benjamin, Lyotard, Rancière.* Santiago: Metales Pesados.

Derrida, J. (2000). Of the Humanities and the Philosophical Discipline: The Right to Philosophy from the Cosmopolitical Point of View (The Example of an International Institution). *Studies in Practical Philosophy, 1*(2), pp. 1–13. https://doi.org/10.5840/studpracphil2000212

Descola, P., & Pálsson, G. (2001). *Naturaleza y sociedad. Perspectivas antropológicas.* México, DF: Siglo XXI editores.

Despret, V. (2018). *¿Qué dirían los animales ... si les hiciéramos las preguntas correctas?* Buenos Aires: Cactus.

Dunne, A., & Raby, F. (2013). *Speculative Everything: Design, Fiction and Social Dreaming.* Cambridge: MIT Press.

Escobar, A. (2016). *Autonomía y Diseño: La realización de lo comunal.* Popayán, CO: Editorial Universidad del Cauca.

Fisher, M. (2016). *Realismo capitalista. ¿No hay alternativa?* Buenos Aires: Caja Negra Editora.

Flusser, V. (1986). The Photograph as Post-Industrial Object: An Essay on the Ontological Standing of Photographs. *Leonardo, 19*(4), pp. 329–332.

Foucault, M. (2001). *Defender la sociedad: Curso en el Collège de France (1975–1976).* Buenos Aires: Fondo de Cultura Económica de Argentina.

Franklin, W., Johnson, W., Sarno, R., & Iriarte, A. (1999). Ecology of the Patagonia puma Felis concolor patagonica in southern Chile. *Biological Conservation, 90,* pp. 33–40.

Fry, T., Dilnot, C., & Stewart, S. C. (2015). *Design and the Question of History* (1st ed.). London: Bloomsbury Academic. https://doi.org/10.5040/9781474245890

Gracía-Reyes, D. (2018). Del Essex a Melville. Reescrituras del mito de la ballena blanca en la novela gráfica Mocha Dick. *Alpha: Revista de Artes, Letras y Filosofía,* (47), 91–104.

Graves, R. (2011). *Los mitos griegos 1.* Madrid: Alianza editorial.

Haraway, D. (2019). *Seguir con el problema: Generar parentesco en el Chthuluceno.* Consonni.

166 *Pablo Hermansen and José Guerra Solano*

Haraway, D., Ishikawa, N., Gilbert, S. F., Olwig, K., Tsing A. L., & Bubandt N. (2016). Anthropologists Are Talking – About the Anthropocene, *Ethnos, 81*(3), pp. 535–564. https://doi.org/10.1080/00141844.2015.1105838

Heckel, W. (2008). *The Conquests of Alexander the Great*. Cambridge: sCambridge University Press.

Hennius, A., Gustavsson, R., Ljungkvist, J., & Spindler, L. (2018). Whalebone gaming pieces: Aspects of marine mammal exploitation in vendel and Viking Age Scandinavia. *European Journal of Archaeology, 21*(4), pp. 612–631.

Hermansen, P., & Tironi, M. (2017). Impugnaciones pedagógicas: prototipado interespecies y encuentros cosmopolíticos. *Diseña, 12*, pp. 196–227.

Hermansen, P., & Tironi, M. (2020). Cosmopolitical Interventions: Prototyping Inter-Species Encounters. In Rucker, S., Roberts-Smith, J., Radzikowska, M. (eds.), *Prototyping Across the Disciplines*. Bristol: Intellect Books, pp. 1–22.

Huizinga, J. (2007). *Homo ludens*. Madrid: Alianza Editorial.

Ingold, T. (2016). On Human Correspondence. *Journal of the Royal Anthropological Institute, 23*, pp. 9–27.

Johnson, C., Reisinger, R., Friedlaender, A., Palacios, D., Willson, A., Zerbini, A., Lancaster, M., Battle, J., Alberini, A., Kelez, S., & Felix, F. (2022). *Protecting Blue Corridors. Challenges and Solutions for Migratory Whales Navigating National and International Seas*. Zenodo. https://doi.org/10.5281/zenodo.6196131

Kaplan, A. (1998). *The Conduct of Inquiry: Methodology for Behavioral Science*. Edison, NJ: Transaction Publishers.

Kirkwood, J. (2019). Los nudos de la sabiduría feminista. (Después del II Encuentro Feminista Latinoamericano y del Caribe, Lima 1983). *Anuario de Filosofía Argentina y Americana, 36*, pp. 187–209.

Latour, B. (1993). *We Have Never Been Modern*. Cambridge: Harvard University Press.

Lausic, S. (1994). *Rostros, mitos y figuras de las etnias patagónicas australes*. Punta Arenas, CL: Fondo de Desarrollo de la Cultura y las Artes.

Lestel, D. (2018). *Hacer las paces con el animal*. Santiago de Chile: Qual Quelle.

Luxemburg, R. (1951). *The Accumulation of Capital*. London: Routledge and Kegan Paul LTD.

Malkiel, Y. (1948). The Etymology of Spanish "Maraña". *Bulletin Hispanique, 50*(2), pp. 147–171.

Martín Juez, F. (2002). *Contribuciones para una antropología del diseño*. Barcelona: Editorial Gedisa Mexicana.

Miller, T. (2021). *Love, Death + Robots. Vol. 2: El gigante ahogado*. Netflix.

Moore, J. (2020). *El capitalismo en la trama de la vida. Ecología y acumulación de capital*. Madrid: Traficantes de sueños.

Mora, M. (2020). *Condiciones materiales para un espacio relacional enriquecido con Huilo y Maqui. Investigación aplicada desde una perspectiva autoetnográfica en el recinto de dos Pumas concolor* [Tesis para optar a título profesional de Diseñador]. Santiago: Pontificia Universidad Católica de Chile.

Morin, E. (1990). *Introducción al pensamiento complejo*. España: Edtorial Gedisa.

Morton, T. (2018). *El pensamiento ecológico*. Barcelona: Paidos.

Morton, T. (2019). *Ecología oscura*. Barcelona: Editorial Planeta.

Pick, A. (2011). *Creaturely Poetics: Animality and Vulnerability in Literature and Film*. New York: Columbia University Press.

Furrowing the Maraña: *designing to sail out of the Anthropocene*   167

Piña, J. (2021). *Mitos y leyendas del pueblo mapuche. Relatos de la tradición oral.* Santiago: Catalonia.

Plumwood, V. (2002). *Environmental Culture: The Ecological Crisis of Reason.* London: Routledge.

Polanyi, M., & Sen, A. (2009). *The Tacit Dimension.* Chicago, IL: University of Chicago Press.

Puig de la Bellacasa, M. (2017). *Matters of Care: Speculative Ethics in More Than Human Worlds.* Minneapolis: University of Minnesota Press.

Rheinberger, H.-J. (2021). *Iteraciones.* Santiago: Pólvora Editorial.

Rousell, D. (2021). *Immersive Cartography and Post-Qualitative Inquiry: A Speculative Adventure in Research-Creation.* London: Routledge.

Sarton, G. (1960). *Ciencia antigua y civilización moderna.* México, DF: Fondo de Cultura Económica.

Serratos, F. (2020). *El capitaloceno: una historia radical de la crisis climática.* México, DF: Universidad Nacional Autónoma de México, Dirección General de Publicaciones y Fomento Editorial y Festina Publicaciones.

Sloterdijk, P. (2010). *Ira y tiempo. Ensayos psicopolítico.* Madrid: Ediciones Siruela.

Sloterdijk, P. (2017). *Esferas I. Burbujas. Microesferología.* Madrid: Ediciones Siruela.

Stengers, I. (2014). La propuesta cosmopolítica. *Revista Pléyade, 14*, pp. 17–41.

Stengers, I. (2017). *En tiempos de catástrofes: Cómo resistir a la barbarie que viene.* Barcelona: Ned Ediciones.

Tafalla, M. (2019). *Ecoanimal. Una estética plurisensocial, ecologista y animalista.* Madrid: Plaza y Valdés.

Tironi, M., Hermansen, P., & Neira, J. (2014). El Prototipo Como Dispositivo cosmopolítico: Etnografía De prácticas De diseño En El Zoológico Nacional De Chile. *Pléyade*, n.° 14 (diciembre), pp. 61–95. https://www.revistapleyade.cl/index.php/OJS/article/view/161

Tironi, M., & Hermansen, P. (2018). Cosmopolitical Encounters: Prototyping at the National Zoo in Santiago, Chile. *Journal of Cultural Economy*, 11(4), pp. 330–347. https://doi.org/10.1080/17530350.2018.1433705

Tironi, M., & Hermansen, P. (2020). Prototyping Coexistence: Design for Interspecies Futures. *ARQ (Santiago)*, (106), pp. 38–47. https://doi.org/10.4067/S0717-69962020000300038

Turner, V. (2007). *La selva de los símbolos: Aspectos del ritual ndembu.* España: Siglo XXI editores.

Vallejo, I. (2019). *El inifinito en un junco: la invención de los libros en el mundo antiguo.* Madrid: Ediciones Siruela.

Vidal, F. (2014). *Puma Araucano: Vida en una dimensión paralela.* Temuco, CL: Ediciones Universidad Santo Tomás de Temuco.

Wendt, H. (1982). *El descubrimiento de los animales. De las leyendas del unicornio hasta la etología.* Bercelona: Editorial Planeta.

Wilkie, A. (2016). Introduction: Aesthetics, Cosmopolitics and Design. In P. Lloyd & E. Bohemia (Eds.), *Proceedings of DRS2016*: Design + Research + Society – Future-Focused Thinking, Volume 3, pp. 873–879. https://doi.org/10.21606/drs.2016.509, ISSN 2398-3132.

Index

Note: *Italic* page numbers refer to figures and page numbers followed by "n" denote endnotes.

aesthetic values 108–109
Akomolafe, B. 48n19
Alexander 23, 106, 143, 145–150, *151*, 153, 158, 163
Aliaga, Valentina 73, 83n2
Amoore, Louise 60
animals-architects co-design: action and reaction plan 98, *100*; beaver experience suit 97, *97*; biodiversity experts 94–95; co-worker suit 97, *97*; design solution 96; destructive behavior 95; last protocol 98, *99*; mitigation and adaptation 92; multispecies architectural practice 93, 98, 101; planetary crisis 92; renaturalisation project 97–98
Anthropocene concept 3, 4, 6, 12, 23, 66, 82, 95, 142, 144, 155, 157, 163
anthropocentrism 23, 45n8, 56, 57, 65
Appadurai, A. 13
Aristotle 145, 146, 149
artificial intelligence (AI) 10–11
Augé, M. 132–133

Barad, K. 144
Benjamin, W. 33
Berns, T. 11
Big Data 11
biofabrication 22, 72–74, 76, 84n3
bioinformatic process 119
Blaser, M. 29, 47n5, 144
Buckley, C. 83
Buen Vivir 17–18

Carrasco, C. 82
Carrasco, Gabriela 77–78, 80, 83n2
Cassirer, Ernst 149
Certeau, M. De 89
Chilean Pavilion 1, 7
Chilet, Marcos 23
Chin, Elizabeth 62
community-based participatory design 61
community-oriented designs 7
community-supported agriculture (CSA) 54–55
contact language 47n4
cosmopolitical diplomacy practice: biodiversity loss 123–124; bostans 114–115, 125, *125*; COVID-19 112; Empathy revisited: designs for more than one 112–113; encounter 116–121; gentrification 123; historical place 113; more-than-human futures 126–127, *127*; shared cosmos 115–116, *117*; Tarlataban 125, *125*; transcalar condition, urban phenomena 124, *124*; ultra-processed food 121
cosmopolitics 8, 24n1, 156
Costanza-Chock, S. 15
Cottom, Tressie McMillan 62
Coupaye, L. 74–75
COVID-19 pandemic 3, 9, 38, 112
Cristi, Nicole 22
cultural innovation 51–52

David Rincón Quijano, Edgard 23
De la Bellacasa, M. P. 10, 17, 55–56, 81

170 Index

De la Cadena, M. 21, 22, 24n1, 30, 32, 48n15, 144
DeCook, Julia R. 66
defuturisation techniques 11, 13
Dekalb Avenue 88, 89
Deleuze, G. 31, 61, 103, 104
Descola, P. 18, 143
design *see individual entries*
design biography 62
design's intimacies: decolonized practices 58; human-centred design 59; indeterminacy 58–61; infrastructures 61–64; pluriversal posthuman 67–68; posthumanism 64–67; sociotechnical systems 59
design theory 72
Despret, V. 94
Dilnot, C. 16
DiSalvo, Carl 16, 22
Dostoyevsky, F. 104

ecofeminism 79, 80
Edgerton, D. 74
Ehrenfeld, Valentina 83n2
Elii 112, 128n4
embodied design 62
encounter: Diplomat 120; with locals 120–121, *122*; microorganisms exchange 116, *118*, *119*; with microworlds 117–120, *121*; Özgürlük Park structure 117, *120*; Turkish kiosk 116
Energy Babble 105, 107–109
energy community 108
energy-demand reduction 108–109
environmental unsustainability 1
ephemeral glimmer 59–60
Escobar, A. 6, 13–15, 21, 22, 67, 132, 158–159
European imperialism 1
Euro-Western design 15

Farías, I. 22–23
Faustino Sarmiento, José 38
Flores, F. 15
Flusser, V. 149
Fogué, Uriel 23
foraging 88–90
Forlano, L. 22, 57n3
Fournier, Lauren 62
Fry, T. 2, 13, 16
futures *see* more-than-human futures
futurological work 10

Galloway, Anne 65
Gaver, W. 104
Gil Lopesino, Eva 23
Gordon, E. 90
Gottlieb Baumgarten, Alexander 106
Graham Ballard, James 156
Graves, R. 144–145
growing materials: biofabrication practices 72; domestic activities 79; ecofeminism 79–80; ecosystem capacities 80; emic categories 81; invisibles activities 75–79; maqui's fermentation 80; micropolitics 72, 82; mixed-method approach 72; tangled technical activities 75–79; as technical activity 73–75; technodiversity 82–83
Gualinga, J. 33
Guattari, F. 31, 103, 104, 106
Guerra Solano, Jose 23
Gutiérrez, A. 42, 43, 48n18

Hallam, E. 74
Haraway, D. J. 65, 66, 79, 131, 132, 163
Heidegger, M. 74, 106
Hellenistic Period 150
Helmreich, S. 9
Hermansen, P. 23, 159
Huerta, Monica 62
Hui, Y. 48n19, 74
Huizinga, J. 148
human-centred design 2, 6–8, 65, 66, 68

idiot tool 103–105
Ingold, T. 4, 17, 74, 156
inverse engineering 2

Jackson, Zekkiyah Iman 67
Jain, S. Llochlain 62
Jameson, Fredric 142
José Besoain, María 73, 77, 78, 80, 83n2

Kafer, Alison 66
Kant, I. 106
Kirkwood, J. 148
Knot, Gordian 23, 143–148, 155, 158
Kusch, R. 34–42, 47n5

LABVA 76, 83n2
Latour, B. 3, 4, 8–10, 12, 20, 21, 24n1, 53, 57, 92

Lausic, S. 152
Luxemburg, R. 157

Malkiel, Y. 143
Manzini, E. 22, 48n19
maraña 148–149; Anthropocene 163–164; civilised-civilisable 141–142; developed-savage 141–142; *enmarañado* and *enmarañándose* 150–154; human-humanisable 141–142; impassable obstacle 147; intricate obstacle 147; knowledge-power 143, 150; more-than-human territories 141; multidimensional planetary ecosystemic crisis 141; mutations 155–163, *160, 162, 163*; precariousness 142–143; vulnerability 142–143; Western civilisational model 142; Western culture 144–145
Mareis, C. 74
Mariano 30
Márquez, Francia 39
Martín Juez, F. 161–162
Mazé, R. 12
Melville, Herman 154
Michael, M. 23, 105
Microbial Fruits of Istanbul (MFoI) 114, *115, 117,* 126 *see also* cosmopolitical diplomacy practice
micropolitics 72, 82
Miller, T. 156
modern-colonial epistemological matrix 2
modern-colonial matrix 18
modern-colonialist system 3
Mora, M. 159–162
more-than-human agencies 7–9, 21, 73
more-than-human design 98
more-than-human entities 7–9, 16
more-than-human futures 13–14, 19, 20, 93, 112, 126–127, *127*; care 55–56; decentring humans 52–53; engendering 53–54; practice to theory 56–57; social innovation 51–52; system reframe 54–55
Morgan, George W. 154
Morin, E. 144, 149
Morton, T. 156
Mugar, M. 90
multispecies approach 93

Münster, U. 93
Mutant Institute of Environmental Narratives (IMNA) 128n4

Nazario 30
neoliberal economic models 51
Neruda, Pablo 48n13

ontological detoxification 2, 22, 44
ontological pluralism 8
Osses, Esteban 83n2

Paim, N. 74
Palacios Rodríguez, Carlos 23
Pallasmaa, J. 93
Pálsson, G. 143
Parisi, Luciana 60
Parra-Agudelo, Leonardo 23
Peronism 37
Phillip, M. 79–80
Pitrou, P. 74–75
planetary disaster design: autonomous design 5; care and reparation design 16–19; COVID-19 pandemic 3; decolonial design 5; decolonial futures 13; decolonising design practices 14–16; design justice 5; ecological damage 4; ecosystemic crisis 3; ecosystem transformation 4; environmental crisis 3–4; fragility 19–21; future prefiguration 12; more-than-human futures 13–14; planetary design 6–10; pluralising future regimes 10–12; transition design 5
planet-oriented design 3, 7, 8, 10
pluriversal design 10–12; African descent 29; Anthropocene–Capitalocene–Plantationocene 32, 34; coloniality 29; contact zones 31–32; designorance 43; excess analytics 30–31; ontological detox 44; political excess 34–38; prefigurative politics 41; propositions of 45–46; Puerto Resistencia 38–41, 48n17; radical interdependence 46n1; radical relational–communal politics 42; Sarayaku territory 33–34; user-human-centred design 44
pluriversal posthuman 67–68

172 Index

politics: cosmopolitics 8, 24n1, 156; micropolitics 72, 82; relational–communal politics 42; prefigurative politics 41
post-extractivist epistemologies 1
posthuman design 65
posthuman failures 63
posthumanism 64–67
Pratt, M. L. 31, 47n4
prefigurative politics 41
Puerto Resistencia 38–41, 48n17

rage concept 164n4
Rancière 39
Reinert, H. 93
Remter, F. 22–23
Rheinberger, H.-J. 149, 161
Rivera Cusicanqui, Silvia 82–83
Rousell, D. 161
Rouvroy, A. 11

Sanchez Criado, T. 22–23
sancocho-style approach 130; boundless connections 133–134; coexistence process 136–138, 137; feelthinking, mycorrhiza 135–136; human concerns 134–135; multispecies ethnography project 132; relational affectation 134; situated lifeworlds 132–133; social transformation 131
Sarayaku territory 33–34
Sarton, G. 149
Savransky, M. 107, 108
Schroer, S. 93
Segato, R. 42
Sehgal, M. 106
Serratos, F. 153

Serres, M. 96
Sigaut, F. 75
Sloterdijk, P. 145
social innovation 51–52, 56, 57, 57n1
socio-environmental changes 2
soma-aesthetic design 62
de Sousa Santos, B. 142, 157
Ståhl, O. 9
Stengers, I. 8, 24n1, 31, 61, 103, 105, 113, 142, 155
Stewart, S. C. 16

Tassinari, Virginia 22
technodiversity 82–83
technology 37, 48n18, 59, 62–65, 67, 72, 74, 81, 109
Telhan, O. 23, 112, 128n4
Thwaites, T. 96
Todd, Zoe 64, 66
Tsing, A. L. 58–59, 88
Turner, V. 152

Ureta Marín, Carola 23
user-centred design 6–7
user-human-centred design 44

van Dooren, A. 93
von Anshelm, K. 131

Wark, McKenzie 62
Weiss, Alejandro 77, 83n2
Whitehead, A. N. 106–107, 109n4
Wilkie, A. 23, 105
Willis, A. M. 15
Winograd, T. 15

Zerwas, S. 131
Žižek, Slavoj 142